There Was a Country

THERE WAS A COUNTRY

A PERSONAL HISTORY
OF BIAFRA

Chinua Achebe

THE PENGUIN PRESS

New York

2012

THE PENGUIN PRESS
Published by the Penguin Group
Penguin Group (USA) Inc., 375 Hudson Street, New York, New York 10014, U.S.A. •
Penguin Group (Canada), 90 Eglinton Avenue East, Suite 700, Toronto, Ontario, Canada M4P 2Y3
(a division of Pearson Penguin Canada Inc.) • Penguin Books Ltd, 80 Strand, London
WC2R 0RL, England • Penguin Ireland, 25 St. Stephen's Green, Dublin 2, Ireland (a division
of Penguin Books Ltd) • Penguin Group Australia, 707 Collins Street, Melbourne,
Victoria 3008, Australia (a division of Pearson Australia Group Pty Ltd) • Penguin Books
India Pvt Ltd, 11 Community Centre, Panchsheel Park, New Delhi – 110 017, India •
Penguin Group (NZ), 67 Apollo Drive, Rosedale, Auckland 0632, New Zealand (a division
of Pearson New Zealand Ltd) • Penguin Books, Rosebank Office Park, 181 Jan Smuts Avenue,
Parktown North 2193, South Africa • Penguin China, B7 Jiaming Center,
27 East Third Ring Road North, Chaoyang District, Beijing 100020, China

Penguin Books Ltd, Registered Offices:
80 Strand, London WC2R 0RL, England

First published in 2012 by The Penguin Press,
a member of Penguin Group (USA) Inc.

Copyright © Chinua Achebe, 2012
All rights reserved

"1966," "Benin Road," "Penalty of Godhead," "Generation Gap," "Biafra, 1969," "A Mother in a Refugee
Camp," "The First Shot," "Air Raid," "Mango Seedling," "We Laughed at Him," "Vultures," and "After
a War" from *Collected Poems* by Chinua Achebe. Copyright © 1971, 1973, 2004 by Chinua Achebe.
Used by permission of Anchor Books, a division of Random House, Inc.

LIBRARY OF CONGRESS CATALOGING IN PUBLICATION DATA
Achebe, Chinua.
There was a country : a personal history of Biafra / Chinua Achebe.
p.   cm.
Includes bibliographical references and index.
ISBN 978-1-59420-482-1
1. Achebe, Chinua.   2. Authors, Nigerian—20th century—Biography.   3. Nigeria—History—Civil War,
1967–1970—Personal narratives.   I. Title.
PR9387.9.A3Z46 2012
823'.914—dc23
[B]
2012005603

Printed in the United States of America
1   3   5   7   9   10   8   6   4   2

Designed by Meighan Cavanaugh

Penguin is committed to publishing works of quality and integrity. In that spirit, we are proud to offer this book to our readers; however, the story, the experiences, and the words are the author's alone.

CONTENTS

PART 2

PART 3

PART 4

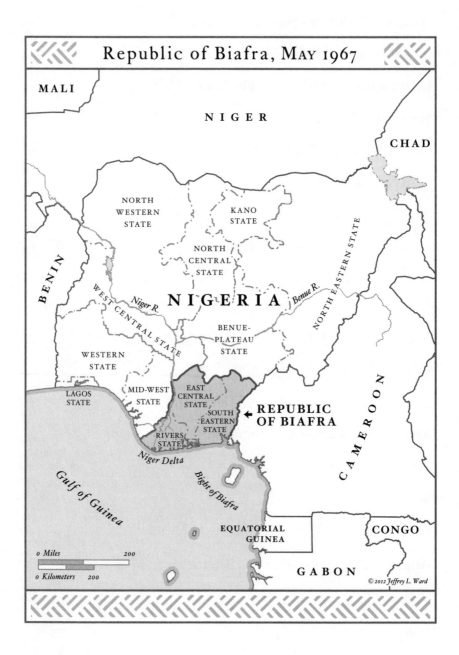

Republic of Biafra, May 1967

MALI

NIGER

CHAD

NORTH
WESTERN
STATE

KANO
STATE

NORTH
CENTRAL
STATE

NORTH EASTERN STATE

BENIN

West Central State

Niger R.

NIGERIA

Benue R.

BENUE-
PLATEAU
STATE

WESTERN
STATE

LAGOS
STATE

MID-WEST
STATE

EAST
CENTRAL
STATE

SOUTH
EASTERN
STATE

**REPUBLIC
OF BIAFRA**

RIVERS
STATE

Niger Delta

CAMEROON

Gulf of Guinea

Bight of Biafra

EQUATORIAL
GUINEA

CONGO

GABON

0 Miles   200

0 Kilometers   200

© 2012 Jeffrey L. Ward

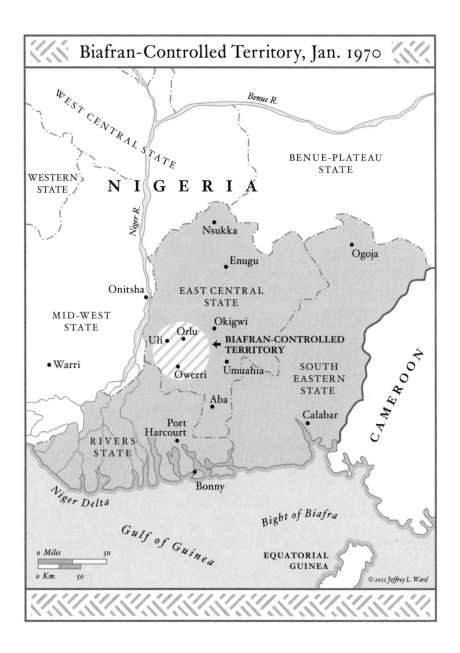

Biafran-Controlled Territory, Jan. 1970

There Was
a Country

INTRODUCTION

An Igbo proverb tells us that a man who does not know where the rain began to beat him cannot say where he dried his body.

The rain that beat Africa began four to five hundred years ago, from the "discovery" of Africa by Europe, through the transatlantic slave trade, to the Berlin Conference of 1885. That controversial gathering of the world's leading European powers precipitated what we now call the Scramble for Africa, which created new boundaries that did violence to Africa's ancient societies and resulted in tension-prone modern states. It took place without African consultation or representation, to say the least.

Great Britain was handed the area of West Africa that would later become Nigeria, like a piece of chocolate cake at a birthday party. It was one of the most populous regions on the African continent, with over 250 ethnic groups and distinct languages. The northern part of the country was the seat of several ancient kingdoms, such as the Kanem-Bornu—which Shehu Usman dan Fodio and his jihadists absorbed into the Muslim Fulani Empire. The Middle Belt of Nigeria was the locus of the glorious Nok Kingdom and its world-renowned terra-cotta sculptures. The southern protectorate was home to some of the region's most sophisticated civilizations. In the west, the Oyo and Ife kingdoms once strode majestically, and in the midwest the incomparable Benin Kingdom elevated artistic distinction to a new level. Across the Niger River in the East, the Calabar and the Nri kingdoms flourished. If the Berlin Conference sealed her fate, then the amalgamation of the southern and northern protectorates inextricably complicated Nigeria's destiny. Animists, Muslims, and Christians alike were held together by a delicate, some say artificial, lattice.[1]

Britain's indirect rule was a great success in northern and western Nigeria, where affairs of state within this new dispensation continued as had been the case for centuries, with one exception—there was a new sovereign, Great Britain, to whom all vassals pledged fealty and into whose coffers all taxes were paid.[2] Indirect rule in Igbo land proved far more challenging to implement. Colonial rule functioned through a newly created and incongruous establishment of "warrant chiefs"—a deeply flawed arrangement that effectively confused and corrupted the Igbo democratic spirit.[3]

Africa's postcolonial disposition is the result of a people who have lost the habit of ruling themselves. We have also had difficulty running the new systems foisted upon us at the dawn of independence by our "colonial masters." Because the West has had a long but uneven engagement with the continent, it is imperative that it understand what happened to Africa. It must also play a part in the solution. A meaningful solution will require the goodwill and concerted efforts on the part of all those who share the weight of Africa's historical burden.

Most members of my generation, who were born before Nigeria's independence, remember a time when things were very different. Nigeria was once a land of great hope and progress, a nation with immense resources at its disposal—natural resources, yes, but even more so, human resources. But the Biafran war changed the course of Nigeria. In my view it was a cataclysmic experience that changed the history of Africa.

There is some connection between the particular distress of war, the particular tension of war, and the kind of literary response it inspires. I chose to express myself in that period through poetry, as opposed to other genres.[4] My Biafran poems and other poetry are collected in two volumes—*Beware, Soul Brother, Poems* (which was published as *Christmas in Biafra and Other Poems* in America) in 1971 and *Collected Poems* in 2004. As a group these poems tell the story of Biafra's struggle and suffering. I have made the conscious choice to juxtapose poetry and prose in this book to tell complementary stories, in two art forms.

It is for the sake of the future of Nigeria, for our children and grandchildren, that I feel it is important to tell Nigeria's story, Biafra's story, our story, my story.

I begin this story with my own coming of age in an earlier and, in some respects, a more innocent time. I do this both to bring readers unfamiliar with this landscape into it at a human level and to be open about some of the sources of my own perspective.

PART I

Pioneers of a New Frontier

My father was born in the last third of the nineteenth century, an era of great cultural, economic, and religious upheaval in Igbo land. His mother had died in her second childbirth, and his father, Achebe, a refugee from a bitter civil war, did not long survive his wife. And so my father was raised by his maternal uncle, Udoh.

It was this maternal uncle, as fate would have it, who received in his compound the first party of English clergy in his town. The new arrivals, missionaries of a new religion, Christianity, had already "conquered" the Yoruba heartland and were expanding their footprint in Igbo land and the rest of southern Nigeria with their potent, irresistible tonic of evangelism and education. A story is told of how Udoh, a very generous and tolerant man, finally asked his visitors to move to a public playground on account of their singing, which he considered too dismal for a living man's compound. But he did not discourage his young nephew from associating with the singers.[1]

My father was an early Christian convert and a good student. By 1904 he was deemed to have received enough education at St. Paul's Teachers College in Awka to be employed as a teacher and an evangelist in the Anglican Mission. He was a brilliant man, who deeply valued education and read a great deal—mainly the Bible and religious books, periodicals, and almanacs from the Church Mission Society.

My mother, Janet Anaenechi Iloegbunam, was an extraordinary woman. As a student of the legendary missionary and evangelist Miss Edith Warner she received a primary school education, which was a phenomenal feat at the time, especially for a woman. My mother joined my father on his travels through much of Igbo land to spread the gospel.

My parents were among the first of their people to successfully integrate traditional values with the education and new religion brought by the Europeans. I still marvel at how wholeheartedly they embraced strangers from thousands of miles away, with their different customs and beliefs.

It is from these two outstanding and courageous individuals that my five siblings—Frank, Zinobia, John, Augustine, and Grace—and I got our deep love for education and the pursuit of knowledge.

The Magical Years

On November 16, 1930, in Nnobi, near my hometown of Ogidi, providence ushered me into a world at a cultural crossroads. By then, a long-standing clash of Western and African civilizations had generated deep conversations and struggles between their respective languages, religions, and cultures.

Crossroads possess a certain dangerous potency. Anyone born there must wrestle with their multiheaded spirits and return to his or her people with the boon of prophetic vision, or accept, as I have, life's interminable mysteries.

My initiation into the complicated world of Ndi Igbo' was at the hands of my mother and my older sister, Zinobia, who furnished me with a number of wonderful stories from our ancient Igbo tradition. The tales were steeped in intrigue, spiced with oral acrobatics and song, but always resolute in their moral message. My favorite stories starred the tortoise *mbe*, and celebrated his mischievous escapades. As a child, sitting quietly, mesmerized, story time took on a whole new world of meaning and importance. I realize, reminiscing about these events, that it is little wonder I decided to become a storyteller. Later in my literary career I traveled back to the magic of the storytelling of my youth to write my children's books: *How the Leopard Got His Claws, Chike and the River, The Drum: A Children's Story,* and *The Flute.*

When I think about my mother the first thing that comes to my mind is how clearly the description "the strong, silent type" fit her. Mother was neither talkative nor timid but seemed to exist on several planes—often quietly escaping into the inner casements of her mind, where she engaged in deep, reflective thought. It was from her that I learned to appreciate the power and solace in silence.

Mother's education prepared her for leadership, and she distinguished herself in the church and as the head of a group of expatriate women from the ancient town of Awka who were married in Ogidi. She always treated others with respect and exuded a calm self-confidence. Mother brought a remarkable, understated elegance to every activity in which she engaged. She had a particularly attractive way of making sure she got her point across without being overbearing or intimidating. It is her peaceful determination to tackle barriers in her world that nailed down a very important element of my development—the willingness to bring about change gently.

We were Christians, though the interreligious struggle was still evident in our time. There were occasions when one would suddenly realize there were sides, and one was on one or another. Perhaps the most important event that illustrates this was what has come to be known in my family as the "Kola nut incident."

The story came out that a neighbor who was a relative of mine and someone the Christians would refer to as "a heathen," was passing on the road one day and watched quietly as my mother pulled down a small Kola nut branch from a tree in her compound and picked a ripe fruit. Now one often forgot that there were taboos about picking Kola nuts. Traditionally no one was allowed to pick them from the tree; they were supposed to ripen, fall, and then be collected from the ground, and by men—not by women. The Kola nut was a sacred fruit and had a very distinct and distinguished role to play in Igbo life and culture.

The neighbor reported this incident to the menfolk, who then exaggerated the "insult to our traditions." But Mother insisted that she had every right to pick the fruit, particularly from a tree in her own compound. I did not think up to that moment that my mother was a fighter. There was pressure to punish my mother, though it did not go anywhere in the end. Looking back, one can appreciate the fact that she had won a battle for Christianity, women's rights, and freedom.

The most powerful memories of my father are the ones of him working as a catechist and a teacher. He read constantly and had a small library. My father also had a number of collages and maps hanging on the walls, and books that he encouraged his children to read. He would often walk us through the house telling stories linked to each prized possession. It was from him that I was exposed to the magic in the mere title of William Shakespeare's *A Midsummer Night's Dream* and to an Igbo translation of John Bunyan's *The Pilgrim's Progress*.

The Bible played an important role in my education. My parents often read passages out loud to us during prayer time and encouraged us, when we were all able, to read and memorize several passages. Sunday school continued this tradition of Christian evangelical education, this time with several other children from the village. Education was so important to my father that he often would sponsor a bright child from an under-privileged background, reminding us that he too, as an orphan, had received providence's benefaction.

The center of our family's activities was St. Philip's Church, Ogidi, a large Gothic-style parish church that my father helped establish. It was constructed on an impressive, open *ilo*, or piece of open grass, on the outskirts of Ogidi. It was an imposing structure for its time, built with wood, cement, mud, and stone. Local lore holds that my father took part in the building of the church from its foundations. My father also helped conduct Sunday service, translate sermons into Igbo, and arrange the sanctuary and vestry. I remember waking up early to help out, carrying his bag for him as we set out at cock crow for the parish church.

Eucharist on Sundays often lasted more than two hours. For those who were not asleep by the end of the proceedings, the fire and brimstone sermons from the pulpit made attendance worthwhile. There was an occasional outburst of uncontrollable laughter, when the rector, an Englishman, enthusiastically drank all the remaining wine at the end of communion, wiping his mouth with the back of his hand. A crowd favorite was the inaccurate translations of Igbo words into English, such as the word *ike*, which is an Igbo word that can mean "strength" or "buttocks" depending on the skill or mischief of the translator!

I can say that my whole artistic career was probably sparked by this tension between the Christian religion of my parents, which we followed in our home, and the retreating, older religion of my ancestors, which fortunately for me was still active outside my home. I still had access to a number of relatives who had not converted to Christianity and were called heathens by the new converts. When my parents were not watching I would often sneak off in the evenings to visit some of these relatives. They seemed so very content in their traditional way of life and worship. Why would they refuse to become Christians, like everyone else around them? I was intent on finding out.

My great-uncle, Udoh Osinyi, was able to bestride both worlds with great comfort. He held one of the highest titles in all of Igbo land—*ozo*. I was very interested in my great-uncle's religion, and talking to him was an enriching experience. I wouldn't give up anything for that, including my own narrow, if you like, Christian background.

In Igbo cosmology there are many gods. A person could be in good stead with one god and not the other—*ogwugwu* could kill a person despite an excellent relationship with *udo*. As a young person that sort of complexity meant little to me. A later understanding would reveal the humility of the traditional religion with greater clarity. Igbo sayings and proverbs are far more valuable to me as a human being in understanding the complexity of the world than the doctrinaire, self-righteous strain of the Christian faith I was taught. This other religion is also far more artistically satisfying to me. However, as a catechist's son I had to suppress this interest in our traditions to some extent, at least the religious component. We were church people after all, helping the local church spread Christianity.

The relationship between my father and his uncle Udoh was instructive to me. There was something deep and mystical about it, judging from the reverence I heard in my father's voice whenever he spoke about his old uncle.

My father was a man of few words, and I have always regretted that I did not ask him more questions. But he took pains to tell me what he thought I needed to know. He told me, for instance, in a rather oblique way of his one attempt to convert his uncle Udoh. It must have been in my father's youthful, heady, proselytizing days! His uncle pointed to the awesome row of insignia of his three titles—*ichi ozo, ido idemili, ime omaalor*. "What shall I do to these?" he asked my father. It was an awesome question. He had essentially asked: "What do I do to who I am? What do I do to history?"

An orphan child born into adversity, heir to the commotions, barbarities, and rampant upheavals of a continent in disarray—it was not at all surprising that my father would welcome the remedy proffered by diviners and interpreters of a new word of God. But my great-uncle, a leader in his community, a moral, open-minded man, a prosperous man who had prepared such a great feast when he took the *ozo* title that his people gave him a praise name for it—was he to throw all that away because some strangers from afar had said so?

At first glance it seemed to me that my father, a deeply religious man, was not tolerant of our ancient traditions and religion. As he got older, however, I noticed that he became more openly accommodating of the old ways of doing things. By this time he had developed quite a reputation as a pious, disciplined, honest catechist. He was widely known as *onye nkuzi* ("the teacher"), and the villagers found him very trustworthy. Strangers would often drop off valuables at our house for Father's safekeeping.

Those two—my father and his uncle—formed the dialectic that I inherited. Udoh stood fast in what he knew, but he also left room for my father to seek other answers. The answer my father found in the Christian faith solved many problems, but by no means all.

As a young person my perspective of the world benefited, I think, from this dichotomy. I wasn't questioning in an intellectual way which way was right, or better. I was simply more interested in exploring the essence, the meaning, the worldview of both religions. By approaching the issues of tradition, culture, literature, and language of our ancient civilization in that manner, without judging but scrutinizing, a treasure trove of discovery was opened up to me.

I often had periods of oscillating faith as I grew older, periods of doubt, when I quietly pondered, and deeply questioned, the absolutist teachings or the interpretations of religion. I struggled with the certitude of Christianity—"I am the Way, the Truth and the Life"—not its accuracy, because as a writer one understands that there should be such latitude, but the desolation, the acerbity of its meaning, the lack of options for the outsider, the other. I believe that this question has subconsciously deeply influenced my writing. This is not peculiar or particularly unique, as many writers, from Du Bois to Camus, Sartre and Baldwin to Morrison, have also struggled with this conundrum of the outsider, the other, in other ways, in their respective locales.

My father had a lot of praise for the missionaries and their message, and so do I. I am a prime beneficiary of the education that the missionaries made a major component of their enterprise. But I have also learned a little more skepticism about them than my father had any need for. Does it matter, I ask myself, that centuries before European Christians sailed down to us in ships to deliver the Gospel and save us from darkness, other European Christians, also sailing in ships, delivered us to the transatlantic slave trade and unleashed darkness in our world?

Every generation must recognize and embrace the task it is peculiarly designed by history and by providence to perform. From where I stand now I can see the enormous value of my great-uncle, Udoh Osinyi, and his example of fidelity. I also salute my father, Isaiah Achebe, for the thirty-five years he served as a Christian evangelist and for all the benefits his work, and the work of others like him, brought to our people. My father's great gift to me was his love of education and his recognition that whether we look at one human family or we look at human society in general, growth can come only incrementally.

A Primary Exposure

I began my formal education at St. Philip's Central School, in 1936 or thereabout. The school had pupils from Ogidi and the surrounding towns. Most who attended classes there had to walk alone several miles every day to get to school. But things were simpler and safer in those days, and there was never a story of child abductions or any unsavory incidents that I can recall.

I enjoyed school a great deal and was a hardworking pupil. I remember looking forward excitedly to new lessons and information from our teachers. Occasionally we received instruction from individuals who were not on the staff of St. Philip's. One particular, humorous event stands out: On a hot and humid day during the wet season our geography teacher decided to move our entire class outside to the cool shade of a large mango tree. After setting up the blackboard he proceeded to give the class a lesson on the geography of Great Britain. The village "madman" came by, and after standing and listening to the teacher's lesson for a short while, walked up to him, snatched the chalk from his hand, wiped the blackboard, and proceeded to give us an extended lesson on Ogidi, my hometown.

Amazingly, the teacher let all this take place without incident. Looking back, it is instructive, in my estimation, that it was a so-called madman whose "clarity of perspective" first identified the incongruity of our situation: that the pupils would benefit not only from a colonial education but also by instruction about their own history and civilization.

The headmaster of St. Philip's Central School was a colorful, extraordinary Igbo man—Jonathan Obimdike Okongwu. He was also known as: *Ara eme ya eme na uno akwukwo Okongwu* or *Ara eme ya eme*, for short.[1] He was one of a handful of Nigerians who had attained the distinction of headmaster of an elementary school. His reputation as a disciplinarian sent chills down the spines of all pupils throughout the Eastern Region. St. Philip's school lore holds that he once spanked every pupil in every class in each form of the entire school in one day—and continued the very next day where he left off![2] Okongwu's unorthodox methods produced top scores on exams, which placed his students in the best boarding schools throughout West Africa, and made him one of the most sought after headmasters in the entire region.[3]

Okongwu was transferred to St. Michael's School, Aba, a well-regarded school in one of the largest commercial cities in eastern Nigeria. Chike Momah and Dr. Francis Egbuonu, who later became students at Government College, Umuahia, completed their elementary school education there. My wife, Christie Okoli, for a brief period, also attended that school. Christie recalls being the only one in her class to evade Mr. Okongwu's cane during a spelling lesson. The word that produced a score of sore bottoms was "because." For every word missed the pupil was "rewarded" with a spanking. The majority of the pupils came up with "becos, becus, or becoz." They never forgot how to spell because ever again.

Okongwu was a pillar of the Igbo community for his time. He was extensively admired for his achievements in education. It is difficult to convey just how important teachers like Okongwu, who were seriously committed to their work, were to the Igbo community, particularly as that is no longer the case today. Education, the white man's knowledge, was a collective aspiration of the entire community. It was the path to individual and family success, and headmaster Okongwu and others like him held the proverbial keys to the kingdom.

Okongwu was a generous man and sponsored a number of children in various schools in Nigeria and abroad. There is a well-known story of how he sent one of his nephews to America to study. He clearly had great expectations for his nephew. In those days, men like Okongwu, who had the means, sent family members abroad to advance their education with the hope that they would return and improve the standard of living of their family and community. Apparently this nephew did quite well and earned his PhD. Sadly, just before he returned to Nigeria, he became quite ill and died. Okongwu was devastated.[4]

The last time I saw Okongwu was at the train station in Enugu, the capital of the Eastern Region. He came there to see his son Sonny Chu Okongwu off to Government College, Umuahia. He was standing, leaning on the railing with his right hand holding on to the bars. He spotted me from a distance and called me over, introduced me to his son, and asked me to "take care of Sonny at Government College." It struck me that the senior Okongwu appeared unhappy. The loss of his nephew clearly had taken a lot out of him.

Leaving Home

For a brief period I spent some time living with my older brother John, who was working at Central School, Nekede, as a teacher. My father had wanted John to follow in his footsteps and become a teacher too. John was a gifted student and successfully fulfilled that dream.

It was John who, quite wisely, thought my own education would be enhanced if I lived with him in a school environment. So I packed up my few belongings and set out with my older brother to Nekede, near the present capital of Imo state, Owerri, about forty-three miles from my ancestral home of Ogidi. That was the first year I spent away from my parents, and at the time Nekede seemed like a distant country.

John enrolled me in Central School, where I prepared for my entrance examination into Government College. The regional center for the exam was St. Michael's School, and John helped me make the trip from Nekede to Aba. Before I arrived Okongwu apparently announced to the students of St. Michael's, in Igbo: *"Onwe nwa onye Ogidi ana akpo Albert Achebe, na akwadobe inene akwukwo-a; oga ama unu nmili."* (The loose translation is: "There is a young man called Albert Achebe from Ogidi, who is coming to take the entrance examination with the students in this school. . . . [H]e will beat all of you in all subjects in the examination.") This, clearly, did not endear me to my fellow pupils at St. Michael's but piqued the interest of future longtime friends, like the brilliant Chike Momah.

Afterward I returned to Nekede for the remainder of the school year. Nekede was a treasure trove of Igbo culture. Our ancient traditions continued to fascinate me, and I sought an alternative education outside the classroom, from the local villagers. The old men in Nekede spoke respectfully about the Otamiri River and the chief deity for which it is named. The Otamiri deity is a female who, according to legend, purified the land of evil and would claim the lives of interlopers who wandered into the area for mischief. It was said that no one had ever drowned in her waters unless they had committed evil deeds or contemplated diabolical acts.

It was in Nekede that I was introduced to *mbari* and the sophistication of Igbo phenomenological thought. The Owerri Igbo, who lived near Owerri township, saw *mbari* as art engaged in the process and celebration of life. A mud house was often built with decorated walls and crowned with either corrugated metal or a thatch roof made of intricately woven palm leaves and spines. Inside, center stage on an elevated mud platform, an observer would find life-size sculptures of the constituent parts of the Owerri Igbo world: Alusi—deities—such as Otamiri and Ani, the earth goddess; and men, women, children, soldiers, animals, crops, and foreigners (mainly Europeans), all seated. The inclusion of the Europeans, a great tribute to the virtues of African tolerance and accommodation, was an example of the positive acknowledgment of strangers who had ventured into their midst. There would also be depictions from ancient mythology, as well as scourges, diseases, and other unpleasant things. The purpose of this art form was to invoke protection from the gods for the people through the celebration of the world these villagers lived in—in other words, through art as celebration.[2]

The Formative Years at Umuahia and Ibadan

It was not long after my foray into the metaphysical world of the Owerri Igbo that I was to leave my traditional classroom in the forests of Nekede for the second stage of my formal education, secondary school. There is a certain sense of mystery that I feel when I look back to those times, because things we encounter in life that leave the greatest impressions on us are usually not clear.

My elder brother John was a very brilliant man. I still say he was the most brilliant of all of us. He was very eloquent, and he would correct my spoken English. I often wondered about John. . . . How did he gain such control of the English language? John had not been to university but had received a secondary school education at Dennis Memorial Grammar School (DMGS) in Onitsha. All my brothers attended this legendary school, which had been built by the Church Mission Society—Frank had attended, John went there, and it was where Augustine was to go. The school was very imposing, with its red earth–brick, limestone-and-wood colonial architecture accentuated by Doric columns, and cathedral-height roofs. And their uniform—the dark red shirt, pants, and cap—was very impressive. DMGS was the place.

In 1944, I took a national entrance examination for the British public schools of the day, and I also was admitted to Dennis Memorial Grammar School and Government College, Umuahia. Now when

John was told that I had been admitted to both Umuahia and his alma mater, with full scholarships to both, he suggested I go to Umuahia. Though Umuahia's location was very remote, its status as a "government college," set up by the colonial government, reassured my parents. Following a period of deliberation and debate, the consensus in my family was that I go to this fairly new school in faraway Umuahia, even though we had no relatives there.

I also privately wished to go to Government College, Umuahia, because I wanted to do something different from my brothers. Umuahia, a new elite boarding school established in 1929, was rapidly developing a reputation as the Eton of the East, and I fancied receiving an education akin to the royals of England!

The Anglican Protestants of the Church Mission Society, as well as the Methodists, Baptists, and Roman Catholics, had built missionary schools throughout the South and Middle Belt of Nigeria. These new government colleges—exemplified by Government College, Umuahia, and Government College, Ibadan—were built to continue the tradition of educational excellence established by even older secondary schools, King's College and Queen's College, both in Lagos. Between these four schools—King's, Queen's, Umuahia, and Ibadan—we had some of the very best secondary schools in the British Empire. As a group, these schools were better endowed financially, had excellent amenities, and were staffed with first-rate teachers, custodians, instructors, cooks, and librarians. Of course today, under Nigerian control, these schools have fallen into disrepair, and are nothing like they were in their heyday.

Shortly after taking the national entrance examination I received a letter in the mail addressed to me explaining that I was under consideration for admission to Umuahia. That had to be the first letter I had ever received in my life.

I traveled to Umuahia to be interviewed by a former principal, a very tall and large man—I believe his name was Mr. Thorp. My interviewer first asked why I did not reply to the letter he wrote me offering me admission. I said I did not know that I was supposed to reply, and he picked up a copy of the letter and read, "Please acknowledge receipt." I did not know the meaning of that phrase, and I said to myself, "Well, I am not getting in at this point." But after a little more conversation he gave me admission to his school.

As the first day of school approached I was overtaken by a sense of excitement and trepidation. I had never been to Umuahia before my interview; in fact, I did not know of anyone who had been to Umuahia. I was to travel first by lorry to Enugu, and then by train to Umuahia.

I arrived at Umuahia railway station alone. A man and his son approached me. The man asked me whether I was going to Umudike, the village where the secondary school was located, and I replied "Yes, sah." He was going there too, with his son. They had hired two bicycles, and he suggested I ride with them. I carried his son, who was considerably smaller than I, on the handlebars of the bicycle to Umudike, which was about three and a half miles from the railway station.

As we sped off, I kept thanking this man for the help. I was completely surprised at the hospitality and warmth that greeted me on my first day in school. His son became a friend, naturally, because he was the first "Umuahian" I had met. Later that semester I would discover that this lad, who would become a renowned physician, Dr. Francis Egbuonu, had come to Umuahia from St. Michael's School, Aba. It was, coincidentally, the very same school that another very close friend of mine, Chike Momah, had attended.

The Umuahia Experience

Government College, Umuahia, was built on a sprawling, parklike campus at the fringes of a tropical forest. The grounds were dotted with large evergreen trees on well-maintained lawns and crisscrossed by hand-crafted stone pathways that were bordered by manicured hedges. The buildings—wood-framed brick-and-stucco bungalows surrounded by wide verandas—were adorned with shuttered windows and crowned with large metal roofs. The vaulted-ceiling design also enhanced ventilation and tempered the tropical heat. Most of the structures rested on elevated foundations or stilts—to protect them from floods and to keep termites, wild animals, serpents, and rodents out.

There were three dormitories at Umuahia—the Niger, Nile, and School houses. I was assigned to Niger house and once there unpacked my few belongings in my dormitory locker. In my time the school had about two hundred students, and our lives were strictly regimented, with literally every hour slated for an activity.

One of the most thrilling peculiarities of the Umuahia experience was the culture of playing cricket. Not all secondary schools in the area played the game; soccer was far more commonplace. Cricket matches were often organized between: Government College, Umuahia; King's College, Lagos; Government College, Ibadan; and a few other elite secondary schools.

Umuahia had a huge cricket field, which had a beautiful grass lawn and a clear sand pitch area with wooden wickets. It was cared for almost more carefully than grass anywhere else in the school. In the afternoons, cricket matches were packed, and the bleachers and grandstands had scarcely an empty spot.

Cricket was not a game that I knew anything about before coming to Umuahia. Over time I began to appreciate that this was a very important global sport, and that it was very popular in literally every part of the British Empire. The schoolmasters referred to the game as one for "gentlemen" and made sure Umuahia athletes played it "properly"—dressed in immaculate white shirts and trousers, gloves, knee-high pads, and helmets. I was not known for my athletic ability, but Chike Momah and Christopher Okigbo were particularly good batsmen and bowlers of the sport.

Christopher Okigbo was a very extraordinary person. He was two years below me, but Christopher was not one to allow two years to get in his way. He quickly became one of my closest friends.

He was born in Ojoto, in Anambra state, and came from a highly talented family, part of the so-called Okigbo trio of intellectual giants that included his older brother, the late legendary economist Dr. Pius Okigbo, and their cousin Professor Bede Okigbo, the renowned agronomist.[1]

Christopher was just somebody you could not ignore or suppress. He struck people because he was so energetic, and so fearless. He was somebody who would walk into a room, sit down, and start learning to play the school piano without any prior exposure. He had an innate understanding of what was required to play the instrument without the regimented, torturous, orthodox lessons. Christopher was a talented artist and a sports hero, and he had a keen mind that won him the admiration of many of the British schoolmasters. He quickly became very popular throughout Umuahia.

His reputation for mischievous exploits preceded him. I think the first time he got the attention of the entire school was when the principal, William Simpson, decided that there was a lot of food waste coming from the kitchen; in other words, it seemed we were being given too much food to eat! Simpson decided to give food not according to one's academic year—the pupils in the higher classes were given more food than those in the junior classes. Simpson felt that this practice was not a very good idea, and that it led to a waste of food. A better arrangement, he thought, was for people to be given food according to their weight. Before we knew what was happening, Christopher, who was slightly built, had talked with the dining prefect, and we noticed that he was now in the food equivalent of heavyweights, receiving more food than his classmates!

There was a strong culture of meritocracy and a very high quality of instruction at Umuahia. I quickly noticed that there were very bright boys in my class, yet there was a sense of friendly competition that pervaded our academic life. I made friends gradually at school, at first mainly with pupils I met in the dormitory, then with a number of others in the classroom, through partnerships that the class master set up for assignments and projects. Benjamin Uzochukwu became one of my closest friends at the beginning of the first semester; he later qualified as an engineer, after studying in Great Britain, and became the director of the Federal Department of Public Works in Lagos.

Ekpo Etien Inyang was another close friend. He was one of my most brilliant classmates—he became a physician—but unfortunately he later committed suicide. We had very different backgrounds, especially in terms of religion. When he arrived at Umuahia, the school officials discovered that he had not been baptized. Most of us did not ask fellow pupils whether they were baptized or not; one just assumed that if you were a Christian you would have been. But Inyang's father was not a particularly religious person. So when he became an upperclassman Inyang decided to be baptized, and after subjecting himself to the religion classes and preparation that were required, he asked me to be his godfather. So I had a godson who was the same age as me. That was quite an extraordinarily moving gesture on his part, to ask me to step in on his behalf in this capacity.

Six of us, including Inyang and me, were promoted to the second-year from the first-year class during our second term at Umuahia. Students with a record of excellent work and who were the best performers in their respective years were combined into a larger second-year class. It was an honor, but it also meant that I began to see a large majority of my contemporaries from my first-year class less often, including my close friends Ben Uzochukwu and Chike Momah.

English was the language of instruction at Government College,

Umuahia. It was at Umuahia that I first truly understood the power and importance of that unifying language. The schoolmasters, well aware that Nigeria had over 250 ethnic groups, had very carefully enrolled students from every nook and cranny of the nation, where possible. While African languages and writing should be developed, nurtured, and preserved, how else, I would wonder later, would I have been able to communicate with so many boys from different parts of the country and ethnic groups, speaking different languages, had we not been taught one language?

Many of our teachers at the time were alumni from Cambridge, the University of London, and other major British institutions of higher learning. They included A. P. L. Slater, who was fondly called "Apples" by his close associates and a few of us who were his former students. Shortly after I left Umuahia, the duo R. H. Stone, a biology instructor, and A. B. Cozens, a onetime principal of the college, arrived. Together Stone and Cozens published a very famous biology textbook called *Biology for Tropical Schools* that was used throughout Africa and beyond.

It was at Umuahia that I continued the introduction to the work of William Shakespeare that my father had first made possible, as well as to Booker T. Washington's *Up from Slavery*, Swift's *Gulliver's Travels*, Dickens's *David Copperfield*, and Stevenson's *Treasure Island*. We were blessed to have had energetic, egalitarian principals such as the Reverend Robert Fisher and W. C. Simpson, who created and encouraged, respectively, the "textbook act"—a time between 4:00 P.M. and 6:00 P.M. when all textbooks had to be put away and novels picked up and read.

Reading these books was a transforming experience, and I have written elsewhere about the influence Umuahia had in educating many of the pioneers of modern African literature—Vincent Chukwuemeka Ike, Christopher Okigbo, Elechi Amadi, I. N. C Aniebo, Chike Momah, Gabriel Okara, and later Ken Saro-Wiwa. Less often stated is the role the school played in producing leaders in the fine arts, such as Ben Enwonwu, and politics, such as Jaja Wachukwu, Nigeria's first speaker of the House of Representatives and later ambassador to the United Nations. Umuahia turned out other stars, such as Okoi Arikpo, Dr. E. M. L. Endeley, and N. U. Akpan. The school also produced respected African intellectuals such as: the agronomist Professor Bede Okigbo; the physician and First Republic Minister of Health J. O. J. Okezie; Chu Okongwu, a former minister of finance; Kelsey Harrison, a renowned professor of obstetrics; and musician and professor Laz Ekwueme, among others.

We went through the designated courses in secondary school, and the last examination that we took was the Cambridge School Certificate exam. There were four classifications of grades: A for distinction, C for credit, P for pass, and F for fail. Most pupils at Umuahia passed all their subjects. I passed my school certificate exam with five distinctions and one credit. Inyang passed with six distinctions and one credit. I narrowly graduated top of the class only because the distinctions that I got were higher in the courses that I took despite the fact that Inyang had more As in more courses. Whatever the case, I held Mr. Inyang in great esteem, especially as he had an A in literature while I had a credit.

As I was completing my secondary school education at Government College, Umuahia, the colonial government announced that it was pre-disposed to building a University College in West Africa. There was some kind of competition—would it be in the Gold Coast (present-day Ghana) or in Nigeria? So a high-powered commission under Walter Elliott was sent to survey the situation on the ground. Such was the reputation of Government College, Umuahia, that the commission paid us a visit and spent a whole weekend at our school. Most of them came to chapel service on Sunday morning, but Julian Huxley, the biologist, roamed our extensive grounds, watching exotic birds with binoculars. The Elliott Commission report led to the foundation of Nigeria's first university institution: a university college at Ibadan in a special relationship with London.

I finished secondary school and literally walked into University College, Ibadan! Well, maybe not walked in. There was a nationwide examination, and I came in first or second in the country. I won what was called a "major" scholarship.[2]

I grew up at a time when the colonial educational infrastructure celebrated hard work and high achievement, and so did our families and communities. Government College, Umuahia, was so proud of my work that they put up a big sign announcing my performance in the national entrance examination. That notice stayed on the wall for years. My family was very pleased with my school performance, from the end of primary school through to this time. No matter that I was not known for my athletic ability; they encouraged me to read voraciously, taking great pleasure in my nickname: Dictionary.

A very distinguished member of the colonial educational system—a British gentleman—who was also the chairman of some important colonial council, heard about my entrance examination result and came to our house to greet me. Now, I had never encountered such a thing before. Surely people of that distinction did not call on children? But here was this man, who was a very important person in the British educational system, who thought that my work deserved encouragement, recognition, and a visit from him. So clearly I had a good beginning.

As a young man, surrounded by all this excitement, it seemed as if the British were planning surprises for me at every turn, including the construction of a new university! It is, of course, only a joke, but I am sure many of my colleagues shared similar feelings. Here we were, a whole generation of students who really could not have had any clear idea of going to university until these events began to unfold.

It was a remarkable group—Chike Momah, Flora Nwapa, Mabel Segun, Ben Obumselu, Emmanuel Obiechina, Kelsey Harrison, Gamaliel Onosode, Wande Abimbola, Iya Abubakar, Adiele Afigbo, Igwe Aja-Nwachukwu, Theophilus Adeleke Akinyele, Grace Alele Williams,

Mohammed Bello, Elechi Amadi. A bit later Wole Soyinka, J. P. Clark, Oluwokayo Oshuntokun, M. J. C. Echeruo, Christopher Okigbo, Ayo Bamgbose, Christine Okoli (my future wife), Emeka Anyaoku, Chukwuemeka Ike, Abiola Irele, Zulu Sofola, and several others. These young men and women came from all over the country—from elite secondary schools modeled on the public schools of England—Government College, Umuahia, Dennis Memorial Grammar School, Government College, Ibadan, and Abeokuta, King's College, Lagos, and Queen's College, Lagos.

THE IBADAN EXPERIENCE

Umuahia had a large contingent of students admitted to University College, Ibadan, with a number of students winning at least minor scholarships.

I received my scholarship to study medicine at Ibadan. I wanted to be in the arts but felt pressure to choose medicine instead. After a year of work I changed to English, history, and theology, but by so doing I lost the bursary and was left with the prospect of paying tuition.

I remember what the dean of the Faculty of Arts, Professor E. A. Cadle, said to me when I went to ask to be moved from the sciences to the arts: in order to get into the arts I had to have taken a school certificate exam in Latin, which was not taught at Umuahia. I was faced with a difficult dilemma and spent some time thinking about the ramifications of taking extra courses in Latin.

But providence had other plans. Soon after my conversation with Professor Cadle an announcement came through from the University of London, our parent institution, indicating that it was dropping the Latin requirement for admission into the Faculty of Arts. The University of London argued that the native languages of students from the British Commonwealth could stand in for the Latin requirement. I was elated.

I went back and asked Professor Cadle for admission into the Arts Faculty. He brought out my file and told me that I was admitted on the basis of my performance in physics and chemistry. He wanted reassurance from me that I would be able to make such a fundamental shift in academic focus and maintain good grades. After a little more conversation, he admitted me to study English, history, and theology, and I moved from medicine to the Arts Faculty.

My older brother Augustine Achebe, an engineer by training, had returned from his studies in England and had landed a good job. On learning that I had lost my bursary, Augustine gave me money he had saved up for his annual leave so that I could pay the university tuition and continue my studies, which I did, very pleasantly.

After graduation I did not have to worry about where I would go next. The system was so well organized that as we left university most of us were instantly absorbed into civil service, academia, business, or industry. We trusted—I did, anyway—the country and its rulers to provide this preparatory education and then a job to serve my nation. I was not disappointed. I went home to my village at the end of the holiday and visited a secondary school within my district, called the Merchants of Light, in Oba, near Ogidi. I asked the principal to give me a job as an English teacher. And he did!

It helped that my colleague J. O. C. Ezeilo had completed a short tenure at the same school and recommended it to me. Ezeilo is often described as Nigeria's leading mathematician, alongside Chike Obi. Ezeilo graduated from University of London in 1953, with a first class honors in mathematics, an amazing feat by any measure, and particularly extraordinary for the time. He would go on to receive his PhD from Queens' College, University of Cambridge, in 1958, and then rise rapidly through the Nigerian academic ranks to become vice chancellor of the University of Nigeria, Nsukka, and several other Nigerian institutions of higher learning.[3]

Meeting Christie and Her Family

The school building at Merchants of Light was in disrepair and had a very small library. I would often encourage my students to read by bringing in a copy of the newspaper or by making a few more books from my own library available to them. Like most young people, they were enthusiastic and interested pupils. I spent about four months at this job. It was known to all that this would be a temporary position, what the Americans call "a summer job," because I had my eyes farther afield.

A few months later, in 1954, I was notified of a job opening at what was then called the Nigerian Broadcasting Service (NBS) in Enugu. I was offered a choice by the search committee of coming to Enugu to interview or having them come to me. I remember feeling quite entitled by this choice and proceeded to enjoy the privilege by asking them to come to me, which they did. The team of mainly Britons left to return to Enugu after an hour or so of interview questions. About a week or so later I received a letter in the mail offering me a job, so I moved to Enugu. I enjoyed my stint at the broadcasting house. Promotions came rapidly, and within a very short period of time I had become the controller of the Nigerian Broadcasting Service, Eastern Region.

At the end of the academic year, during the long vacation, the NBS offered summer jobs to college students on vacation. They did not pay very well but provided young people with exposure to the world of journalism, broadcasting, and news reporting.

NBS was inundated with a large number of applicants during this particular long vacation—not only students from my alma mater, University College, Ibadan, but from those returning from studies abroad. A few weeks later one could hear the unmistakable banter of young people as they milled about the normally quiet halls of the Nigerian Broadcasting Service. As the controller I had very little interaction with the students. I found all this excited commotion amusing and got on with my work.

But soon after I was told by my secretary that a delegation of university students wanted to speak with me about a matter of great importance. The students trooped into my office led by their leader, Christie Okoli. She was a beautiful young woman and very articulate, and when she spoke she caught my attention. I was spellbound. In grave tones she announced the complaint of the students: There was one student whose salary was higher than all the others, and they wanted "equal pay for equal time." I was kindly disposed toward them and made sure that all of the students received the same remuneration for the work that they did.

My interest in Christie grew rapidly into a desire to get to know her better. I discovered, for instance, that she was from the ancient town of Awka, the present-day capital of Anambra state. Awka held a soft spot in my heart because it was my mother's hometown, and it was known throughout Igbo land and beyond for its skilled artisans and blacksmiths, who fashioned bronze, wood, and metal carvings of a bold and haunting beauty.

Two years into our friendship, Christie and I were engaged.

Christie was from a very prominent Awka family. She was the daughter of one of the most formidable Igbo men of the early twentieth century, Timothy Chukwukadibia Okoli, and Mgboye Matilda Mmuo, who unfortunately died not long after Christie was born.

"T. C. Okoli," as he was widely known, was the son of a famous *dibia*, or traditional medicine man, known from Arochukwu to Nri and from Onitsha to Ogoja for skills that encompassed herbal medicine, mysticism, divination, and magic. After a lifetime in the service of the ancient medical practice, Okoli gave his son the name Chukwukadibia, which means "God is greater than a traditional medicine man." He encouraged his newborn son to seek a Christian life.

An early convert to Christianity in Igbo land, T. C. Okoli was one of the few educated men of his time to attain the position of senior post-master in the colonial Posts and Telecommunications (P&T) Department. He was a profoundly generous man, and used his resources—which were quite outstanding for a Nigerian at that time—to sponsor the education of gifted children from scores of families in Awka. When he died at 102, in the mid-1980s, all thirteen villages of the town celebrated his life for several days, through both traditional and Christian rites and festivities.

Meeting Christie's father for the first time was a great thrill for me. His compound in Awka was always full of laughter. People visited constantly, some to drink and make merry, others for favors and to pay their respects. I belonged to the latter category.

We arrived, and Christie promptly took me to meet her dad.

"Papa" she said, "meet Chinua Achebe."

We shook hands, and then the pleasantries gave way to a brief interview: "Where are you from, young man?" "What do you do?" "Where did you go to school?" "Who are your parents?" I quickly discovered that T. C. Okoli was an Anglophile: He took pleasure in reciting passages in English from scripture, Shakespeare, and poetry; and he had sent several of his children off to England to advance their education. He was also a deeply respectful and kind man who left me with a lasting lesson that I have never forgotten.

Christie and I were talking one evening when Okoli walked into the living room. We exchanged greetings. He sat down and listened to our conversation while sipping wine, watching the two of us talk. By this time I could say confidently that he liked me. We got along very well. But in the course of the conversation he missed something Christie said and asked for clarification. At this prompting I responded by saying jestfully

in Igbo: "*Rapia ka ona aghaigha agba*," or in English, "Don't mind her . . .
wagging her jaw. . . ."

T. C. Okoli sat up and rebuked me. He said: "Don't say or imply that
what someone else has to say or is saying is not worth attending or listening to." It immediately struck me that I had to be careful about the way I
handled someone else's words or opinions, especially Christie's. Even
when there was strong disagreement, one had to remember to be discor-
dant with respect.

Discovering *Things Fall Apart*

Soon after this educational encounter with my future father-in-law I
moved to Lagos to interview for a new position at the headquarters of
what was now called the Nigerian Broadcasting Corporation (NBC). The
Talks Department hired me to maul over scripts and prepare them for
broadcast. A tedious job, it nevertheless honed my skill for writing realistic dialogue, a gift that I gratefully tapped into when writing my novels.

In my second or third year at University College, Ibadan, I had
offered two short stories, "Polar Undergraduate" and "Marriage Is a Private Affair," to the *University Herald*, the campus magazine. They were
accepted and published. I published other stories during that time,
including "The Old Order in Conflict with the New" and "Dead Men's
Path." In my third year I was invited to join the editorial committee of
the journal. A bit later I became the magazine's editor.

At the University College, Ibadan, I was in contact with instructors
of literature, of religion, and of history who had spent several years teaching in England. Studying religion was new to me and interesting because
the focus went beyond Christian theology to encompass wider
scholarship—West African religions. One of my professors in the Department of Religion, Dr. Parrinder, was a pioneer in the area. He had done

extensive research in West African religions and cosmology, particularly in Dahomey, present-day Republic of Benin. For the first time I was able to see the systems—including my own—compared and placed side by side, which was really exciting. I also encountered another professor, James Welch, in that department, an extraordinary man, who had been chaplain to King George VI, chaplain to the BBC, and all kinds of high-powered things before he came to University College, Ibadan.

My professors were excellent people and excellent teachers, but they were not always the ones I needed. James Welch said to me, "We may not be able to teach you what you need or what you want. We can only teach you what we know." I thought that was wonderful. Welch helped me understand that they were not sent there to translate their knowledge to me in a way that would help me channel my creative energies to tell my story of Africa, my story of Nigeria, the story of myself. I learned, if I may put it simply, that my story had to come from within me. Finding that inner creative spark required introspection, deep personal scrutiny, and connection, and this was not something anybody could really teach me.[1]

I have written elsewhere of how I fared when I entered a short story competition in the Department of English, and how my teacher, who supervised this competition, announced the result, which was that nobody who entered the competition was good enough. I was more or less singled out as someone with some promise, but the story I submitted lacked "form." Understandably, I wanted to find out more about what the professor meant by form. It seemed to me that here was some secret competence that I needed to be taught. But when I then applied some pressure on this professor to explain to me what form was, it was clear that she was not prepared—that she could not explain it to me. And it dawned on me that despite her excellent mind and background, she was not capable of teaching across cultures, from her English culture to mine.

It was in these circumstances that I was moved to put down on paper the story that became *Things Fall Apart*. I was conscripted by the story, and I was writing it at all times—whenever there was any opening. It felt like a sentence, an imprisonment of creativity. Through it all I did not neglect the employment for which I earned a salary. Additional promotions came at NBC, and very swiftly, particularly after most of the British returned to England; I was appointed director of external broadcasting.

I worked on my writing mostly at night. I was seized by the story and I found myself totally ensconced in it. It was almost like living in a parallel realm, a dual existence not in any negative sense but in the way a hand has two surfaces, united in purpose but very different in tone, appearance, character, and structure. I had in essence discovered the writer's life, one that exists in the world of the pages of his or her story and then seamlessly steps into the realities of everyday life.

The scribbling finally grew into a manuscript. I wanted to have not just a good manuscript but a good-looking manuscript, because it seemed to me that that would help to draw readers' and publishers' attention to the work. So I decided, on the strength of a recommendation of an advertisement in a British magazine or journal that described a company's ability to transform a manuscript through typing into an attractive document, to send it off for "polishing."

What I did next, in retrospect, was quite naïve, even foolish. I put my handwritten documents together, went to the post office, and had them parcel the only copy of the manuscript I had to the London address of the highly recommended typing agency that was in the business of manuscript preparation. A letter came from this agency after a few weeks. They confirmed that they had received my document and wrote that the next thing I should do was send them thirty-two pounds, which was the cost of producing my manuscript. Now, thirty-two pounds was a lot of money in 1956, and a significant slice of my salary, but I was encouraged by the fact that I had received this information, this feedback, and that the people sounded as if they were going to be of great value to me. So, I sent off the payment as instructed.

What happened next was a near catastrophe. The typing agency, obviously having received the money I sent, went silent. One week passed, then two, three, four, five, six weeks, and I began to panic. I wrote two letters inquiring about the status of the manuscript preparation and I got no answer.

One had a great deal of confidence and faith in the British system that we had grown up in, a confidence and faith in British institutions. One trusted that things would get where they were sent; postal theft, tampering, or loss of documents were unheard-of. Today one would not even contemplate sending off materials of importance so readily, either abroad or even locally, by mail.

The good luck was that at that point in my career I was working very closely with a British former BBC Talks producer, Angela Beattie. Beattie was seconded to the Nigerian Broadcasting Corporation, for which she served as head of our two-person department. She was the head of Talks and I was the Talks producer, and we had a secretary, I believe, also from the BBC. It was to Beattie that I now went to and told my story about the British typing agency. Ms. Angela Beattie was shocked—she was a no-nonsense person.

"Give me their name and address," she insisted.

Fortunately, she was about to go to England on leave, so she became the perfect vehicle to carry my anguish to the typists in London. And she did it in her distinctive way.

She arrived at the offices of the typing agency and asked to speak to the manager, who showed up swiftly. Angela Beattie asked the manager sternly what she had done with the manuscript that her colleague in Lagos, Nigeria, had sent. Here, right before them, armed with a threat, was a well-connected woman who could really make trouble for them.

The people there were surprised and shaken. "Now, I am going back to Nigeria in three weeks," Angela Beattie said as she left the agency's office, "and when I get there, let us hope that the manuscript you took money to prepare has been received by its owner, or else you will hear more about it." A few weeks later I received a handsome package in the mail. It was my manuscript. I look back now at those events and state categorically that had the manuscript been lost I most certainly would have been irreversibly discouraged from continuing my writing career.

Later that year, in the fall of 1956 or thereabouts, I was selected to travel to the British Broadcasting Corporation school in London where its staff were trained. Bisi Onabanjo, a good friend of mine and the future governor of Ogun state, was also among the small group of Nigerians attending this course. I had not up to this time traveled outside Nigeria. In those days such trips were done by boat, as commercial air flights from Lagos were not commonplace. London was a brand-new and pleasant experience. I took advanced technical production skills courses during my time at the BBC staff school, and in between my classes was able to take in the sights and sounds of London, a city that remains one of my favorite international capitals.

I took along my typed manuscript, hoping to bump into a number of writers and publishers who could provide me with some advice about how best to get the book published. I was fortunate to meet and make the acquaintance of Gilbert Phelps, a British writer, who read the manuscript and was quite enthusiastic about its literary merit and prospects for publication. When Mr. Phelps kindly suggested that I hand over the manuscript to him to pass on to some publishers he knew; I hesitated and told him that I needed some more time to work on the novel. I was still wondering whether to publish it in three parts or divide the work into three separate books.[2]

About a year later I wrote Gilbert Phelps and informed him that my novel, *Things Fall Apart*, was ready, and he happily sent the manuscript off to a number of publishers. There were several of instant rejections. Some did not even bother to read it, jaundiced by their impression that a book with an African backdrop had no "marketability." Some of the responders found the very concept of an African novel amusing. The book's fortunes changed when it got into the hands of Alan Hill and Donald McRae, executives of Heinemann. McRae had extensive experience traveling throughout Africa and encouraged Heinemann to publish the novel with a powerful recommendation: "This is the best first novel I have read since the war."[3]

It was under Alan Hill's guidance that *Things Fall Apart* received immediate and consistent support. The initial publication run from Heinemann was two thousand hardcover copies. *Things Fall Apart* got some of its earliest endorsements and positive reviews from Canada, where critics such as G. D. Killam and the novelist Jean Margaret Laurence embraced it. Later the postcolonial literary critics Bill Ashcroft, Gareth Griffiths, and Helen Tiffin helped introduce the book into the Australian and British literary establishments. Michael Thelwell, Bernth Lindfors, Priscilla Tyler, Charles Larson, and Catherine Lynnette Innes were some of the first intellectuals in America to pick up the novel and present it to an American audience.

In England the book received positive reviews from the *Observer, Time and Tide*, and *The Times Literary Supplement*, among other publications. But not all the reviews were as kind or positive. Some failed to understand "the point of African Literature" and what I and others were trying to achieve by telling our own stories. It did the work a great deal of good, however, that the distinguished novelist Angus Wilson and the well-respected literary critic Walter Allen wrote positively about my first novel.

In Nigeria there was a mixed bag of responses. Some of my old teachers at Ibadan found the idea of my publishing a novel "charming," but many African intellectuals saw both literary and political merit in the work.

When I wrote *Things Fall Apart* I began to understand and value my traditional Igbo history even more. I am not suggesting that I was an expert in the history of the world. I was a very young man. I knew I had a story, but how it fit into the story of the world—I really had no sense of that. After a while I began to understand why the book had resonance. Its meaning for my Igbo people was clear to me, but I didn't know how other people elsewhere would respond to it. Did it have any meaning or relevance for them? I realized that it did when, to give just one example, the whole class of a girls' college in South Korea wrote to me, and each one expressed an opinion about the book. And then I learned something: They had a history that was similar to the story of *Things Fall Apart*—the history of colonization. This I didn't know before. Their colonizer was Japan. So these people across the waters were able to relate to the story of dispossession in Africa. People from different parts of the world can respond to the same story if it says something to them about their own history and their own experience.[4]

A Lucky Generation

It has often been said that my generation was a very lucky one. And I agree. My luck was actually quite extraordinary. And it began quite early. The pace of change in Nigeria from the 1940s was incredible. I am not just talking about the rate of development, with villages transforming into towns, or the coming of modern comforts, such as electricity or running water or modes of transportation, but more of a sense that we were standing figuratively and literally at the dawn of a new era.

My generation was summoned, as it were, to bear witness to two remarkable transitions—the first the aforementioned impressive economic, social, and political transformation of Nigeria into a midrange country, at least by third world standards. But, more profoundly, barely two decades later we were thrust into the throes of perhaps Nigeria's greatest twentieth-century moment—our elevation from a colonized country to an independent nation.

The March to Independence

The general feeling in the air as independence approached was extraordinary, like the building anticipation of the relief of torrential rains after a season of scorching hot Harmattan winds and bush fires. We were all looking forward to feeling the joy that India—the great jewel of the British Empire—must have felt in 1948, the joy that Ghana must have felt years later, in 1957.

We had no doubt where we were going. We were going to inherit freedom—that was all that mattered. The possibilities for us were endless, at least so it seemed at the time. Nigeria was enveloped by a certain assurance of an unbridled destiny, of an overwhelming excitement about life's promise, unburdened by any knowledge of providence's intended destination.

Ghana was a particularly relevant example for us subjects in the remaining colonies and dominions of the British Empire. There was a growing confidence, not just a feeling, that we would do just as well parting ways with Her Majesty's empire. If Ghana seemed more effective, as some of our people like to say, perhaps it was because she was smaller in size and neat, as if it was tied together more delicately by well-groomed, expert hands.

So we had in 1957 an extraordinary event. I remember it vividly. It was not a Nigerian event. Ghana is three hundred or more miles away from us, but we saw her success as ours as well. I remember celebrating with Ghanaian and Nigerian friends in Lagos all night on the eve of Ghana's independence from Britain, ecstatic for our fellow Africans, only to wake up the next morning to find that we were still in Nigeria. Ghana had made it, leaving us all behind. But our day came, finally, three years after hers.

Now let it be said: There was a subtle competition between the two countries. There was a sense in which one could say that Ghana and Nigeria resented each other and competed for supremacy in every sphere—politics, academia, sports, you name it. It is possible that Nigerians were less accurate in thinking of our "rival neighbor" as being perhaps "too small to matter." Of course Ghanaians came right back by saying that "Nigeria is bigger than Ghana in the way in which threepence was bigger than sixpence." If one were to look at the various denominations of coins in those days, one would discover that threepence was very huge, much larger than sixpence, and the quality of metal used in making the smaller denomination was clearly of inferior value and had less purchasing power in the marketplace, where it mattered most. So the relationship between Ghana and Nigeria has always been very important. Ghanaian nationalists were heavily influenced by their Nigerian counterparts.

The father of African independence was Nnamdi Azikiwe. There is no question at all about that. Azikiwe, fondly referred to by his admirers as "Zik," was the preeminent political figure of my youth[1] and a man who was endowed with the political pan-Africanist vision. He had help, no doubt, from several eminent sons and daughters of the soil.

When Azikiwe came back from his university studies in the United States of America, in 1934 or thereabout, he did not return to Onitsha, his hometown. He settled at first in Accra, in the Gold Coast (present-day Ghana), where he worked as the editor of the *African Morning Post*, a new daily newspaper. There were stories of inter-ethnic friction in the Gold Coast, so he moved to Lagos. Despite initial problems in Ghana,

Azikiwe had acquired admirers, especially young aspiring freedom fighters, including Kwame Nkrumah, the greatest of them all. Nkrumah was still a student in Ghana, but he was motivated to go to America to study largely as a result of Azikiwe's influence. Zik opened the historically black college in the United States that he attended—Lincoln University—to other West Africans and Nigerians. Quite a number of young Africans who left the country for America did so because of Azikiwe. It didn't hurt that Azikiwe wrote glowingly about America in his newspaper articles on almost a daily basis. America, you see, seemed to a number of those young people to provide an escape from the chains of colonialism.[2]

Soon after Azikiwe arrived in Lagos he established his own paper, *The West African Pilot*. At this time there were two or three families of newspapers: Azikiwe's and an even older group from Freetown, Sierra Leone; *The Accra Herald* from the Gold Coast; *The Anglo African*; *Iwe Ihorin* (a prominent Yoruba newspaper) in Lagos; and Herbert Macauley's *The Daily News*. These newspapers had different traditions. There used to be a joke about the quality of newspapers that were founded by aristocratic Lagosians.[3] Some of these papers went out of their way to be highbrow; it was said that occasionally large chunks of the editorials of some were written in Latin.

In contrast to his competition Azikiwe's newspaper was written in accessible, stripped-down English—the type of prose educated members of society often snickered at. And that was Azikiwe's intention, to speak directly to the masses. His strategy was an incredible success. *The West African Pilot*'s anticolonial message was spread very quickly, widely, and effectively. From the time of its establishment through the 1940s and 1950s, *The West African Pilot* was the most influential publication of its type throughout British West Africa—from Sierra Leone through Ghana to Nigeria.

Azikiwe wanted to remain financially autonomous from the British, so he established the African Continental Bank in 1944 and invited wealthy and influential Nigerians such as Sir Louis Odumegwu Ojukwu to join the board. Azikiwe also started newspaper outposts in Lagos, Ibadan, Kano, Port Harcourt, and the market town of Onitsha. I remember in particular that traders in Onitsha and other markets throughout Nigeria relished *The West African Pilot*'s daily political analysis and editorials. Many learned to read with the help of *The Pilot*. The traders, in their eagerness to read Azikiwe's paper, often ignored early-morning customers who visted their stalls.

The West African Pilot served other purposes. It became the nurturing ground for top journalistic and future political talent. Anthony Enahoro, who became the paper's editor, and Akinola Lasekan, the legendary political cartoonist, are just two examples that come to mind. *The West African Pilot* enjoyed an exponential level of commercial as well as critical success after it supported striking Nigerian workers against the British government in the 1940s. Its circulation was in the tens of thousands. That was an outstanding achievement for its time.[4]

The Cradle of Nigerian Nationalism

Here is a piece of heresy: The British governed their colony of Nigeria with considerable care. There was a very highly competent cadre of government officials imbued with a high level of knowledge of how to run a country. This was not something that the British achieved only in Nigeria; they were able to manage this on a bigger scale in India and Australia. The British had the experience of governing and doing it competently. I am not justifying colonialism. But it is important to face the fact that British colonies, more or less, were expertly run.

There was a distinct order during this time. I recall the day I traveled

from Lagos to Ibadan and stayed with Christopher Okigbo that evening.
I took off again the next morning, driving alone, going all the way from
Lagos to Asaba, crossing the River Niger, to visit my relatives in the east.
That was how it was done in those days. One was not consumed by fear
of abduction or armed robbery. There was a certain preparation that the
British had undertaken in her colonies. So as the handover time came, it
was done with great precision.

As we praise the British, let us also remember the Nigerian
nationalists—those who had a burning desire for independence and
fought for it. There was a body of young and old people that my parents'
generation admired greatly, and that we later learned about and deeply
appreciated. Herbert Macauley, for instance, often referred to as "the
father of Nigerian nationalism,"[1] was a very distinguished Nigerian born
during the nineteenth century and the first president of the Nigerian
National Democratic Party (NNDP), which was founded in 1922.[2]

The dawn of World War II caused a bit of a lull in the organized independence struggles that had been centered mainly in the Western Region
of the country up to that time. Across the River Niger, in Eastern Nigeria, I was entering my teenage years, bright-eyed and beginning to grapple with my colonial environment. At this time most of the world's
attention, including Nigeria's, was turned to the war. Schools and other
institutions were converted into makeshift camps for soldiers from the
empire, and there was a great deal of local military recruitment. A number of my relatives quickly volunteered their services to His Majesty's
regiments. The colonies became increasingly important to Great Britain's war effort by providing a steady stream of revenue from the export
of agricultural products—palm oil, groundnuts, cocoa, rubber, etc. I
remember hearing stories of valiant fighting by a number of African soldiers in faraway places, such as Abyssinia (today's Ethiopia), North
Africa, and Burma (today's Myanmar).[3]

The postwar era saw an explosion of political organization.

Newspapers, newsreels, and radio programs were full of the exploits of Nnamdi Azikiwe and the National Council of Nigeria and the Cameroons (NCNC, which later became the National Council of Nigerian Citizens) that was founded in 1944. Azikiwe built upon lessons he had learned from earlier forays in political activism and successfully persuaded several active members of the Nigerian Youth Movement to form an umbrella group of all the major Nigerian organizations.

By the time I became a young adult, Obafemi Awolowo had emerged as one of Nigeria's dominant political figures. He was an erudite and accomplished lawyer who had been educated at the University of London. When he returned to the Nigerian political scene from England in 1947, Awolowo found the once powerful political establishment of western Nigeria in disarray—sidetracked by partisan and intra-ethnic squabbles. Chief Awolowo and close associates reunited his ancient Yoruba people with powerful glue—resuscitated ethnic pride—and created a political party, the Action Group, in 1951, from an amalgamation of the Egbe Omo Oduduwa, the Nigerian Produce Traders' Association, and a few other factions.[4]

Over the years Awolowo had become increasingly concerned about what he saw as the domination of the NCNC by the Igbo elite, led by Azikiwe. Some cynics believe the formation of the Action Group was not influenced by tribal loyalties but a purely tactical political move to regain regional and southern political power and influence from the dominant NCNC.

Initially Chief Obafemi Awolowo struggled to woo support from the Ibadan-based (and other non-Ijebu) Yoruba leaders who considered him a radical and a bit of an upstart. However, despite some initial difficulty, Awolowo transformed the Action Group into a formidable, highly disciplined political machine that often outperformed the NCNC in regional elections. It did so by meticulously galvanizing political support in Yoruba land and among the riverine and minority groups in the Niger

Delta who shared a similar dread of the prospects of Igbo political domination.[5]

When Sir Ahmadu Bello, the Sardauna of Sokoto,[6] decided to create the Northern People's Congress (NPC) in the late 1940s, he knew that the educationally disadvantaged North did not have as rich a source of Western-educated politicians to choose from as the South did. He overcame this "shortcoming" by pulling together an assortment of leaders from the Islamic territories under his influence and a few Western-educated intellectuals—the most prominent in my opinion being Aminu Kano and Alhaji Tafewa Balewa, Nigeria's first prime minister. Frustrated by what he saw as "Ahmadu Bello's limited political vision,"[7] the incomparable Aminu Kano, under whom I would serve as the deputy national president of the Peoples Redemption Party decades later, would leave the NPC in 1950 to form the left-of-center political party, the Northern Elements Progressive Union (NEPU).[8]

Sir Ahmadu Bello was a schoolteacher by training. He was a contentious and ardently ambitious figure who claimed direct lineage from one of the founders of the Islamic Sokoto Caliphate—Shehu Usman dan Fodio. It was also widely known that he had "aspired to the throne of the Sultan of Sokoto." By midcentury, through brilliant political maneuvering among the northern ruling classes, Sir Ahmadu Bello emerged as the most powerful politician in the Northern Region, indeed in all of Nigeria.

Sir Ahmadu Bello was able to control northern Nigeria politically by feeding on the fears of the ruling emirs and a small elite group of Western-educated northerners. His ever-effective mantra was that in order to protect the mainly feudal North's hegemonic interests it was critical to form a political party capable of resisting the growing power of Southern politicians.

Ahmadu Bello and his henchmen shared little in terms of ideological or political aspirations with their southern counterparts. With the South split between Azikiwe's National Council of Nigerian Citizens (NCNC) and Awolowo's Action Group, his ability to hold the North together meant that the NPC in essence became Nigeria's ruling party. A testament to its success is the fact that the NPC later would not only hold the majority of seats in the post-independence parliament, but as a consequence would be called upon to name the first prime minister of Nigeria.[9]

The minorities of the Niger Delta, Mid-West, and the Middle Belt regions of Nigeria were always uncomfortable with the notion that they had to fit into the tripod of the largest ethnic groups that was Nigeria—Hausa/Fulani, Yoruba, and Igbo. Many of them—Ijaw, Kanuri, Ibibio, Tiv, Itsekiri, Isang, Urhobo, Anang, and Efik—were from ancient nation-states in their own right. Their leaders, however, often had to subsume their own ethnic ambitions within alliances with one of the big three groups in order to attain greater political results.

The British were well aware of the inter-ethnic tensions and posturing for power among the three main ethnic groups. By 1951 they had divided the country into the Northern, Eastern, and Western Regions, with their own respective houses of assembly, to contain this rising threat.[10] There was also what many thought was an inane house of chiefs—a poor copy of the House of Lords of the British Parliament. Clear-eyed pundits saw this mainly as a political ploy to appease the Northerners and Westerners who wanted their traditional rulers to play a greater role in Nigerian affairs.

Initially the British resisted any agitations for independence, often by handing out stiff jail terms for "sedition" to the "disturbers of the peace." They knew the value of their colonies, and the natural resources they possessed—in Nigeria's case oil, coal, gold, tin, columbite, cocoa, palm oil, groundnuts, and rubber, as well as the immense human resources and intellectual capital. Surely Great Britain had no plans to hand all these riches over without a fight.

Over time, however, it became clear to the colonizers that they were engaged in a losing battle. By the end of World War II Great Britain was financially and politically exhausted. This weakness was exploited by Mohandas Gandhi and his cohorts in India during their own struggle against British rule. Nigerian veterans from different theaters of the war had acquired certain skills—important military expertise in organization, movement, strategy, and combat—during their service to the king. Another proficiency that came naturally to this group was the skill of protest, which was quickly absorbed by the Nigerian nationalists.

Post-Independence Nigeria

By the late 1950s the British were rapidly accepting the inevitability of independence coming to one of their major colonies, Nigeria. Officers began to retire and return home to England, vacating their positions in Nigeria's colonial government. They left in droves, quietly, amiably, often at night, mainly on ships, but also, particularly the wealthier ones, on planes. The British clearly had a well-thought-out exit strategy, with handover plans in place long before we noticed.

Literally all government ministries, public and privately held firms, corporations, organizations, and schools saw the majority of their expatriate staff leave. Not everyone left, however; some, particularly in the commercial sector and the oil businesses, stayed. The civilized behavior of their brethren made this an acceptable development.

While this quiet transition was happening a number of internal jobs, especially the senior management positions, began to open up for Nigerians, particularly for those with a university education. It was into these positions vacated by the British that a number of people like myself were placed—a daunting, exhilarating inheritance that was not without its anxieties. Most of us felt well prepared, because we had received an out-standing education. This is not to say that there were not those racked with doubt, and sometimes outright dread. There were. But most of us were ready to take destiny in our own hands, and for a while at least, it worked quite well.

This "bequest" was much greater than just stepping into jobs left behind by the British. Members of my generation also moved into homes in the former British quarters previously occupied by members of the European senior civil service. These homes often came with servants—chauffeurs, maids, cooks, gardeners, stewards—whom the British had organized meticulously to "ease their colonial sojourn." Now following the departure of the Europeans, many domestic staff stayed in the same positions and were only too grateful to continue their designated salaried roles in post-independence Nigeria. Their masters were no longer European but their own brothers and sisters. This bequest continued in the form of new club memberships and access to previously all-white areas of town, restaurants, and theaters.

This account about the handover of power I have just provided is perhaps too wonderful to be absolutely true. History teaches us that people who have been oppressed—this is the language of the freedom fight, and it was a fight—are often too ready to let bygones be bygones. Clearly it was more complicated than that; it was a long struggle. Having said that, I think most who were there would admit that when the moment came, it was handled quite well.

One example that I will give to illustrate the complexity of that moment of transition occurred at the very highest level of government. When Britain decided to hand over power to Nigeria, they also decided to change the governor general. They brought a new governor general from the Sudan, Sir James Robertson, to take the reins in Nigeria. Now

that Independence Day was approaching a number of onlookers were
wondering why there was a new posting from Britain, and no provision
made for a Nigerian successor. It became clear that Sir James was going
to be there on Independence Day and, as it turned out, wanted to stay on
as governor general for a whole year into the period of freedom. One
wondered how he was going to leave. Would it be in disgrace? Would he
be hiding, or something of the sort?

It is now widely known that Sir James Robertson played an important
role in overseeing the elections (or lack thereof) at independence, throw-
ing his weight behind Abubakar Tafawa Balewa, who had been tapped to
become Nigeria's first prime minister.

I remember hearing Azikiwe comment years later on those events.
He was asked in a small gathering: "Why did Sir James Robertson not go
home, like the other people who were leaving?"

Azikiwe made light of the question: "Well, when he told me that he
was going to stay on, I said to him, Go on, stay as long as you like." The
laughter that followed did not obscure the greater meaning of his
statement.

Later it was discovered that a courageous English junior civil servant
named Harold Smith had been selected by no other than Sir James Robertson to oversee the rigging of Nigeria's first election "so that its compliant friends in [Northern Nigeria] would win power, dominate the
country, and serve British interests after independence." Despite the
enticements of riches and bribes (even a knighthood, we are told), Smith
refused to be part of this elaborate hoax to fix Nigeria's elections, and he
swiftly became one of the casualties of this mischief. Smith's decision
was a bold choice that cost him his job, career, and reputation (at least
until recently).[1]

In a sense, Nigerian independence came with a British governor general in command, and, one might say, popular faith in genuine democracy was compromised from its birth.

The Decline

Within six years of this tragic colonial manipulation Nigeria was a cesspool of corruption and misrule. Public servants helped themselves freely to the nation's wealth. Elections were blatantly rigged. The subsequent national census was outrageously stage-managed; judges and magistrates were manipulated by the politicians in power. The politicians themselves were pawns of foreign business interests.[1]

The social malaise in Nigerian society was political corruption. The structure of the country was such that there was an inbuilt power struggle among the ethnic groups, and of course those who were in power wanted to stay in power. The easiest and simplest way to retain it, even in a limited area, was to appeal to tribal sentiments, so they were egregiously exploited in the 1950s and 1960s.

The original idea of one Nigeria was pressed by the leaders and intellectuals from the Eastern Region. With all their shortcomings, they had this idea to build the country as one. The first to object were the Northerners, led by the Sardauna, who were followed closely by the Awolowo clique that had created the Action Group. The Northern Peoples Congress of the Sardaunians was supposed to be a national party, yet it refused to change its name from Northern to Nigerian Peoples Congress, even for the sake of appearances. It refused right up to the end of the civilian regime.

The prime minister of Nigeria, Sir Abubakar Tafawa Balewa, who had been built up into a great statesman by the Western world, did nothing to save his country from impending chaos. The British made certain on the eve of their departure that power went to that conservative element in the country that had played no real part in the struggle for independence. This was the situation in which I wrote my novel *A Man of the People*.

Nigerian artists responded to these events in a variety of ways. The irrepressible Wole Soyinka put on the stage a devastating satire, *Before the Blackout*, which played to packed houses night after night in Ibadan. The popular traveling theater of Hubert Ogunde and his many wives began to stage a play clearly directed against the crooked premier of Western Nigeria. The theater group was declared an unlawful society and banned in Western Nigeria. Things were coming to a head in that region. Violence erupted after an unbelievable election swindle, as a result of the anger and frustration of Western Nigerians. It was in these circumstances that Wole Soyinka was charged with holding up the Ibadan radio station and removing the premier's taped speech!

Creative writers in independent Nigeria found themselves with a new, terrifying problem on their hands: They found that the independence their country was supposed to have won was totally without content. In the words of Dr. Nnamdi Azikiwe, Nigeria was given her freedom "on a platter of gold." We should have known that freedom should be won, not given on a plate. Like the head of John the Baptist, this gift to Nigeria proved most unlucky.

The Role of the Writer in Africa

What then were we to do as writers? What was our role in our new country? How were we to think about the use of our talents? I can say that when a number of us decided that we would be writers, we had not thought through these questions very clearly. In fact, we did not have a clue what we were up against. What I can say is that it was clear to many of us that an indigenous African literary renaissance was overdue. A major objective was to challenge stereotypes, myths, and the image of ourselves and our continent, and to recast them through stories—prose, poetry, essays, and books for our children. That was my overall goal.

When a number of us decided to pick up the pen and make writing a career there was no African literature as we know it today. There were of course our great oral tradition—the epics of the Malinke, the Bamana, and the Fulani—the narratives of Olaudah Equaino, works by D. A. Fagunwa and Muhammadu Bello, and novels by Pita Nwana, Amos Tutuola, and Cyprian Ekwensi.

Across the African continent, literary aficionados could savor the works of Egyptian, Nubian, and Carthaginian antiquity; Amharic and Tigrigna writings from Ethiopia and Eritrea; and the magnificent poetry and creation myths of Somalia. There was more—the breathtakingly beautiful Swahili poetry of East and Central Africa, and the chronicles, legends, and fables of the Ashanti, Dogon, Hutu, Kalanga, Mandingo, Ndebele, Ovambo, Shona, Sotho, Swazi, Tsonga, Tswana, Tutsi, Venda, Wolof, Xhosa, and Zulu.

Olive Schreiner's nineteenth-century classic *Story of an African Farm* and works by Samuel Mqhayi and Thomas Mofolo, Alan Paton, Camara Laye, Mongo Beti, Peter Abrahams, and Ferdinand Oyono, all preceded our time. Still, the numbers were not sufficient.[1]

And so I had no idea when I was writing *Things Fall Apart* whether it would even be accepted or published. All of this was new—there was nothing by which I could gauge how it was going to be received.

Writing has always been a serious business for me. I felt it was a moral obligation. A major concern of the time was the absence of the African voice. Being part of that dialogue meant not only sitting at the table but effectively telling the African story from an African perspective—in full earshot of the world.

The preparation for this life of writing, I have mentioned, came from English-system-style schools and university. I read Shakespeare, Dickens, and all the books that were read in the English public schools. They were novels and poems about English culture, and some things I didn't know anything about. When I saw a good sentence, saw a good phrase from the Western canon, of course I was influenced by it. But the story itself—there weren't any models. Those that were set in Africa were not particularly inspiring. If they were not saying something that was antagonistic toward us, they weren't concerned about us.

When people talk about African culture they often mean an assortment of ancient customs and traditions. The reasons for this view are quite clear. When the first Europeans came to Africa they knew very little of the history and complexity of the people and the continent. Some of that group persuaded themselves that Africa had no culture, no religion, and no history. It was a convenient conclusion, because it opened the door for all sorts of rationalizations for the exploitation that followed. Africa was bound, sooner or later, to respond to this denigration by resisting and displaying her own accomplishments. To do this effectively her spokesmen—the writers, intellectuals, and some politicians, including Azikiwe, Senghor, Nkrumah, Nyerere, Lumumba, and Mandela—engaged Africa's past, stepping back into what can be referred to as the "era of purity," before the coming of Europe. We put into the books and poems what was uncovered there, and this became known as African culture.

This was a very special kind of inspiration. Some of us decided to tackle the big subjects of the day—imperialism, slavery, independence, gender, racism, etc. And some did not. One could write about roses or the air or about love for all I cared; that was fine too. As for me, however, I chose the former.

Engaging such heavy subjects while at the same time trying to help create a unique and authentic African literary tradition would mean that some of us would decide to use the colonizer's tools: his language, altered sufficiently to bear the weight of an African creative aesthetic, infused with elements of the African literary tradition. I borrowed proverbs from our culture and history, colloquialisms and African expressive language from the ancient griots, the worldviews, perspectives, and customs from my Igbo tradition and cosmology, and the sensibilities of everyday people.

It was important to us that a body of work be developed of the highest possible quality that would oppose the negative discourse in some of the novels we encountered. By "writing back" to the West we were attempting to reshape the dialogue between the colonized and the colonizer. Our efforts, we hoped, would broaden the world's understanding, appreciation, and conceptualization of what literature meant when including the African voice and perspective.[2] We were clearly engaged in what Ode Ogede aptly refers to as "the politics of representation."[3]

This is another way of stating the fact of what I consider to be my mission in life. My kind of storytelling has to add its voice to this universal storytelling before we can say, "Now we've heard it all." I worry when somebody from one particular tradition stands up and says, "The novel is dead, the story is dead." I find this to be unfair, to put it mildly. You told your own story, and now you're announcing the novel is dead. Well, I haven't told mine yet.[4]

There are some who believe that the writer has no role in politics or the social upheavals of his or her day. Some of my friends say, "No, it is too rough there. A writer has no business being where it is so rough. The writer should be on the sidelines with his notepad and pen, where he can observe with objectivity." I believe that the African writer who steps aside can only write footnotes or a glossary when the event is over. He or she will become like the contemporary intellectual of futility in many other places, asking questions like: "Who am I? What is the meaning of my existence? Does this place belong to me or to someone else? Does my life belong to me or to some other person?" These are questions that no one can answer.

Ali Mazrui famously restated this position in his novel *The Trial of Christopher Okigbo* in which he takes my friend, the great poet, to task for, as Mazrui believes, "wasting his great talent on a conflict of disputable merit: 'The Nigerian Civil War and all its ramified implications [can be] compressed in the single poetic tragedy of the death of Christopher Okigbo.'"[5] In Mazrui's fiction Christopher Okigbo finds himself charged with "the offence of putting society before art in his scale of values. . . . No great artist has a right to carry patriotism to the extent of destroying his creative potential."[6]

Christopher Okigbo believed, as I do, that art and community in Africa are clearly linked. African art as we understand it has not been distilled or purified and refined to the point where it has lost all traces of real life, lost the vitality of the street, like art from some advanced societies and academic art tend to be. In Africa the tendency is to keep art involved with the people. It is clearly emphasized among my own Igbo people that art must never be allowed to escape into the rarefied atmosphere but must remain active in the lives of the members of society.

I have described earlier the practice of *mbari*, the Igbo concept of "art as celebration." Different aspects of Igbo life are integrated in this art form. Even those who are not trained artists are brought in to participate in these artistic festivals, in which the whole life of the world is depicted. Ordinary people must be brought in; a conscious effort must be made to bring the life of the village or town into this art. The Igbo culture says no condition is permanent. There is constant change in the world. Foreign visitors who had not been encountered up to that time are brought in as well, to illustrate the dynamic nature of life. The point I'm trying to make is that there is a need to bring life back into art by bringing art into life, so that the two can hold a conversation.

In a novel such as Amos Tutuola's *The Palm-Wine Drinkard* you can see this vitality put to work on the written page. There is no attempt to draw a line between what is permissible and what is not, what is possible and what is not possible, what is new and what is old. In a story that is set in the distant past you suddenly see a telephone, a car, a bishop—all kinds of things that don't seem to tie in. But in fact what you have is the whole life of the community, not just the community of humans but the community of ancestors, the animal world, of trees, and so on. Everything plays a part.

My own assessment is that the role of the writer is not a rigid position and depends to some extent on the state of health of his or her society. In other words, if a society is ill the writer has a responsibility to point it out. If the society is healthier, the writer's job is different.

We established the Society of Nigerian Authors (SONA) in the mid-1960s as an attempt to put our writers in a firm and dynamic frame. It was sort of a trade union. We thought it would keep our members safe and protect other artists as well. We hoped that our existence would create an environment in Nigeria where freedom of creative expression was not only possible but protected. We sought ultimately through our art to create for Nigeria an environment of good order and civilization—a daunting task that needed to be tackled in a country engulfed in crisis.

The notion of beneficent fiction is simply one of defining storytelling as a creative component of human experience, human life. It is something griots have done in Africa from the dawn of time—pass down stories that have a positive purpose and a use for society, from generation to generation. Some people flinch when you talk about art in the context of the needs of society, thinking you are introducing something far too common for a discussion of art. Why should art have a purpose and a use? Art shouldn't be concerned with purpose and reason and need, they say. These are improper. But from the very beginning, it seems to me, stories have indeed been meant to be enjoyed, to appeal to that part of us which enjoys good form and good shape and good sound. Still I think that behind it all is a desire to make our experience in the world better, to make our passage through life easier. Once you talk about making things better you're talking about politics.

I believe that it is impossible to write anything in Africa without some kind of commitment, some kind of message, some kind of protest. In my definition I am a protest writer, with restraint. Even those early novels that look like very gentle re-creations of the past—what they were saying, in effect, was that we had a past. That was the protest, because there were people who thought we didn't have a past. What I was doing was to say politely that we did—here it is. So commitment is nothing new. Commitment runs through my work. In fact, I should say that all of our writers, whether they're aware of it or not, are committed writers. The whole pattern of life demanded that one should protest, that you should put in a word for your history, your traditions, your religion, and so on.[7] The question of involvement in politics is really a matter of definition. I think it is quite often misunderstood. I have never proposed that every artist become an activist in the way we have always understood political activity. Some will, because that's the way they are. Others will not, and we must not ask anyone to do more than is necessary for them to perform their task.

At the same time it is important to state that words have the power to hurt, even to denigrate and oppress others. Before I am accused of prescribing a way in which a writer should write, let me say that I do think that decency and civilization would insist that the writer take sides with the powerless. Clearly there is no moral obligation to write in any particular way. But there is a moral obligation, I think, not to ally oneself with power against the powerless. An artist, in my definition of the word, would not be someone who takes sides with the emperor against his powerless subjects.[8] If one didn't realize the world was complex, vast, and diverse, one would write as if the world were one little county, and this would make us poor, and we would have impoverished the novel and our stories.

The reality of today, different as it is from the reality of my society one hundred years ago, is and can be important if we have the energy and the inclination to challenge it, to go out and engage with its peculiarities, with the things that we do not understand. The real danger is the tendency to retreat into the obvious, the tendency to be frightened by the richness of the world and to clutch what we always have understood. The writer is often faced with two choices—turn away from the reality of life's intimidating complexity or conquer its mystery by battling with it. The writer who chooses the former soon runs out of energy and produces elegantly tired fiction.[9]

The Igbo believe that art, religion, everything, the whole of life are embodied in the art of the masquerade. It is dynamic. It is not allowed to remain stationary. For instance, museums are unknown among the Igbo people. They do not even contemplate the idea of having something like a canon with the postulate: "This is how this sculpture should be made, and once it's made it should be venerated." No, the Igbo people want to create these things again and again, and every generation has a chance to execute its own model of art. So there's no undue respect for what the last generation did, because if you do that too much it means that there is no need for me to do anything, because it's already been done.[10]

One thing that I find a little worrying, though, is the suggestion that perhaps what was done in the 1960s, when African literature suddenly came into its own, was not as revolutionary as we make it out to be. That African literature without a concerted effort on the part of the writers of that era would still have found its voice. You find the same kind of cynicism among young African Americans who occasionally dismiss the contributions of the civil rights activists of that same period. Many of these same critics clearly did not know (or maybe do not want to be told) what Africa was like in the 1940s, back when there was no significant literature at all.

There are people who do not realize that it was a different world than the world of today, one which is far more open. This openness and the opportunities that abound for a young intellectual setting out to carve a writing career for him- or herself are in fact partly a result of the work of that literature, the struggles of that era. So even though nobody is asking the new writer or intellectual to repeat the stories, the literary agenda or struggles of yesteryear, it is very important for them to be aware of what our literature achieved, what it has done for us, so that we can move forward.

As I write this I am aware that there are people, many friends of mine, who feel that there are too many cultures around. In fact, I heard someone say that they think some of these cultures should be put down, that there are just too many. We did not make the world, so there is no reason we should be quarreling with the number of cultures there are. If any group decides on its own that its culture is not worth talking about, it can stop talking about it. But I don't think anybody can suggest to another person, Please drop your culture; let's use mine. That's the height of arrogance and the boast of imperialism. I think cultures know how to fight their battles; cultures know how to struggle. It is up to the owners of any particular culture to ensure it survives, or if they don't want it to survive, they should act accordingly, but I am not going to recommend that.

My position, therefore, is that we must hear all the stories. That would be the first thing. And by hearing all the stories we will find points of contact and communication, and the world story, the Great Story, will have a chance to develop. That's the only precaution I would suggest—that we not rush into announcing the arrival of this international, this great world story, based simply on our knowledge of one or a few traditions. For instance, in America there is really very little knowledge of the literature of the rest of the world. Of the literature of Latin America, yes. But that's not all that different in inspiration from that of America, or of Europe. One must go further. You don't even have to go too far in terms of geography—you can start with the Native Americans and listen to their poetry.

Most writers who are beginners, if they are honest with themselves, will admit that they are praying for a readership as they begin to write. But it should be the quality of the craft, not the audience, that should be the greatest motivating factor. For me, at least, I can declare that when I wrote *Things Fall Apart* I couldn't have told anyone the day before it was accepted for publication that anybody was going to read it. There was no guarantee; nobody ever said to me, Go and write this, we will publish it, and we will read it; it was just there. But my brother-in-law, who was not a particularly voracious reader, told me that he read the novel through the night and it gave him a terrible headache the next morning. And I took that as an encouraging endorsement![11]

The triumph of the written word is often attained when the writer achieves union and trust with the reader, who then becomes ready to be drawn deep into unfamiliar territory, walking in borrowed literary shoes so to speak, toward a deeper understanding of self or society, or of foreign peoples, cultures, and situations.[12]

1966

absentminded
our thoughtless days
sat at dire controls
and played indolently

slowly downward in remote
subterranean shaft
a diamond-tipped
drill point crept closer
to residual chaos to
rare artesian hatred
that once squirted warm
blood in God's face
confirming His first
disappointment in Eden[1]

January 15, 1966, Coup

On Saturday, January 15, 1966, a pivotal day in the history of Nigeria, members of the Society of Nigerian Authors happened to be gathered for a meeting. The venue was an office building on Kingsway Road in Ikoyi, Lagos. There were about ten of us living in Lagos at the time: John Pepper Clark-Bekederemo (aka J. P. Clark), Wole Soyinka, Onuora Nzekwu, and a few others. A few members were sitting at a table that looked out onto the Lagos Lagoon. We were engaged in polite conversation, delaying the start of the meeting as some of our members trickled in.

It happened that my new novel, *A Man of the People*, was about to be published in London, and I was communicating with my publisher, Heinemann. I knew that the book was going to be problematic for me because of its criticism of Nigerian politics—very severe criticism. The novel, after all, climaxes in a military coup.

I had sent one copy of the novel to J. P. Clark on a Wednesday, two days earlier. When J.P. arrived at the meeting his voice rang out from several hundred feet away.

"Chinua, you know, you are a prophet. Everything in this book has happened except a coup!"

That very evening, unbeknownst to us, a military coup was being launched that would change Nigeria forever.

The next day I got a message from Heinemann, a cable or telex, asking me whether they should go ahead and publish the book. Why would they send this message? I wondered. I was unaware that a coup had happened the night before. I told the gentleman who carried this message—I think from the British embassy—to tell my publisher to go ahead and publish the novel. I was not particularly afraid, even though I had concerns. I thought, Who was likely to misunderstand? My sentiment

changed from incredulity to dread when we heard details and the surrounding events of the coup.

In those days we went to work on Saturdays and worked till noon.
When I got to my office that Saturday there were soldiers everywhere,
surrounding Broadcasting House. The soldiers stopped me and interro-
gated me until they were satisfied that I worked there, and then let me
pass through. The announcement of a coup on the radio had not been
made. Some people had their suspicions, because soldiers in military
vehicles were seen being deployed throughout the city, and roadblocks
with barbed wire were being erected everywhere.

News began to seep through. We heard that the prime minister was
missing. Then came news from Kaduna that the Sardauna,[1] Sir Ahmadu
Bello, the most powerful of the premiers, had been killed. We then heard
that Samuel Akintola, the premier of Western Nigeria, had also been
killed. Those of us working in broadcasting in the coming days would
get a more detailed list of those killed, imprisoned, or detained during the coup. These events thrust Nigeria into a state of shock for a
long time.

Nigeria was not ready or willing to face her problems. If her leaders had
approached their duty with humility, they all might have realized long
before the coup that the country was in deep trouble. Nigeria was rocked
by one crisis after another in the years that followed independence. First
the Nigerian census crisis of 1963–64 shook the nation, then the federal
election crisis of 1964, which was followed by the Western Nigeria election crisis of 1965—which threatened to split the country at its seams. At
that point most of us, the writers at least, knew that something was very
wrong in Nigeria. A fix was long overdue.

When the artist's imagination clashes with life's very reality it creates
a heavy conundrum. The story Nigeria had of herself was that something

like a military coup would never happen; Nigeria was too stable for that. We were utterly unprepared for such an event, and for the magnitude of the dislocation that ensued.

Despite my fictional warning I never expected or wanted the form of violent intervention that became the military coup of January 15, 1966. I had hoped that the politicians would sort things out for our new nation. Any confidence we had that things could be put right was smashed as we watched elements from the military take control. The coup was led by a group of junior officers, most of them Igbo, and it would be known widely as the Nzeogwu coup after Major Chukwuma Nzeogwu, the ringleader, who was from the northern city of Kaduna. That night of January 15, 1966, is something Nigeria has never really recovered from.

The Dark Days

On January 16, 1966, the day after the Nzeogwu coup, my wife, Christie, took our first child, Chinelo, to the movies to catch the matinee. Chinelo was full of energy—always running all over the place. My wife's doctor, Dr. Okoronkwo Ogan, who became our daughter's godfather, called her "quicksilver."[1] On their way home, my wife decided to drop by and see me in the office, so that our daughter could tell me all about the movie they had watched. I believe it was the Disney classic *Dumbo*, about the flying elephant. As they approached the Nigerian Broadcasting Corporation they saw the soldiers around but did not know what was happening. They were not scared, even though they found the commotion a bit peculiar.

As they walked to my office someone yelled at my wife: "Where are you going? Don't you know what is happening?" So she walked more briskly, because she wanted to find out whether I was alive. A soldier stopped them and asked them to leave. They returned home and tuned into the radio station to find out what was going on.

People were standing on the streets in small groups, listening to the radios of street newspaper vendors. There had been a coup, the radio announcers said, at which point there was an initial period of spontaneous, overt jubilation. The story of the coup and how it happened started leaking out, first from the military barracks and then from the international media. There was a great deal of anxiety among the general populace. Everyone wanted to find out exactly what had happened in Kaduna, Lagos, Ibadan, and elsewhere the night before, though apparently not much action had been seen in Enugu, the capital of the Eastern Region. The initial vacuum of information was filled with gossip, innuendo, and fabricated accounts that magnified the confusion throughout the country. A second story got around that the military coup, which at first had been so well received, was in fact a sinister plot by the ambitious Igbos of the East to seize control of Nigeria.

In a country in which tribalism was endemic, the rumor of an "Igbo coup" began to find acceptance. Before long many people were persuaded that their spontaneous jubilation in January had been a mistake. A Nigerian poet who had dedicated a new book "to the heroes of January 1966" had second thoughts after the countercoup of July, and he sent a frantic cable to his publishers to remove the dedication.

Those who knew Nigeria were not very surprised, because part of the way to respond to confusion in Nigeria is to blame those from the other ethnic group or the other side of the country. One found some ethnic or religious element supporting whatever one was trying to make sense of. This angle grew stronger and stronger as the days passed, mainly because the state of confusion was not really dispelled satisfactorily by the authorities.

The weeks following the coup saw Easterners attacked both randomly and in an organized fashion. There seemed to be a lust for revenge, which meant an excuse for Nigerians to take out their resentment on the Igbos who led the nation in virtually every sector—politics, education, commerce, and the arts. This group, the Igbo, that gave the colonizing British so many headaches and then literally drove them out of Nigeria was now an open target, scapegoats for the failings and grievances of colonial and post-independence Nigeria.

It was a desperate time. Soldiers were being used by elements in power to commit a number of crimes against Igbos, Nigerian citizens. Military officers were rounding people up and summarily executing them, particularly in the North, we were told by victims fleeing the pogroms. There was a story of hoodlums looking to hunt down and kill Dr. Okechukwu Ikejiani, who was the chairman of the Nigerian Coal Corporation.[2] Dr. Ikejiani escaped the grasp of these thugs by dressing up as a woman and crossing the Nigeria border to Dahomey (today's Republic of Benin)!

In Lagos, where we lived, soldiers were also used in targeted raids of certain people's homes, including our own. It happened that my wife and I had moved recently from Milverton Street to Turnbull Road, after my promotion to director of external broadcasting. Fortunately for us the soldiers went to Milverton Street, to our old house, to search for me.

Some may wonder why soldiers would be after me so fervently. As I mentioned, it happened that I had just written *A Man of the People*, which forecast a military coup that overthrows a corrupt civilian government. Clearly a case of fact imitating fiction and nothing else, but some military leaders believed that I must have had something to do with the coup and wanted to bring me in for questioning.

Eventually my family and I left our Turnbull Road house, a painful decision. We had moved into it after we were married. It was located in Ikoyi, a nice section of town, overlooking the lagoon. I remember receiving important visitors in our home, such as the great African American poet Langston Hughes, who stopped by during one of his famous African tours. I have a favorite picture of the two of us from that period, standing near a palm tree on the lawn of that lovely residence.

We found refuge in an old friend's house—Frank Cawson, the British Council representative in Lagos, whose intervention literally saved our lives. He housed us for a number of days. Mr. Cawson had been the British Council representative in Accra, Ghana, and had invited me to give a lecture there before he came to Lagos. I delivered a lecture, entitled, "The African Writer and the English Language." So when Mr. Cawson was transferred to Nigeria, he was already known to me.

He was monitoring local and international radio and newspapers to get a sense of what was happening. He took a number of precautionary steps to enhance our safety. First he took his car out of the garage and put our own there instead, so that no one would see it. It was a very tense, anxiety-plagued period for my wife and me and our two children, Chinelo, who was five years old, and Ike, who was two. Making matters worse was the fact that Frank Cawson was quite ill—I think with malaria.

For about a week, lying hidden in Mr. Cawson's house in Lagos, I still simply thought that things had temporarily gotten out of hand, and that everything would soon be all right. Then, suddenly, I discovered that I had been operating on a false and perhaps naïve basis all along. The soldiers located us after we had been hiding about a week. It became clear to me that I had to send my family away.

As many of us packed our belongings to return east some of the people we had lived with for years, some for decades, jeered and said, "Let them [Igbos] go; food will be cheaper in Lagos." That kind of experience is very powerful. It is something I could not possibly forget. I realized suddenly that I had not been living in my home; I had been living in a strange place. There were more and more reports of massacres, and not only in the North, but also in the West and in Lagos. People were hounded out of their homes, as we were in Lagos, and returned to the East. We expected to hear something from the intellectuals, from our friends. Rather, what we heard was, "Oh, they had it coming to them," or words to that effect. There were many others from other parts of Nigeria who did not jeer but suffered with us at this sudden discovery that a section of the large, diverse Nigerian family was not welcome in this new country.

A lot of this hot-blooded anger was fanned by British intellectuals and some radical Northern elements in places like Ahmadu Bello University. They were aided by a few in the expatriate population from outside Nigeria, who easily influenced the mostly self-satisfied and docile Northern leadership to activate a weapon that has been used repeatedly in Nigeria's short history—a fringe element known as "area boys" or the "rent-a-crowd types"—to attack Igbos in an orgy of blood.

As we reached the brink of full-blown war it became clear to me that the chaos enveloping all of us in Nigeria was due to the incompetence of the Nigerian ruling class. They clearly had a poor grasp of history and found it difficult to appreciate and grapple with Nigeria's ethnic and political complexity. This clique, stunted by ineptitude, distracted by power games and the pursuit of material comforts, was unwilling, if not incapable, of saving our fledgling new nation.

I arranged to smuggle Christie and the children out of Lagos on a cargo ship from the port. Christie reports that it was one of the most horrendous voyages she has ever undertaken. She remembers the seasickness heightened on this particular trip as a result of her pregnancy. She and the children and other refugees from the bloodshed were placed in a section of the ship that was in the open, without any shelter from the elements. There was vomiting, nausea; it was just awful. After the harrowing sea journey, Christie, Chinelo, and Ike were received safely in Port Harcourt in Eastern Nigeria by her brother, Dr. Samuel Okoli, an obstetrician-gynecologist, who served gallantly during the war effort.

I found it difficult to come to terms with the fact that Nigeria was disintegrating, that I had to leave my house, leave Lagos, leave my job. So I decided to sneak back into our Turnbull Road residence and return to work. People were disappearing right and left. . . . There was a media report of someone from the senior service whose body was found the night before. At this point the killings had reached the peak figure of hundreds a week.

Victor Badejo, the director general of Nigerian Broadcasting Corporation, saw me on the premises, stopped me, and said, "What are you still doing here?" And then he said, "Life has no duplicate"[3] and provided further clarification of the situation. Badejo confirmed a story I had heard of drunken soldiers who came to my office "wanting to find out which was more powerful, their guns or my pen." He was quite anxious on my behalf and advised me to leave my Turnbull Road residence immediately.[4]

Philip Ume-Ezeoke was the controller of education programming at the Nigerian Broadcasting Corporation. We were both from the Eastern Region and got on rather well. He and I decided together that the time had come for us to travel back to the East. Relatives were sending messages from there begging their loved ones in Lagos to return. There were a number of people like us who did not really want to see this come about . . . did not believe this was happening. Ume-Ezeoke came to my house and suggested we go in a two-car convoy back to Eastern Nigeria. We agreed on a time that we would leave Lagos the following morning.

I got to Ume-Ezeoke's house the next morning very early, exactly at the agreed-upon time, but no one was there. He was already gone. Unfortunately, Philip Ume-Ezeoke is no longer alive. If he were, it would be interesting to know what happened. In any case, I set out on my own, wondering what would come up at any point. The highway was full of police roadblocks along the way. I was stopped once or twice and had to show my papers—what Nigerians call my "particulars."

I was one of the last to flee Lagos. I simply could not bring myself to accept that I could no longer live in my nation's capital, although the facts clearly said so. My feeling toward Nigeria was one of profound disappointment. Not only because mobs were hunting down and killing innocent civilians in many parts, especially in the North, but because the federal government sat by and let it happen.

The problems of the Nigerian federation were well-known, but I somehow had felt that perhaps this was part of a nation's maturation, and that given time we would solve our problems. Then, suddenly, this incredible, horrific experience happened—not just to a few people but to millions, together. I could not escape the impact of this trauma happening to millions of people at the same time. Suddenly I realized that the only valid basis for existence is one that gives security to you and your people. It is as simple as that.[5]

When I finally got to Benin City, which is located roughly halfway from Lagos to Igbo land in the Mid-West Region, there was a distinct atmospheric change. The fact that the Mid-West was a neighbor of the East meant that at this point there were Mid-Western Igbo policemen. It is important to recall that during this period in Nigerian history the Igbos had large numbers in the police force but not in the army, where their numbers were concentrated in the officer corps. Crowds of policemen recognized me when I got to Benin City and cheered, saying, "Oga, thank you!," and let me through to continue my journey without incident to Onitsha Bridge, and over the Niger River to the East.

It is pertinent to note that within the military there had been for at least half a decade preceding the coup a great sense of alienation from and disillusionment with the political class in Nigeria. They shared that feeling with a growing number of ordinary Nigerians, and clearly with the writers and intellectuals. The political class, oblivious of the growing disenchantment permeating literally every strata of Nigerian society, was consumed with individual and ethnic pursuits, and with the accumulation of material and other resources. Corruption was widespread, and those in power were "using every means at their disposal, including bribery, intimidation, and blackmail, to cling to power."[6]

Many within the military leadership were increasingly concerned that they were being asked to step in and set things right politically. In the first six years of its post-independence existence Nigeria found itself calling on the armed forces to quell two Tiv riots in the Middle Belt, crush the 1964 general strike, and reestablish order following regional elections in the Western Region in 1965. In hindsight, it seems as though President Azikiwe may have been aware of the sand shifting beneath the feet of the political class, and he tried to gain the support of the military brass during the constitutional crisis following the 1964 federal general election. The failure of Azikiwe's attempt perhaps should have been the first sign to many of us that trouble lay ahead for our young nation.[7]

BENIN ROAD

Speed is violence
Power is violence
Weight violence

The butterfly seeks safety in lightness
In weightless, undulating flight

But at a crossroads where mottled light
From old trees falls on a brash new highway
Our separate errands collide

I come power-packed for two
And the gentle butterfly offers
Itself in bright yellow sacrifice
Upon my hard silicon shield.[1]

A History of Ethnic
Tension and Resentment

I have written in my small book entitled *The Trouble with Nigeria* that
Nigerians will probably achieve consensus on no other matter than their
common resentment of the Igbo. The origin of the national resentment
of the Igbo is as old as Nigeria and quite as complicated. But it can be
summarized thus: The Igbo culture, being receptive to change, individualistic, and highly competitive, gave the Igbo man an unquestioned
advantage over his compatriots in securing credentials for advancement
in Nigerian colonial society. Unlike the Hausa/Fulani he was unhindered
by a wary religion, and unlike the Yoruba he was unhampered by traditional hierarchies. This kind of creature, fearing no god or man, was
custom-made to grasp the opportunities, such as they were, of the white
man's dispensations. And the Igbo did so with both hands. Although the
Yoruba had a huge historical and geographical head start, the Igbo wiped
out their handicap in one fantastic burst of energy in the twenty years
between 1930 and 1950.[1]

Had the Igbo been a minor ethnic group of a few hundred thousand
their menace might have been easily and quietly contained. But their
members ran in the millions. As in J. P. Clark's fine image of "ants filing
out of the wood," the Igbo moved out of their forest home, scattered, and
virtually seized the floor.[2]

Paul Anber explains:

> With unparalleled rapidity, the Igbos advanced fastest in the shortest
> period of time of all Nigeria's ethnic groups. Like the Jews, to whom they
> have frequently been likened, they progressed despite being a minority in
> the country, filling the ranks of the nation's educated, prosperous upper

classes.... It was not long before the educational and economic progress
of the Igbos led to their becoming the major source of administrators,
managers, technicians, and civil servants for the country, occupying
senior positions out of proportion to their numbers. Particularly with
respect to the Federal public service and the government statutory corporations, this led to accusations of an Igbo monopoly of essential services to the exclusion of other ethnic groups.

The rise of the Igbo in Nigerian affairs was due to the self-confidence
engendered by their open society and their belief that one man is as good
as another, that no condition is permanent. It was *not* due, as non-Igbo
observers have imagined, to tribal mutual aid societies. The Igbo Town
Union that has often been written about was in reality an extension
of the Igbo individualistic ethic. The Igbo towns competed among
themselves for certain kinds of social achievement, like the building
of schools, churches, markets, post offices, pipe-borne water projects,
roads, etc. They did not concern themselves with pan-Igbo unity nor
were they geared to securing an advantage over non-Igbo Nigerians. The
Igbo have no compelling traditional loyalty beyond town or village.[3]

There were a number of other factors that spurred the Igbos to educational, economic, and political success. The population density in Igbo
land created a "land hunger"—a pressure on their low-fertility, laterite-
laden soil for cultivation, housing, and other purposes, factors that led
ultimately to migration to other parts of the nation: "In Northern Nigeria there were less than 3,000 Igbos in 1921; by 1931 the number had
risen to nearly 12,000 and by 1952 to over 130,000."[4]

The coastal branches of the Yoruba nation had some of the earliest
contact with the European missionaries and explorers as a consequence
of their proximity to the shoreline and their own dedication to learning.
They led the entire nation in educational attainment from the late nineteenth to the early twentieth centuries. By the time the Church Mission

Society and a number of Roman Catholic orders had crossed the Niger River and entered Igbo land, there had been an explosion in the numbers of young Igbo students enrolled in school. The increase was so exponential in such a short time that within three short decades the Igbos had closed the gap and quickly moved ahead as the group with the highest literacy rate, the highest standard of living, and the greatest proportion of citizens with postsecondary education in Nigeria. The Igbo, for the most part (at least until recently), respected the education that the colonizers had brought with them. There was not only individual interest in the white man's knowledge, but family, community, and regional interest. It would not surprise an observer that the "Igbos absorbed western education as readily as they responded to urbanization."[5]

I will be the first to concede that the Igbo as a group is not without its flaws. Its success can and did carry deadly penalties: the dangers of hubris, overweening pride, and thoughtlessness, which invite envy and hatred or, even worse, that can obsess the mind with material success and dispose it to all kinds of crude showiness. There is no doubt at all that there is a strand in contemporary Igbo behavior that can offend by its noisy exhibitionism and disregard for humility and quietness.[6]

Having acknowledged these facts,[7] any observer can clearly see how the competitive individualism and the adventurous spirit of the Igbo could have been harnessed by committed leaders for the modernization and development of Nigeria. Nigeria's pathetic attempt to crush these idiosyncrasies rather than celebrate them is one of the fundamental reasons the country has not developed as it should and has emerged as a laughingstock.[8]

The ploy in the Nigerian context was simple and crude: Get the achievers out and replace them with less qualified individuals from the desired ethnic background so as to gain access to the resources of the state. This bizarre government strategy transformed the federal civil service, corporations, and universities into centers for ethnic bigotry and petty squabbles.[9] It was in this toxic environment that Professor Eni Njoku, an Igbo who was vice chancellor of the University of Lagos, was forced out of office. An exasperated Kenneth Onwuka Dike, an ethnic Igbo and the vice chancellor of the University of Ibadan facing similar bouts of tribal small-mindedness, famously lamented during this crisis that "intellectuals were the worst peddlers of tribalism."[10]

One of the first signs I saw of an Igbo backlash came in the form of a 1966 publication from Northern Nigeria called *The Nigerian Situation: Facts and Background.* In it the Igbo were cast as an assertive group that unfairly dominated almost every sector of Nigerian society. No mention was made of the culture of educational excellence imbibed from the British that pervaded Igbo society and schools at the time. Special attention instead was paid to the manpower distribution within the public services, where 45 percent of the managers were Igbo "and it is threatening to reach 60 percent by 1968. Moreover, regrettably though, [the] North's future contribution"[11] was credited with only 10 percent of the existing posts.

Of particular dismay to the authors of the report were the situations in the Nigerian Railway Corporation, in which over half of the posts were occupied by Igbos; the Nigerian Ports Authority; and the Nigerian Foreign Service, in which over 70 percent of the posts were held by Igbos. Probably the pettiest of the accusations was the lamentation over the academic success of Easterners who graduated in larger numbers in the 1965–66 academic year than their counterparts from the West, Mid-West, and North.[12]

By the time the government of the Western Region also published a white paper outlining the dominance of the ethnic Igbo in key government positions in the Nigerian Railway Corporation and the Nigerian Ports Authority, the situation for ethnic Igbos working in Western Nigeria in particular, but all over Nigeria in general, had become untenable. This government-sanctioned environment of hate and resentment created by self-serving politicians resulted in government-supervised persecutions, terminations, and dismissals of Nigerian citizens based on their ethnicity.

In most other nations the success of an ethnic group as industrious as the Igbo would stimulate healthy competition and a renaissance of learning and achievement. In Nigeria it bred deep resentment and both subtle and overt attempts to dismantle the structures in place for meritocracy in favor of mediocrity, under the cloak of a need for "federal character"—a morally bankrupt and deeply corrupt Nigerian form of the far more successful affirmative action in the United States.[13]

The denial of merit is a form of social injustice that can hurt not only the individuals directly concerned but ultimately the entire society. The motive for the original denial may be tribal discrimination, but it may also come from sexism, from political, religious, or some other partisan consideration, or from corruption and bribery. It is unnecessary to examine these various motives separately; it is sufficient to state that whenever merit is set aside by prejudice of whatever origin, individual citizens as well as the nation itself are victimized.[14,15]

The Army

Before I go further an effort should be made to explain the nature of the dynamics at work within the Nigerian military at the time of the January 15, 1966, coup and the events that followed. Striking a balance between a level of detail that will satisfy readers who still feel the impact of these events deeply and that which will be palatable, if not to say comprehensible, to a less well-informed reader is an impossibility, but I will strive to do so nonetheless.

Historians have argued incessantly about the makeup of the January 15, 1966, coup and its meaning. It was led by the so-called five majors, a cadre of relatively junior officers whose front man of sorts was Chuk-wuma Nzeogwu. Very few people outside military circles (with the exception of the poet Christopher Okigbo) knew very much about him. What I heard of him was what his friends or those who happened to know him were telling us. He seemed to be a distant, mysterious figure.[1]

Nzeogwu had a reputation as a disciplined, no-nonsense, nonsmok-ing, nonphilandering teetotaler, and as an anticorruption crusader. This reputation, we were told, served him well as the chief instructor at the Nigerian Military Training College (NMTC) in Kaduna,[2] and in recruit-ing military "intellectuals."

In the wee hours of January 15, 1966, in a broadcast to the nation, Nzeogwu sought to explain "the coup attempt." It happened that some journalists had approached him to clarify the situation. Apparently the plan of the coup plotters was to take control of the various military com-mands in Kaduna, Lagos, and Enugu and to make a radio announcement from Lagos. Unbeknown to Nzeogwu, who was still in Kaduna, the Lagos operation had failed, and most information available to the popu-lation was coming from the BBC. Nzeogwu hastily put together a speech that became notorious for its attacks on the political class, bribery, and corruption.[3]

But by killing Sir Ahmadu Bello, Nzeogwu and the other coup plot-ters had put themselves on a collision course with the religious, ethnic, and political ramifications of such an action, something they had clearly not thought through sufficiently.[4]

Superficially it was understandable to conclude that this was indeed "an Igbo coup." However, scratch a little deeper and complicating factors are discovered: One of the majors was Yoruba, and Nzeogwu himself was Igbo in name only. Not only was he born in Kaduna, the capital of the Muslim North, he was widely known as someone who saw himself as a Northerner, spoke fluent Hausa and little Igbo, and wore the Northern traditional dress when not in uniform. In the end the Nzeogwu coup was crushed by the man who was the highest-ranking Igbo officer in the Nigerian army, Major-General Aguiyi-Ironsi.[5]

We were to learn later that Aguiyi-Ironsi was also on the list of those to be murdered. Ironsi got wind of the plot and mounted a successful resistance in Lagos, ultimately breaking the back of the coup.[6]

Major-General Aguiyi-Ironsi emerged as Nigeria's new head of state in late May 1966. In a broadcast to the nation on May 24, 1966, Ironsi banned all political parties and imposed what he called Decree No. 34 on a bewildered country. The widely unpopular decree eliminated Nigeria's federal structure and put in place a unitary republic, which seemed to threaten more local patronage networks. For the first time in history a federal military government was in control of Nigeria.[7]

There was growing anger and dissatisfaction among officers from Northern Nigeria, who wanted revenge for what they saw[8] as an Igbo coup. Aguiyi-Ironsi, a mild-mannered person, was reluctant to execute the Nzeogwu coup plotters, who were serving stiff prison sentences. Nzeogwu was imprisoned at the Kirikiri Maximum Security Prison in Lagos. It didn't help matters that all the coup plotters were eventually transferred to the Eastern Region, which at that time was under the jurisdiction of Colonel Odumegwu Ojukwu, son of Sir Louis Odumegwu Ojukwu.[9]

Countercoup and Assassination

Throughout this time there was a sense of great unease and tension across the country, and multiple rumors of military insurrection in the offing. Prior to Major-General Aguiyui-Ironsi's ascension in May 1966, there were reports of riots in Northern Nigeria. There are many reports of the genesis of these spontaneous riots.[1] Marauding Northern youths armed with machetes, knives, and other instruments of death attacked unsuspecting civilians, mostly Igbos. The mainly Igbo and other Easterners who fled to the Eastern Region from the North during the May riots were persuaded to return to their livelihoods in the North by Aguiyi-Ironsi, the head of state, and Odumegwu Ojukwu, the military governor of Eastern Nigeria. These calls were predicated upon assurances from the Northern Region's governor, Hassan Katsina, that no harm would befall them.[2]

By June several meetings had taken place among the Northern Nigerian ruling elite. They sent representatives to meet with now general Ironsi, handing him a list of their demands that included the revocation of the unpopular Decree 34; the courts-martial and punishment of the leaders of the January 15, 1966, coup; and the discontinuation of any plans to investigate the underpinnings of the May 1966 massacres in the North.[3]

Ironsi was alarmed that Northern leaders had been meeting without his knowledge for several months, and he sensed a great deal of anger bubbling beneath the surface. He made the ill-advised determination that, as Nigeria's head of state, he could appease and soothe concerns if he met with the leaders of the regions.[4] Ironsi embarked on a nationwide tour to calm growing fears of a permanently fractured nation and to promote his notion of a unitary republic. He stopped over in Ibadan as the guest of the military governor of Western Nigeria, Lieutenant Colonel Adekunle Fajuyi. A close friend and confidant, Fajuyi made Ironsi aware of rumors of a pending mutiny in the army.[5]

There are several accounts of what transpired next. What I was told by those close to the army was that on July 29, 1966, Ironsi was arrested by Nigerian army captain Theophilus Y. Danjuma, a Northerner, who wanted to know if Ironsi was linked to the death of the Sardauna of Sokoto. There are divergent accounts of what happened next. What is well known is that in a matter of hours the bullet-ridden bodies of

Ironsi and Fajuyi were discovered in the bush.[6] These executions would prove to be part of a larger and particularly bloody coup by Northern officers led by Murtala Muhammed.[7]

The Pogroms

Looking back, the naively idealistic coup of January 15, 1966, proved a terrible disaster. It was interpreted with plausibility as a plot by the ambitious Igbo of the East to take control of Nigeria from the Hausa/Fulani North. Six months later, I watched horrified as Northern officers carried out a revenge coup in which they killed Igbo officers and men in large numbers. If it had ended there, the matter might have been seen as a very tragic interlude in nation building, a horrendous tit for tat. But the Northerners turned on Igbo civilians living in the North and unleashed waves of brutal massacres that Colin Legum of *The Observer* (UK) was the first to describe as a pogrom. Thirty thousand civilian men, women, and children were slaughtered, hundreds of thousands were wounded, maimed, and violated, their homes and property looted and burned—and no one asked any questions. A Sierra Leonean living in Northern Nigeria at the time wrote home in horror: "The killing of the Igbos has become a state industry in Nigeria."[1]

What terrified me about the massacres in Nigeria was this: If it was only a question of rioting in the streets and so on, that would be bad enough, but it could be explained. It happens everywhere in the world. But in this particular case a detailed plan for mass killing was implemented by the government—the army, the police—the very people who were there to protect life and property. Not a single person has been punished for these crimes. It was not just human nature, a case of somebody hating his neighbor and chopping off his head. It was something far more devastating, because it was a premeditated plan that involved careful coordination, awaiting only the right spark.

Throughout the country at this time, but particularly in Igbo intellectual circles, there was much discussion of the difficulties of coexisting in a nation with such disparate peoples and religious and cultural backgrounds. As early as October 1966, some were calling for outright war.[2] Most of us, however, were still hoping for a peaceful solution. Many talked of a confederation, though few knew how it would look.

In the meantime, the Eastern Region was tackling the herculean task of resettling the refugees who were pouring into the East in the hundreds of thousands. It was said at the time that the number of displaced Nigerian citizens fleeing from other parts of the nation back to Eastern Nigeria was close to a million.

PENALTY OF GODHEAD

The old man's bed
of straw caught a flame blown
from overnight logs by harmattan's
incendiary breath. Defying his age and
sickness he rose and steered himself
smoke-blind to safety.

A nimble rat appeared at the
door of his hole looked quickly to left and
right and scurried across the floor
to nearby farmlands.

Even roaches that grim
tenantry that nothing discourages
fled their crevices that day on wings they
only use in deadly haste.

Household gods alone
frozen in ritual black with blood
of endless tribute festooned in feathers
perished in the blazing pyre
of that hut.[1]

The Aburi Accord

The absence of a concerted plan to address the eruption of violence throughout Nigeria against Easterners, mainly Igbos, and the inaction around the refugee problem amplified the anger and tensions between the federal government, now led by Lieutenant Colonel Yakubu Gowon, and the Eastern Region. Calls in the East for independence grew louder, and threats from the deferral government grew more ominous, in a vicious cycle.

A last-ditch summit was held from January 4 to January 5, 1967, to discuss the areas of conflict. Great optimism was expressed that this would be the instrument to bring lasting peace to Nigeria. Aburi, in Ghana, was chosen as the venue, as a concession to Ojukwu, who had asked for a neutral site outside Nigeria for this meeting, but also to impart a sense of impartiality and credibility to the summit. A document memorializing the areas of shared understanding was produced after two days of meetings. It would be known as the Aburi Accord.[1]

The gathering was attended by senior military and police officials[2] and government secretaries.[3] Topics for discussion included: a committee to work out a constitutional future for Nigeria; the back payment of salaries to Igbo government employees who were forced to leave their posts as a result of the disturbances; the need for a resolution renouncing the use of force; and the refusal of the Eastern Region to recognize Lieutenant Colonel Yakubu Gowon as supreme commander. The predicament of displaced persons following the pogroms in the North, the fate of soldiers involved in disturbances on January 15, 1966, and the planned distribution of power between the federal military government and the regional governments also required urgent attention.[4]

The goal of the Gowon-led Nigerian government was to emerge from these deliberations with Nigeria intact as a confederation of the regions. Many intellectuals and key members of Ojukwu's cabinet in the East had been battling with solutions to these issues for months before the Aburi meetings, thinking through various possible answers to these key questions: What is a confederation? How would it work in the Nigerian setting? How much power would be delegated to the central federal government as opposed to the regions? In my estimation there was not as much rigorous thought given by Gowon's federal cabinet and the powerful interests in the North. The two parties therefore left Aburi with very different levels of understanding of what a confederation meant and how it would work in Nigeria.[5]

By March 1967, two months after the summit in Aburi, Ghana, the Aburi Accord resolutions had yet to be implemented, and there was growing weariness in the East that Gowon had no intention of doing so. The government of the Eastern Region warned Gowon that his repeated failure to act on issues pertaining to Nigerian sovereignty could lead to secession.

Gowon responded by issuing a decree, Decree 8, which called for the resurrection of the proposals for constitutional reform promulgated during the Aburi conference. But for reasons hard to explain other than as egotistical self-preservation, members of the federal civil service galvanized themselves in energetic opposition to the agreements of the Aburi Accord. Seeing this development as a strategic political opening, the Yoruba leader, Obafemi Awolowo, the West's political kingpin, heretofore nursing political trouble himself, including prior imprisonment for sedition, insisted that the federal government remove all Northern military troops garrisoned in Lagos, Ibadan, Abeokuta, and throughout the Western Region—a demand similar to those Ojukwu had made earlier, during the crisis.[6]

Awolowo warned Gowon's federal government that if the Eastern Region left the federation the Western Region would not be far behind.

This statement was considered sufficiently threatening by Gowon and the federal government to merit a complete troop withdrawal.

There were increasing indications that Northern leaders never had any intention of implementing the settlement negotiated at Aburi. Ojukwu at this point was exasperated by what he saw as purposeful inaction from Gowon. During March through April 1967 he responded by instituting a systematic process that severed all Biafran ties to Nigeria: First he froze all official communication with Lagos, and he then followed this swiftly by disconnecting the "Eastern regional government's administration and revenues from those of the federal government."[7]

I was in Lagos at the time. This event was so big that I cannot even in retrospect fully explain exactly what was happening. People were confused. I was confused myself. People who are confused in such a situation generally act with great desperation, emotion—some would say without logic.

The movement toward a declaration of independence was very clear and sharp, because it was a result of a particular group of Nigerian citizens from the Eastern Region attempting to protect themselves from the great violence that had been organized and executed by arms of the government of the Federal Republic of Nigeria. There was a strong sense that Nigeria was no longer habitable for the Igbo and many other peoples from Eastern Nigeria.

That epiphany made us realize that Nigeria "did not belong we," as Liberians would put it. "This country belong we" was the popular pidgin English mantra from their liberation struggle. That was not the case for Igbo people and many others from Eastern Nigeria. Nigeria did not belong to us. It was now clear to many of us that we, the Nigerian people, were not what we had thought we were. The Nigeria that meant so much to all of us was not reciprocating the affection we had for it. The country had not embraced us, the Igbo people and other Easterners, as full-fledged members of the Nigerian family. That was the predicament that the Igbo and many peoples from Eastern Nigeria found themselves in, and one that informed Ojukwu's decisions, I believe, on the eve of civil war.

The first part of May 1967 saw the visit of the National Reconciliation Commission (NRC) to Enugu, the capital of the Eastern Region. It was led by Chief Awolowo and billed as a last-minute effort at peace and as an attempt to encourage Ojukwu and Eastern leaders to attend peace talks at a venue suitable to the Easterners. Despite providing a friendly reception, many Igbo leaders referred to the visit disdainfully as the "chop, chop, talk, talk, commission." A majority of Easterners by this time had grown contemptuous of Gowon's federal government for its failure to bring the culprits of the mass murders in the North to justice, and they saw this as the latest in a series of insincere overtures. Senior Igbo military officers were also openly voicing their concern that Gowon was an illegitimate leader, because he was not the most senior officer in the chain of military command, and so had no right to be head of state.

There were a number of distinguished and well-meaning Nigerians on the National Reconciliation Commission, but they were meeting with leaders of an emotionally and psychologically exhausted and disillusioned Igbo people. Many of these same Igbo leaders had been at the vanguard of independence struggles, and after years of spearheading the "one Nigeria" mantra, had very little to show for it. Clearly the situation had become untenable.[8]

On May 24, 1967, in the midst of this chaos, my wife went into labor. I sent my close friend, the poet Christopher Okigbo, to the hospital she had been admitted to to find out when the birth would take place, and then to call me at home, where I had briefly returned to rest and take a shower. In characteristic Okigbo fashion, he waited for the delivery, went to the nursery to see the baby, and then drove back to convey the news to me that my wife had delivered our third child, Chidi—"There is a God"—and that the way his baby locks were arranged, he looked like he had had a haircut and was ready to go to school! The baby's arrival was a great joy, but I couldn't but feel a certain amount of apprehension for this infant, indeed for all of us, as the prospect of civil war cast a dark shadow over our lives.

GENERATION GAP

A son's arrival
is the crescent moon
too new too soon to lodge
the man's returning. His
feast of reincarnation
must await the moon's
ripening at the naming
ceremony of his
grandson.[1]

The Nightmare Begins

May the twenty-sixth saw an emergency meeting of Ojukwu's special Advisory Committee of Chiefs and Elders in Enugu. The consensus was building across his cabinet that secession was the only viable path. "On May 27, the Consultative Assembly mandated Colonel Ojukwu to declare, at the earliest practicable date, Eastern Nigeria a free sovereign and independent state by the name and title of the Republic of Biafra."[1]

It is crucial to note that the decision of an entire people, the Igbo people, to leave Nigeria, did not come from Ojukwu alone but was informed by the desires of the people and mandated by a body that contained some of the most distinguished Nigerians in history: Dr. Nnamdi Azikiwe, Nigeria's, former governor-general and first ceremonial president; Dr. Michael I. Okpara and Sir Francis Ibiam, former premier and governor of Eastern Nigeria, respectively; and Supreme Court justice Sir Louis Mbanefo. Others included: the educator Dr. Alvan Ikoku; first republic minister Mr. K. O. Mbadiwe; as well as Mr. N. U. Akpan; Mr. Joseph Echeruo; Ekukinam-Bassey; Chief Samuel Mbakwe; Chief Jerome Udoji; and Chief Margaret Ekpo.

In a speech to the nation on May 27, 1967, Gowon responded to Ojukwu's "assault on Nigeria's unity and blatant revenue appropriation," as the federal government saw it, by calling a state of emergency and dividing the nation into twelve states.[2]

The official position from the federal government was that the creation of new states was an important move to foster unity and stability in Nigeria. Many suspect a more Machiavellian scheme at work here.[3] Gowon, understanding inter-ethnic rivalry, suspected that dividing the East into four states, landlocking the Igbos into the East Central State and isolating the oil-producing areas of Nigeria outside Igbo land, would weaken secessionist sentiments in the region and empower minority groups that lived in oil-producing regions to stand up to what they had already dreaded for years—the prospects of Igbo domination.[4]

On May 30, 1967, Ojukwu, citing a variety of malevolent acts directed at the mainly Igbo Easterners—such as the pogrom that claimed over thirty thousand lives; the federal government's failure to ensure the safety of Easterners in the presence of organized genocide; and the direct incrimination of the government in the murders of its own citizens— proclaimed the independence of the Republic of Biafra from Nigeria, with the full backing of the Eastern House Constituent Assembly.[5] By taking this action Ojukwu had committed us to full-blown war. Nigeria would never be the same again.

PART 2

The Nigeria-Biafra War

To fully comprehend some of the competing positions during the Nigeria-Biafra War, it may be useful to begin with an examination of the local and international response to Biafra.

THE BIAFRAN POSITION

Beginning with the January 15, 1966, coup d'état, through the counter-coup (staged mainly by Northern Nigerian officers, who murdered 185 Igbo officers[1]) and the massacre of thirty thousand Igbos and Easterners in pogroms that started in May 1966 and occurred over four months—the events of those months left millions of other future Biafrans and me feeling terrified. As we fled "home" to Eastern Nigeria to escape all manner of atrocities that were being inflicted upon us and our families in different parts of Nigeria, we saw ourselves as victims. When we noticed that the federal government of Nigeria did not respond to our call to end the pogroms, we concluded that a government that failed to safeguard the lives of its citizens has no claim to their allegiance and must be ready to accept that the victims deserve the right to seek their safety in other ways—including secession.

THE NIGERIAN ARGUMENT

Nigeria's position on Biafra, as I understand it, was hinged on the premise that if Biafra was allowed to secede then a number of other ethnic nationalities within Nigeria would follow suit.[2] The Nigerian government, therefore, had to block Biafra's secession to prevent the dissolution of Nigeria.[3]

THE ROLE OF THE ORGANIZATION OF AFRICAN UNITY

The Organization of African Unity (OAU) attempted to facilitate a number of "peace meetings" throughout the conflict. The umbrella body of sovereign African nations lacked credibility in this effort, in my opinion, as it harbored a strong One Nigeria bias from the very beginning of the war. The OAU's initial attempts to bring about peace talks—with meetings slated for Kampala, the capital of Uganda, in May 1968, and Addis Ababa, Ethiopia (at the OAU headquarters), in July 1968—were ineffectual, and quickly disintegrated into fiascos of confusion.[4]

Facing international pressure and ridicule for failing to mediate effectively between the two warring parties,[5] the OAU's consultative committee, which was made up of diplomats from Liberia, Ghana, Niger, Ethiopia, the Congo, and Camaroon, quickly re-sent invitations to the heads of state of Nigeria and Biafra—Yakubu Gowon and Emeka Ojukwu—for talks in Niamey, the capital of Niger, Nigeria's northern neighbor.[6]

The summit, from what I later learned, became a case of "sliding doors," with Gowon arriving and meeting with OAU principals ahead of the visit by Ojukwu. This treatment, meant to avoid confrontation, created the opposite effect and played no small part in diminishing the possible results that the first president of the Republic of Niger, Hamani Diori, was attempting to moderate. Professor Eni Njoku, the chief negotiator from Biafra, gallantly attempted to salvage what was left of that Nigeria-Biafra summit. He arranged a meeting with the leader of the Mid-West Region government's delegation, Chief Anthony Ena-horo, that closed in an impasse.[7]

Ojukwu saw an opportunity to speak to a world audience at the next summit and agreed to attend; it was planned for August in the Ethiopian capital of Addis Ababa. He treated the gathered delegates to a speech of over two hours in length, and made the case for Biafran independence. He pointed out the great irony of the conflict, one that most of us in Biafra were already aware of: Having spearheaded the fight for Nigerian independence, Biafrans were later driven out by the rest of Nigeria, which waged war with the secessionist republic to conserve the very sovereignty of a nation (Nigeria) within whose walls Biafrans did not feel free, safe, or desired.[8]

In my opinion, Gowon's absence at these meetings was telling, because it clearly suggested that he had a different agenda. This suspicion would be confirmed by his announcement of a surge in the Nigerian offensive that would increase exponentially the numbers dying and starving to death in the coming months.

Most African countries adhered to the doctrines of the Organization of African Unity, which supported Nigeria for the same reasons espoused by the great powers: "[A]llowing Biafra to secede would result in the destabilization of the entire continent."[9] There were a few prominent nations in Africa that openly declared support for the Biafran cause for humanitarian, ethical, and moral reasons. Tanzania's Nyerere, one of the few survivors of the cold war tussle on the continent and a towering African statesman of the era, saw Biafra's attempts to secede through the lens of "the Jews seeking a homeland following the Holocaust in Nazi Germany and elsewhere in Europe."[10]

President Julius Nyerere was the first African head of state to recognize Biafra. His statement was published by the government printer in

Tanzania's capital, Dar es Salam, on April 13, 1968. The day we heard that
Tanzania had recognized Biafra "was a fantastic day." I remember it vividly. "I was sitting in my home with my wife; we were feeling very
depressed, I don't know why, then suddenly somebody ran in and told us
[the good news], and we said, 'Don't be silly,' because we [did not believe
him]. And then we heard [the same news] on the BBC [British Broadcasting Corporation], and my wife rushed up" to tell me. She was so elated and

> said she was going to teach in Tanzania. Soon after that the streets were
> filled with people dancing and singing. For the first time in months you
> found dancing again, and the radio was playing Tanzanian music. People
> were reassured again that there was justice in the world, because we were
> already becoming quite cynical about the outside world, saying, "Don't
> imagine anyone would come to your rescue—they know you're right, but
> it doesn't pay, so they won't do anything." We were more or less per-
> suaded that we would have to fight on our own. [Nyerere's] gesture meant
> nothing in military or material terms but it assured us—the effect it had
> on us—was electric.[11]

Other African leaders—Zambia's Kenneth Kaunda, Gabon's Omar
Bongo, and Ivory Coast's Houphouët-Boigny—also officially recognized
Biafra. I later learned that Boigny was ideologically opposed to large
African states and helped develop France's well-planned decolonization
policy in West Africa during his days as a parliamentarian in Paris.[12]
Boigny could have very well convinced a sympathetic Charles de Gaulle
to support Biafra in order to achieve this ideological vision. Whatever
his agenda was, it was to Houphouët-Boigny's Ivory Coast that Ojukwu
would escape after the fall of Biafra in January 1970.

There were other attempts to garner recognition for secessionist Biafra
beyond the African continent, including wide international ones. Those
who followed our story were aware of the shared history between Biafra

and several Caribbean nations, where descendants of former Igbo slaves now lived. That historical connection was employed by Biafran emissaries with some success. Biafra's diplomatic delegation, led by Dr. Okechukwu Ikejiani and Mr. Chukwuma Azikiwe, met with Dr. François Duvalier, president of Haiti, at the presidential palace in Port-au-Prince in February 1969. Following that visit, on March 22, 1969, Biafra secured the only non-African full diplomatic recognition—from the Haitian people.[13]

The Triangle Game: The UK, France, and the United States[1]

Great Britain's official response to the conflict, we were told, was predicated upon the fact that as our "former colonial master," she would not stand for the breakup of one of her prized colonies, especially one she had worked hard to develop. Michael Leapman's report in *The Independent* in 1998 uncovers a far more cynical attitude. This paragraph confirmed what a number of us in Biafra already suspected about Harold Wilson's government:

> Cabinet papers for [1967], just released, show how the decision to continue arming Nigeria was not based on arguments for or against secession, or on the interests of its people, but on backing the likely winner. It is a case study in realpolitik. As one Commonwealth Office briefing document to the prime minister put it: "The sole immediate British interest is to bring the [Nigerian] economy back to a condition in which our substantial trade and investment can be further developed."[2]

The BBC's Rick Fountain, in a story on Monday, January 3, 2000, called "Secret Papers Reveal Biafra Intrigue," confirms that oil interests and competition between Britain, France, and the United States played a far more important role than the "unified Nigeria" position:

> At first Biafra was successful and this alarmed Britain, the former colonial power, anxious for its big oil holdings. It also interested the Soviet Union which saw a chance to increase its influence in West Africa. Both sent arms to boost the federal military government, under General Yakubu Gowon.
>
> But France, the other big former colonial power in the region, also took a hand. . . . Although Paris repeatedly denied arming the Biafrans, the newly released papers reveal intelligence reports showing that very large weapon shipments were reaching Biafra via two neighboring Francophone states, Ivory Coast and Gabon. The UK intelligence services warned that Soviet penetration was growing but that this did not much trouble Paris. The British reports say the French objective "appears to be the breakup of Nigeria, which threatens, by its size and potential, to overshadow France's client Francophone states in West Africa."[3]

I was aware from my contacts in England that many Britons were not pleased with the unsolicited leadership role Harold Wilson's government was playing in the bloody conflict in their former African colony. Emotional antipathy among the British public grew sufficiently as the conflict progressed to threaten the British Labor government's reelection chances. British journalists, writers, and intellectuals found the situation appalling as well. "The Times of London complain[ed] that Britain's Nigerian policy is a failure. . . . [T]here is a serious loss of touch in the conduct of British foreign policy."[4]

Harold Wilson's government soon found itself awash in a public relations nightmare at home and abroad.[5] Wilson personally accused Ojukwu of attempting to garner sympathy by exploiting the casualties of a war to which his government was supplying arms![6] The bombing of civilian targets in Biafra by the Nigerian air force made the evening news and appeared in the major newspapers in Great Britain and "stirred a hornet's nest" of outrage from the British people. Things were so tense that British dockworkers reportedly refused to load ships with British arms heading for Lagos, protesting that they were being used to kill "Biafran babies."

By the time the Nigerian air force shot down a Swedish Red Cross plane carrying humanitarian supplies and medicines to the sick and dying in Biafra, killing all aboard, there was, understandably, an "outbreak of public anguish" in Britain. That distress grew even worse shortly after this, with the awful news that the International Red Cross's director, Dr. August Lindt, and his aides were detained for nearly sixteen hours following their arrival in Lagos for a tour of humanitarian relief sites in Biafra and talks with Nigerian government officials.[7]

Across the English Channel, there was uplifting news. On July 31, 1968, Biafran diplomacy reached a milestone when the French Council of Ministers released a statement of approbation in support of Biafra, though it fell short of a full recognition of the secessionist republic:

> The Government [of France] considers that the bloodshed and suffering endured for over a year by the population of Biafra demonstrate their will to assert themselves as a people. Faithful to its principles, the French Government therefore considers that the present conflict should be solved on the basis of the right of peoples to self-determination and should include the setting in motion of appropriate international procedures.[8]

There was great excitement about this news in Biafra. Charles de Gaulle was a widely respected European leader who fought the Nazis valiantly during World War II from his base in Africa. I personally hoped that de Gaulle's extensive knowledge of the continent's history and political affairs would result in a sophisticated response to the crisis. I was encouraged when I heard that he was toying with the possibility of an outright statement of recognition of the Republic of Biafra. Also buoyed by this news, the Biafran head of state, Ojukwu, sent emissaries to Paris to lobby for full French credence, which we all mistakenly assumed was in the bag, but also for de Gaulle to help persuade the United States government to support the Biafran cause.[9]

I discovered later that Jacques Foccart—described as "the most powerful man in the fifth republic" by eminent French journalist Pierre Péan—was the chief architect of French policy on the African continent. It was Foccart, I understand, who convinced the French parliament and de Gaulle to respond forcefully to the humanitarian disaster in Biafra.[10]

De Gaulle needed little persuasion. It was well-known that he bore a deep resentment of the British for what he saw as their unhelpful role in the French resistance (*La Résistance française*) during World War II. Foccart, in his memoirs, informs us that Paris increased this Anglo-French rivalry by making aggressive diplomatic inroads into Ghana (a former British colony, which was surrounded by the former French colonies Benin, Togo, Burkina Faso, and Ivory Coast).[11] Some Africanists believe that the Gaullist objective seemed to be to neutralize Ghana and diminish Nigeria as a regional power, and thereby contract Great Britain's sphere of influence in West Africa.

There were other French interests that later came to light: Paris wanted the French oil company Elf Aquitaine (which had a smaller market share in Nigeria's oil industry) to have a greater footprint in the West African region consistent with Jacques Foccart's vision of French dominance.[12] Whatever French motivations might have been, we were grateful in Biafra to be receiving their support.

The United States of America was officially "neutral" during the conflict, which meant that it overtly supported neither the Nigerians nor the Biafrans.[13] Those of us who wanted a more aggressive pro-Biafra stance from America, particularly on humanitarian grounds, were deeply disappointed, to put it mildly. Covertly, however, it was alleged that Washington under President Lyndon Johnson, before he left office in January 1968, was aiding the Nigerian war effort, in cooperation with the British. His government also had a number of run-ins with Biafran authorities over the role of the International Red Cross, America's chief humanitarian organ for getting relief to the needy in Biafra, particularly after Gowon and his government imposed a blockade.

Several months into the conflict, however, the Nixon administration, initially toeing the Johnson administration's line of "neutral engagement in support of a one Nigeria," took a more proactive role and called for the cessation of hostilities. It was the government of the much maligned Richard Nixon that raised concerns about Nigerian military strategy and levied the charges of ethnic cleansing and genocide against the Nigerian forces. Despite what some of us saw as a cynical disinterest on the part of the American government, the American people were characteristically generous and magnanimous in spirit; they sent millions of humanitarian dollars to ease the suffering of the innocent caught between the belligerents.[14]

The leaders of the African American civil rights community were understandably horrified by the breakdown in law and order in Nigeria. The black intelligentsia—colleagues of Martin Luther King and Rosa Parks—were scholars of the nonviolence movement. On several occasions they came out forcefully against all forms of ferocity during the Nigeria-Biafra conflict, reacting with dismay at the magnitude of the human suffering in Biafra. They sent numerous forms of communication both to Ojukwu and Gowon to put an end to the bloody civil war. They were particularly appalled by the widespread hunger and starvation of Biafrans and by the millions of stranded refugees, all of which they reiterated was "unacceptable to civilized world opinion."[15]

The National Association for the Advancement of Colored People (NAACP) was particularly critical of the brutality of the conflict. The leader of the influential civil rights group, Roy Wilkins, implored the Nigerians especially to be more humane in their treatment of the Biafrans. He made a moral argument to end the food blockade by reminding Gowon that the need to save the lives of the thousands starving daily "outweighed any military or political considerations."[16] My admiration of the African American civil rights community was due not only to their moral positions on racial equality and the quest for peaceful coexistence of all peoples, but also on their arbitration during the Biafran struggle— an intervention that brought succor to millions and helped place a moral lens on the atrocities taking place in my homeland.

The Soviet Union had no significant presence in the region prior to 1966 but progressively took greater interest in Nigerian affairs after the Aguiyi-Ironsi coup d'état and the emergence of Nigeria as an important oil exporter. The initial neutrality of the USSR's Western rivals, including Britain and the United States in particular, I gather, provided an opening for the Soviets to send MiG fighters and technical assistance to the Nigerians, thereby including the region in the cold war theater.[17]

There were other reasons for the ever-growing Soviet presence in Nigeria in 1969.[18] The Soviets had announced their intention to expand their bilateral trade agreements with Nigeria to include military and economic assistance. They had their eyes on a truly large prize: a contract to build one of the largest steel mills in all of Africa, at a cost of a then astonishing $120 million.[19] That steel investment later became the Ajaokuta Steel Mill in northern Nigeria—the poster child of corruption and white elephant projects in Africa—that went on to gulp over $4.6 billion of the Nigerian taxpayers' money although very little steel was produced.[20]

The Portuguese, it should be made clear, had a more nebulous role with regard to Biafra. Portugal did not overtly back one side over the other during the conflict, which generated a great deal of talk and speculation. The extent of the Biafran relationship with Portugal was quite simply one that said, We will support you quietly. . . . Your planes can land in our territory—São Tomé. Rajat Neogy of *Transition* magazine probed to find out from me whether there was more to our relationship. My position at the time was understandably passionate:

> I am not interested in what motives Portugal may have. If the devil himself had offered his air facilities we would have taken it, and I would have supported it. Portugal was very clever when it realized we were about to be exterminated, and said, "You can land at my airport," and that, as far as I know, is the extent of Biafran association with Portugal. Portugal has not given us any arms. We buy arms on the black market. What we cannot get elsewhere, we try and make.[21]

The Chinese entered the contest late, albeit on the side of the Biafrans. Reports of Chinese technical and military assistance have been widely cited. Nevertheless, all told, the callous interference of the great powers led to great despair and a prolongation of the tragedy.[22]

The Writers and Intellectuals

Some of the leading international thinkers of the era were so appalled by the Biafran tragedy that they took it upon themselves to pay the breakaway republic a visit and get a firsthand look at the suffering, the destitution, and the starvation. Auberon Waugh came and afterward wrote a devastating book on Harold Wilson's duplicitous policy. He also named his newborn child Biafra Waugh! There was a small group of American writers—Kurt Vonnegut,[1] Herbert Gold, and Harvey Swados—who came to show solidarity with me and other beleaguered Biafran writers.[2]

Vonnegut was so devastated following his trip that he cried for weeks. Todd Davis reports that

Vonnegut's response to his trip to Biafra was not suicide, but tears. He recounts his return to Manhattan, where he checked in to [*sic*] the Royalton Hotel (his family was skiing in Vermont): "I found myself crying so hard I was barking like a dog. I didn't come close to doing that after World War II" [*Fates* 174]. [His experiences in] Biafra and Mozambique, quite obviously, play a part in the author's consistent plea that we respect one another, an action that must involve our participation in meeting the needs of the global community.[3]

Kurt left in the seminal essay "Biafra: A People Betrayed" a glowing testament to his observations.

Geoffrey Hill, the British poet, Douglas Killam, the Canadian literary critic and scholar, Stanley Diamond, and the amiable Conor Cruise O'Brien all visited Biafra. Diamond brought something additional—a long-standing scholarly interest and expertise in the territory.[4] This world-renowned anthropologist became an "intellectual Biafran warrior,"[5] galvanizing a formidable American and Canadian intellectual response to the tragedy.

Diamond's knowledge of Nigeria came from having done extensive fieldwork in parts of the country right from the last days of the British raj, and he followed its affairs closely through independence, and after. He understood the ideological dimension of the Nigeria-Biafra conflict. He was not fooled by the strenuous effort of Britain to pass off her former colony as a success story of African independence, when in fact it had only passed, with Britain's active collaboration, from colonial to neocolonial status. He saw the bloody civil war not as Harold Wilson and other apologists for Nigeria presented it—that is, as progressive nationalism fighting "primitive" tribalism—but as the ruining of a rare and genuine national culture at the moment of its birth.

It was advantageous to the federal Nigerian case to stigmatize Biafra for its alleged links with South Africa and Portugal. Diamond pointed out that it was the Czechoslovakians and the Chinese, not South Africans or Portuguese, who supplied the bulk of Biafra's arms in the first year of the war, and that the Czech source dried up after the Prague spring reform movement was crushed by Soviet tanks and the fall of Alexander Dubček in 1968.

The moment has come for Nigerians and the world to ask the proper questions and draw the right inferences about what happened in those terrible years. Stanley Diamond's perceptions will, no doubt, be a great help to us. They are rooted in prodigious learning and a profoundly humane sensibility. I am happy that this remarkable man, who has searched far, who has found and reclaimed the uncluttered vision of the "primitive" at the crossroads of science and song, has bestowed on my country the benefit of his deep scholarly, humanistic, and spiritual meditation.

The New York Review of Books of May 22, 1969, carried a long article, "Biafra Revisited," by Conor Cruise O'Brien on the second visit he made with Diamond to the secessionist enclave. It was accompanied by a poem I had just written in memory of Christopher Okigbo, Africa's greatest modern poet, who had recently died on the Biafran battlefield. It also carried a profoundly moving poem, "Sunday in Biafra," by Stanley Diamond that, like all his poetry, combines startling substantiality with haunting ease and inevitability, and it stamps on the mind like an icon of Africa's tragedy an image and logic that nothing will remove.[6]

Nigerian author Enzwa-Ohaeto later wrote, "O'Brien was convinced that the 'survival of Biafra' would be 'a victory for African courage, endurance, and skill, and an opportunity for the further development of African creativity.' In his report on that visit in *The New York Review of Books*, he points out that of the 'two best known writers, . . . Achebe is a convinced Biafran patriot and the other, the playwright Wole Soyinka (a Yoruba) is a prisoner in Northern Nigeria.'"[7] Of critical importance to the entire debate around the Biafran affair was O'Brien's conclusion: "'[N]o one seriously interested in African literature, in its relation to African social and political life, can have failed to ponder the meaning of the choices and fates of these two men.'"[8]

The War and the Nigerian Intellectual

The war came as a surprise to the vast majority of artists and intellectuals on both sides of the conflict. We had not realized just how fragile, even weak, Nigeria was as a nation. Only a few Nigerians, such as the poet Christopher Okigbo, had early and privileged insights into the Nigerian-Biafran crisis.

We, the intellectuals, were deeply disillusioned by the ineptitude of Nigeria's ruling elite and by what we saw taking place in our young nation. As far as their relationship with the masses was concerned, Nigerian politicians, we felt, had slowly transformed themselves into the personification of Anwụ—the wasp—a notorious predator from the insect kingdom. Wasps, African children learn during story time, greet unsuspecting prey with a painful, paralyzing sting, then lay eggs on their body, which then proceed to "eat the victim alive."

Intellectuals had other reasons to despair: We were especially disheartened by the disintegration of the state because we were brought up in the belief that we were destined to rule. Our Northern Nigerian brethren had similar sentiments, but those feelings came from a totally different understanding of the world.

This opinion may explain why so many intellectuals played an active role in various capacities during the war years. Some of us evolved into "public intellectuals" through the period of the national crisis leading up to the war and exposed distortions and misrepresentations within the political system. Once the war began, however, many, particularly those of us in Biafra, drew upon the teachings of our ancient traditions.

Nri philosophy implores intellectuals to transform themselves into "warriors of peace" during periods of crisis, with a proclivity for action over rhetoric. Many of our finest writers and thinkers were armed with this ancient wisdom and worked toward a peaceful resolution to the hostilities.

Cyprian Ekwensi was one of the pioneers of the West African literary renaissance of the twentieth century. He was the author of numerous works, such as *An African Night's Entertainment*, *The Passport of Mallam Ilia*, *Burning Grass*, *The Drummer Boy*, and *Jagua Nana*. When the war broke out Ekwensi left his job as director of the Nigerian Ministry of Information and served the Biafran cause in the Bureau of External Publicity, and as a roving ambassador for the people of the enclave. During the war years I traveled with Ekwensi and Gabriel Okara on several diplomatic voyages on behalf of the people of Biafra.

Wole Soyinka was already regarded by this time as Africa's foremost dramatist. He had published *The Swamp Dweller*, *The Lion and the Jewel*, and *The Trials of Brother Jero* as well as collections of poetry. *The Road* is considered by many to be his greatest play. *A Dance of the Forest*, a biting criticism of Nigeria's ruling classes, was the first of what was to become his signature role—as one of the most consistent critics of misrule from his generation. His 1964 novel, *The Interpreters*, as well as ventures into recording, film, and poetry, showcased his versatility. Soyinka's attempts to avert a full-blown civil war by meeting with Colonel Ojukwu and Victor Banjo, as well as with then lieutenant colonel Olusegun Obasanjo, would earn him enemies in the Nigerian federal government and a twenty-two-month imprisonment.

The story I was told about this incident was that Wole, fed up with the federal government's unsuccessful treatment of the Biafra issue, had traveled to secessionist Biafra in an attempt to appeal for a cease-fire to the hostilities. He planned to set up an antiwar delegation made up of intellectuals, artists, and writers from both sides of the conflict—and from around the world—to achieve his aim. When he returned to Nigeria the authorities arrested him and accused him of assisting Biafra in the purchase of weapons of war.[1] There was no evidence to corroborate their case, and Wole was imprisoned without bail. Later, to justify holding him without evidence, the federal government accused Wole of being a Biafran agent or spy, trumped-up charges that he categorically denied. I remember relating my disgust about Soyinka's predicament to the editors of *Transition* in 1968 during the war: "I have no intention of being placed in a Nigerian situation at all. I find it intolerable. I find the Nigerian situation untenable. If I had been a Nigerian, I think I would have been in the same situation as Wole Soyinka is—in prison."[2]

There was great concern for Wole's health and safety as time went on. For many of the months he was in prison he was held in solitary confinement and moved from one prison to another. Most of us in Biafra were appalled. PEN International and many major writers of the time— Norman Mailer comes to mind—led a vigorous protest on his behalf, but he was not released until close to the very end of the war.

Professor Kenneth Onwuka Dike inspired us all very greatly and deserves special attention. He was a pioneer in so many respects. He was one of the first pupils to attended Dennis Memorial Grammar School. After that he traveled to the Gold Coast to attend Achimota College, and then went farther afield to Sierra Leone to attend Fourah Bay College before proceeding to England for undergraduate studies. He received his bachelor of science degree at the Durham University, England, and his master of arts degree from the University of Aberdeen, in Scotland. After a few years of study at Oxford, he earned his PhD in history from the University of London and returned to Nigeria, first to join the faculty, but later to become the first indigenous vice chancellor of University College, Ibadan.

In the late 1960s, the Ford and Rockefeller foundations decided to set up the International Institute of Tropical Agriculture somewhere in Nigeria, under the leadership of the former president of North Dakota State University, Fargo, Dr. Herbert R. Albrecht; Dike, along with Dr. T. A. Lambo, were among the Nigerians consulted. Dike suggested the prestigious institute be founded on a twenty-three-hundred-acre campus, in a loose affiliation with University College, Ibadan. And so it was. Dike was involved in several of these kinds of projects. For example, he was also instrumental in the establishment of the Nigerian National Archives.

Everyone who knew him will acknowledge that Dike was one of the most "detribalized" Nigerians of his generation. This point requires emphasis. A man of this ilk, a rare breed indeed, watched horrified at the disintegration of the nation that he and so many others had fought to establish. His sentiments would change to despair and anger following the massacre of thirty thousand Easterners and the rising hostility toward him and his family in Ibadan.[3]

Dike resigned as vice chancellor of Ibadan in December 1966 and returned to Eastern Nigeria, where he served as vice chancellor of the University of Biafra for a brief period. When the war broke out Dike was appointed by Ojukwu to be a roving ambassador for Biafra. He and other roving ambassadors[4] traveled extensively throughout the world, speaking on behalf of the secessionist republic. Dike was particularly effective in this role, and his appearances attracted vigorous media attention. I remember reading several articles in the *Washington Post* following his appearance at the National Press Club. One article in particular, called "Biafra Explains Its Case" and published on April 13, 1969, was especially influential.

Before our time, Dike had already established an international reputation for academic excellence as a historian. He taught at Harvard University after the war as the first Mellon Professor of African History. In 1978, at the dawn of Nigeria's Second Republic, this towering international academic returned to Nigeria to help set up the Anambra State University of Technology (ASUTECH). It is a disservice to this wonderful man, to his achievements and contribution to Nigeria's development, that he died in 1983 from a blood infection that would not have been difficult to cure had he stayed in the United States![5]

Vincent Chukwuemeka Ike also supported the Biafran cause and served the Biafran people in several bureaucratic positions. Later, through prolific literary output, Ike took a well-deserved place at the vanguard of the continent's leading novelists.

The literary harvest from Africa today owes a great debt to female African intellectual forerunners. These griots, orators, and later writers played an indispensable role in recording, molding, and transmitting the African story. By boldly mixing numerous African and Western literary traditions in a cauldron, seasoning them with local color, and spicing their tales with the complexity of the human condition, modern women wordsmiths have deepened our understanding of our world. Florence Nwanzuruahu Nwapa (Flora Nwapa) belongs to this important school of African female literary progenitors.

Five years before the war, in 1962, Flora Nwapa informed me that she was working on a manuscript to be called *Efuru*. After some editorial work, *Efuru* was published in 1966, on the eve of the war, to great fanfare. It was a monumental event, as it was, as far as I could tell, the first novel published by a Nigerian woman. It was also important because it was a book ahead of its time, with an assuredly feminist plot and perspective.[6]

Around the same period, as providence would have it, Alan Hill, the publishing executive at Heinemann Publishers in England, asked me to become the first editor of the African Writers Series. Alan and I, with James Currey and a few others, developed a vision of gathering much of Africa's literary talent under this series rubric in order to showcase the best of postcolonial African literature. We had a fascinating beginning, and ended up publishing Christopher Okigbo from Nigeria, Ayi Kwei

Armah from Ghana, al-Tayyib Salih from Sudan, Ngũgĩ wa Thiong'o from Kenya, Bessie Head from Botswana, Nadine Gordimer from South Africa, and Nelson Mandela, along with several other major African writers.[7]

Flora Nwapa aided the Biafran war effort in various capacities, and after the conflict was over continued her service to her people in the Ministry of Health and Social Welfare, the Ministry of Lands, Survey and Urban Development, and the Ministry of Establishment. She is remembered for her bold efforts at reconstructing many institutions that had been destroyed during the Nigeria-Biafra War.[8]

It is important to point out that a number of writers were neutral and quietly, as far as I could tell, apolitical during the conflict between Nigeria and Biafra. They did not align themselves with or provide overt support to either belligerent during the war. One such individual was Amos Tutuola, who was a talented writer. His most famous novels, *The Palm-Wine Drinkard*, published in 1946, and *My Life in the Bush of Ghosts*, in 1954, explore Yoruba traditions and folklore. He received a great deal of criticism from Nigerian literary critics for his use of "broken or Pidgin English." Luckily for all of us, Dylan Thomas, the Welsh poet and writer, was enthralled by Tutuola's "bewitching literary prose" and wrote glowing reviews that helped Tutuola's work attain international acclaim. I still believe that Tutuola's critics in Nigeria missed the point. The beauty of his tales was fantastical expression of a form of an indigenous Yoruba, therefore African, magical realism. It is important to note that his books came out several decades before the brilliant Gabriel García Márquez published his own masterpieces of Latin American literature, such as *One Hundred Years of Solitude*.

I first met Mabel Segun (nee Aig-Imoukhuede), another prominent literary figure, who was in the second set of students admitted to University College, Ibadan, around 1949. She was a bright and energetic student from Sabongida Ora in Edo State. I was the editor of the university paper, the *University Herald*, and when it came time to appoint a deputy editor and advertisement manager, she was a natural choice. In 1965, African University Press, a formidable outfit at the time, published her children's book, *My Father's Daughter.*

Bolanle Awe, Dr. Tai Solarin, S. J. Cookey, Gabriel Okara, Ola Rotimi, Ade Ajayi, and Emmanuel Obiechina were other towering figures of that era who I admired.

The Life and Work of Christopher Okigbo

I have written and been quoted elsewhere as saying that Christopher Ifekandu Okigbo was the finest Nigerian poet of his generation, but I believe that as his work becomes better and more widely known in the world, he will also be recognized as one of the most remarkable anywhere in our time. For while other poets wrote good poems, Okigbo conjured up for us an amazing, haunting, poetic firmament of a wild and violent beauty.[1] Forty years later I still stand by that assessment.

Christopher and I kept in touch after we graduated from Government College, Umuahia, and our friendship grew during our time at University College, Ibadan. He studied the classics and took classes in Latin—a subject that was not available at Government College, Umuahia. A rumor I heard at the time was that a teacher at Yaba Higher College who had been Pius Okigbo's teacher (Christopher's senior brother), Professor E. A. Cadle, had wanted Pius to study classics, but Pius did not want to, and instead traveled to America to study economics at Northwestern University. Pius later became arguably the continent's leading thinker in that field. By the time Christopher got to University College, Ibadan,

Professor Cadle was now a professor of the classics and later dean of the Faculty of Arts. He persuaded Christopher to take a major in the classics. Christopher did, although he had a myriad of other interests. He was involved in all aspects of campus life and had a very active social calendar. He was a member of every cultural, literary, intellectual and political organization, club, and association. He and I were founding members of the notable Mbari Club, which was led by Ulli Beier, our professor. Okigbo was also the editor in chief of the *University Weekly*, the campus newspaper.

His legendary creative work was first noted at Umuahia, where the teachers encouraged this budding talent. Later, at the University College, Ibadan, he published a number of poems in *Horn*, the university magazine edited by J. P. Clark. He also published his work in Wole Soyinka's *Black Orpheus* and *Transition*, and then produced a number of critically acclaimed poetry collections, including the groundbreaking classics *Heavens Gate* and *Labyrinths*.[2]

After graduation, his reputation as a talented intellectual spread like a savannah bush fire. He was highly sought after. He rapidly ran up a list of jobs that read like a manual of careers: civil servant, businessman, teacher, librarian, publisher, industrialist, and soldier. I am told that Chike Momah, a professional librarian, was somewhat scandalized when Okigbo announced that he was going to Nsukka to be interviewed for a position in the library of the new university. Reminded that he knew nothing about librarianship, Okigbo blithely replied that he had bought a book on the subject, which he intended to read during the four-hundred-mile journey to the interview. And he got the job![3]

Christopher could not enter or leave a room unremarked, yet he was not extravagant in manner or appearance. There was something about him not easy to define, a certain inevitability of drama and event. There was a day, back when my family still lived in Lagos, when my wife,

Christie, overheard some people talking quite early in the morning on our patio. Startled and a bit frightened, she wondered what was going on. A few minutes later she smelled the aroma of food, and at this point her curiousity was piqued. "What was the cook doing so early in the morning?" she thought out loud. She put on her robe and went to find out. It turned out that it was Christopher Okigbo. There he was sitting on the kitchen table with the food that the cook had prepared for him, munching away. He had arrived very early in the morning, went to the "boys' quarters," and woke up the cook, described what he wanted him to cook, and said, "Don't tell them anything." That was quintessential Okigbo.

Christopher's vibrancy and heightened sense of life touched everyone he came into contact with. It is not surprising, therefore, that the young poet Kevin Echeruo should have celebrated him as an Ogbanje—one of those mysterious, elusive, and highly talented beings who hurry to leave the world and to come again. Equally profound was the fact that Pol Ndu, who died in a road disaster he had predicted every gory detail of in a poem five years earlier, proclaimed Christopher a seer.[4]

Christopher never took antimalarial drugs, because he rather enjoyed the cozy, delirious fever he had when malaria got him down, about once a year. He relished challenges, and the more unusual or difficult, the better it made him feel. Although he turned his hand to many things, he never did anything badly or half-heartedly.[5]

The experiences of the Igbo community from the pogroms onward had different effects on different people. There were a multitude of reactions—anger, loathing, sorrow, concern, depression, etc. These sentiments in Christopher's case somehow transformed into a very strong pro-Biafra feeling. He had no doubt at all in his mind about Biafra and the need for the country to be a free and separate nation. That strong stance was something new for Christopher.

The intensity of Christopher's dedication to the Biafran cause was so deep that I remember hearing him get into a raucous debate with his elder brother Pius.[6] Apparently the cause of the flare-up of emotions was a discussion about Biafran sovereignty and its importance for the Easterners, particularly the Igbo, to create a state of their own and secede from the federal republic of Nigeria. Pius Okigbo was not, at least initially, very strong in his support of the idea of separation. This position outraged the much younger Christopher, who rebuked Pius by saying: "Don't let what happened to Ironsi repeat itself," implying that Pius, in his determination to preserve One Nigeria, should be careful not to be destroyed by Nigeria like Ironsi was during the time he was trying to appease extremists. Pius was so shocked by the rebuke that he turned to me, raised his hands in disbelief, and said, "Uncle Chris!"[7] in a sarcastic tone. Pius Okigbo was a very senior economist and part of the diplomatic corps representing Nigeria in several capacities, so he was a bit wary about what was going on in the East, and in Nigeria as a whole, and rightfully so. Later, as the atrocities against the Igbos in particular intensified, Pius Okigbo's position solidified squarely on Biafra's side. At that point the pressure of war was being felt. Now unbeknownst to us, Christopher had joined the army. Whereas I did not find the army particularly exciting or interesting, for whatever reason Okigbo was enthralled by the military. He would keep you up at night telling stories of what Nzeogwu and the other officers said.[8]

When Okigbo decided to join the army he went to great lengths to conceal his intention from me, for fear, no doubt, that I might attempt to dissuade him. I probably would have tried. He made up an elaborate story about an imminent and secret mission he was asked to undertake to Europe that put me totally off the scent. But to make absolutely certain, he borrowed my traveling bag and left his brown briefcase with me. When I saw him again two weeks later he was a major, by special commission, in the Biafran army, though I never saw him in uniform.[9]

The Major Nigerian Actors in the Conflict: Ojukwu and Gowon

A number of individuals played key roles during the Nigeria-Biafra War.[1] The principal actors in 1967, however, were both young Sandhurst-trained soldiers—Odumegwu Ojukwu, who was thirty-three, and Yakubu Gowon, who was thirty-two. One was from a highly privileged background and the other was the so-called darling of the British establishment.[2]

THE ARISTOCRAT

General Chukwuemeka (Emeka) Odumegwu Ojukwu was born on November 4, 1933, in Zungeru, in Northern Nigeria, to Sir Louis Odumegwu Ojukwu and Grace Oyibonanu. The senior Ojukwu was already a legendary figure while I was growing up in Eastern Nigeria, known far and wide for his great wealth and success in business. Indeed, by midcentury Sir Louis Odumegwu Ojukwu had established himself as one of West Africa's leading entrepreneurs, with business interests spanning several sectors of the Nigerian and West African economies—agriculture, mining, transportation, and banking.

Sir Louis Ojukwu at some time or other sat on the boards of a number of the largest corporations of the time—Shell BP, United Africa Company (UAC), Nigerian Coal Corporation, and African Continental Bank. For his services to the empire, Louis Odumegwu Ojukwu was knighted by Queen Elizabeth II during her official visit to Enugu in 1956.

It was in this privileged environment that General Emeka Ojukwu was raised. Like a number of other children of privilege, Ojukwu was educated at one of the leading secondary schools in the nation, King's

College, Lagos. Later he was sent to Epsom College, England, and then on to Lincoln College—University of Oxford.[3]

When Emeka Ojukwu returned to Nigeria after his studies in England, he spent a short time "finding himself." Against the wishes of his father, who wanted him to attend law school and join the family business in some capacity, the young Ojukwu decided to first work in the Eastern Nigeria civil service as an assistant district officer (ADO). Then, in a move likely designed to enrage his father even further, the young Ojukwu joined the colonial armed forces known as the Queen's Own Nigeria Regiment. Emeka Ojukwu's decision caused quite a sensation at the time, because most educated Nigerians, particularly those of privileged birth like him, sought jobs in the business, academic, or civil service sectors, but not in the army. The Nigerian army did have educated officers, but they were few in number.

Emeka Ojukwu went back to England to attend the Royal Military Academy Sandhurst and returned shortly after to Nigeria, where he joined the officer corps and rapidly rose through the military ranks. He was accorded a great deal of respect by his military colleagues, who admired his pedigree and education.[4] Frederick Forsyth, Ojukwu's close friend, who would become a close Biafran ally during the war, reports of his days in England: "[H]e developed a private philosophy of total self-reliance, an unyielding internal sufficiency that requires no external support from others."[5] This trait would bring Ojukwu in direct collision with some senior Biafrans, such as Dr. Nnamdi Azikiwe, Michael Okpara, Dr. Okechukwu Ikejiani, and a few others who were concerned about Ojukwu's tendency toward introversion and independent decision making.

Emeka Ojukwu received a mixed reception among the expatriate, mainly British, population in Nigeria. Many admired him for his background, as well as for his oratorical skills, and took great pride in the fact that he had been educated extensively in England. There is a magnificent story of how Emeka Ojukwu's professors at Oxford enjoyed taking a spin or two in his sports car while he was a student there. Others, in contrast, felt that Ojukwu was some sort of spoiled rich kid. This impression made it more difficult for him to be cast as a sympathetic figure in the Western media when the war broke out. Complicating this image problem was the fact that some important wartime actors and observers, such as Sir David Hunt, the British ambassador to Nigeria during the conflict, and the eminent British journalist John de St. Jorre, believed Ojukwu looked down on Gowon. Ojukwu felt, they believed, that as an Oxford man he was far better prepared for leadership.[6] Those of us who knew Ojukwu did not feel he harbored such sentiments. Whatever the case may be, Ojukwu's background and temperament, for good or ill, influenced the decisions and choices that he made throughout the crisis and during much of what many believed was "a personal war and collision of egos"[7] with Gowon.

The Gentleman General

Yakubu Gowon was born on October 19, 1934, in Pankshin, Plateau State, under circumstances very different from those of his military nemesis Emeka Ojukwu. Yakubu Gowon's parents were Christian missionaries. His family spent several years during his early development in Zaria in Hausa land, where he received his early education and learned to speak the language of the dominant Hausa/Fulani fluently.[8] Yakubu Gowon then received military training in Ghana and Eaton Hall in England before proceeding to the legendary officer training school in Sandhurst. "He then attended Young Officers' College, Hythe Warminster, in 1957, Staff College, Camberley, England (1962), and Joint Services College, Latimer, England (1965)."[9] He returned to Nigeria soon thereafter and became a star officer; his ability to assimilate would serve him well as he advanced rapidly in the Nigerian army.

Alexander Madiebo recounts the perception of Gowon's contemporaries in the army:

Gowon for unknown reasons has always been very popular with the British authorities, both during his training in Britain and throughout his military service in Nigeria. For this reason, his progress in the army was so remarkable and extraordinary that even his fellow Northern officers were beginning to grumble. For instance, when he was chosen to attend the Camberley Staff College, England in January 1962, Major Pam, a Jos [Joint Service] Officer senior to him, called him a "sneaky sucker."[10]

Yakubu Gowon was a particular favorite of the queen and other members of Britain's royal family, a fact that he relished immensely.[11] "[He] impressed the British monarchy as a sincere God-fearing leader who was determined to work for the development of his country under conditions of international peace and stability." He did not fail to impress Britain's cousins across the Atlantic either, at any opportunity. Henry Luce, the wealthy and highly influential American publisher of *Time* magazine, found Gowon

[a] spit-and-polish product of Britain's Royal Military Academy at Sandhurst. Gowon is sometimes dismissed as "Jack the Boy Scout" in Lagos diplomatic circles. He neither smokes nor drinks, and keeps his 5-ft. 10-in. frame trim at 140 lbs.[12]

Whether or not one can ascribe this resentment held by his fellow officers toward Gowon to soldiers' envy isn't clear, but what was evident was that Gowon was a charismatic, eloquent, personable soldier who utilized a number of his skills to impress the rich and powerful. General Aguiyi-Ironsi, who became Nigeria's first military head of state following the failed coup d'état of January 15, 1966, was one of many who were fond of Gowon, and the general appointed him chief of army staff. While I was watching events unfold in Nigeria in 1966, I found it instructive that when Ironsi was killed in the counter–coup d'état of young Northern officers on July 29, 1966, it was Yakubu Gowon who was chosen to become head of the federal military government and commander in chief of the armed forces.

Gowon's elevation to head of state was a tactical compromise to assuage most ethnic groups that Nigeria was not coming under an Islamic Hausa/Fulani leadership intent on Christian and Southern domination. It did not help matters that many officers did not feel that Gowon was the most qualified to be in the role of head of state. In the *Nigerian Outlook* of March 21, 1967, Ojukwu revealed the sentiments of many military officers in Eastern Nigeria:

> The point here and the crux of the whole matter is the fact that the North wants to dominate. . . . Gowon is not capable of doing anything. He is only a front man for the whole NPC/NNDP coalition. . . . [I]n fact the officers and men who took part in the July massacre were being used as tools. . . . But the NNDP/NPC coalition which master-minded this pogrom definitely wanted to continue the old policy of the North, that is to dominate and dictate.[13]

Behind the scenes, Murtala Muhammed was nursing his wounds. It was well-known that Muhammed, a favorite son of the Muslim Hausa/Fulani military establishment, was initially tapped to be head of state—an idea that was quickly shelved in favor of Gowon, the charismatic Christian and ethnic minority candidate from Plateau State. This snub was not lost on Muhammed, who harbored an unrelenting resentment toward Gowon and would later, in 1975, mount the decisive coup that ousted him from office.

In what was widely seen as an attempt to soothe growing ethnic hostility, particularly in Eastern Nigeria, Gowon appointed Emeka Ojukwu, a fellow Sandhurst alumnus, to the post of military governor of the Eastern Region, a post similar to that which he had held within

Aguiyi-Ironsi's Supreme Military Council. It was said that Emeka Ojukwu served in this new capacity reluctantly, because of what he believed was Gowon's unclear role in the coup that led to the assassination of General Aguiyi-Ironsi and nearly two hundred Igbo officers. The relationship between the two men, shaky from the start of Gowon's new government, suffered several other setbacks in the months to come, particularly following the series of pogroms that left over thirty thousand Easterners, mainly Igbo, murdered, and nearly one million fleeing to their ancestral homes in 1966.[14]

There are a number who believe that neither Gowon nor Ojukwu were the right leaders for that desperate time, because they were blinded by ego, hindered by a lack of administrative experience, and obsessed with interpersonal competition and petty rivalries.[15] As a consequence, according to this school of thought, these two men failed to make appropriate and wise decisions throughout the conflict and missed several opportunities when compromise could have saved the day.[16]

No small number of international political science experts found the Nigeria-Biafra War baffling, because it deviated frustratingly from their much vaunted models. But traditional Igbo philosophers, eyes ringed with white chalk and tongues dipped in the proverbial brew of prophecy, lay the scale and complexity of our situation at the feet of ethnic hatred and *ekwolo*—manifold rivalries between the belligerents. Internal rivalries, one discovers, between personalities, across ethnic groups, and within states, often fuel the persistence of conflicts.[17] Conflicts are not just more likely to last longer as a result of these rivalries but are also more likely to recur, with alternating periods of aggression and peace of shorter and shorter duration.[18] A "lock-in period"—the intensification of war with ever-shortening times of peace—is also classically seen.[19]

The internal rivalries that existed between Gowon and Ojukwu, and

the pathological intraethnic dynamics that plagued the Nigerian military and wartime government, contributed in no small measure to the
scale of the catastrophe that was the Nigeria-Biafra War. The fractured
respect and unenthusiastic reception Gowon received following his
ascendancy to the position of head of state was only the beginning. There
was a stifling anger at the dissolution of the Nigerian state, with all its
ramifications. These sentiments were borne particularly by the Easterners overlooked by the young general at the helm of Nigerian affairs, with
disastrous consequences.

There are a few other factors that merit consideration. There was an
obsessive tendency by both belligerents—Gowon and Ojukwu—to seek
positions of strength and avoid looking weak throughout the conflict. I
am not referring to the propaganda statements, however over the top,
which one expects in times of war, but to the ego-driven policies that
were clearly not about the conflict at hand. Some of Ojukwu's and
Gowon's civilian advisers aggravated the crisis by transforming themselves into sycophants. Rather than encourage their respective leader on
each side of the conflict to consider a cease-fire, they massaged their egos
and spurred them on to ever-escalating hostility.[20]

The longer the war dragged on, the more difficult it was for both sides
to give in to anything that might lead to a peaceful resolution. In Biafra
there was a widely held belief that "a cease-fire would lead to genocide
or retribution of equal magnitude, or at least the relinquishing of
self-determination and freedom." Biafrans widely believed that the
gap between our ideological position and that of our Nigerian brethren
had simply grown too wide to bridge.[21] Complicating matters was the
fact that most intellectuals in Biafra viewed Nigeria, now under military
dictatorship, as a neocolonial state under the iron grasp of its former
colonial master, Great Britain, with a very willing steward at the helm.

There are some scholars who believe that the Igbo turned to Emeka
Ojukwu by virtue of the fact that he was the governor of the Eastern

Region of Nigeria at the time of the crisis—the "man in power" theory. Others have gone as far as to suggest that the war would have been prevented if there was a leader other than Ojukwu in place. The first statement will be debated for generations. As for the second, I believe that following the pogroms, or rather, the ethnic cleansing in the North that occurred over the four months starting in May 1966, which was compounded by the involvement, even connivance, of the federal government in those evil and dastardly acts, secession from Nigeria and the war that followed became an inevitability.

To be sure, there were a number that harbored alternative points of view. One of those people was the distinguished diplomat Raph Uwechue, who served as Biafra's envoy to Paris up until 1968, and then later as Nigeria's ambassador to Mali. Uwechue published a well-known personal memoir called *Reflections on the Nigerian Civil War: Facing the Future* in 1969, in which he unleashed a scathing criticism of Ojukwu and the leadership he provided for Biafra:

> In Biafra two wars were fought simultaneously. The first was for the survival of the Ibos [*sic*] as a race. The second was for the survival of Ojukwu's leadership. Ojukwu's error, which proved fatal for millions of Ibos [*sic*], was that he put the latter first.[22]

Many who share Uwechue's point of view cite as an example Ojukwu's refusal to accept $600,000 from the British for relief supplies; they see this as evidence of a beleaguered albeit committed adversary who made ideological rather than practical or pragmatic decisions. Uwechue's conclusions about the Biafran people are, however, far more controversial, in my opinion:

> The Biafran masses, enslaved by an extremely efficient propaganda network and cowed by the iron grip of a ruthless military machine, had

neither the facts nor the liberty to form an independent opinion. The case of the elite was different. . . . Those who had access to the facts knew that the time had come to seek a realistic way to end the war. . . . In private they expressed this view but proved too cowardly to take a stand and tell Ojukwu the truth.[23]

The late Senator Francis Ellah, a close friend of mine who helped set up the Biafran mission in London, and then served Biafra in several capacities, provides much more of a middle-ground analysis. He does, however, come down on the side of the many who believed that the Biafrans, not just the Nigerians, missed a number of opportunities to compromise and end the war earlier than they did:

I think the circumstances that led to Biafra were very unique; I remember that when I heard news of the secession on the radio I almost broke down . . . the causes were quite traumatic. I think once secession had been declared, the efforts made to fight the war were staggering. We were highly impressed by the solidarity shown by the Eastern Region. Then we had a cause we were fighting for.

I think that around March 1968, when we were in a position to achieve a confederation, we should have accepted the chance or opportunity. When we were insisting that Biafran sovereignty was not negotiable, as the government thought at the time, we ought to have considered the tragedy of the situation, because this country would have been much better if we had a confederation of four to six states, other than what we have now. Around the time of the Kampala talks there were definite signs that a confederation could be achieved. The Biafran side was adamant on the fact of sovereignty being nonnegotiable.[24]

THE FIRST SHOT

That lone rifle-shot anonymous
in the dark striding chest-high
through a nervous suburb at the break
of our season of thunders will yet
steep its flight and lodge
more firmly than the greater noises
ahead in the forehead of memory.[1]

The Biafran Invasion
of the Mid-West

The Nigeria-Biafra War began soon after Emeka Ojukwu's proclamation of secession. Gowon decided to first use the federal army's First Command in what he termed a "police action,"[1] in an attempt to "restore federal government authority in Lagos and the break-away Eastern region." The move to capture the Biafran border towns of Ogoja and Nsukka proved to be a declaration of war. Following this, in July 1967, Nigerian troops attempted to cross the Niger Bridge into Biafra. The Biafran army was able to halt its advance and disperse them.[2]

That Biafran response became an advance, leading to the taking of a large swath of the Mid-Western Region in a surprise maneuver that the Nigerian federal troops had not anticipated. Ojukwu explained his ambitious plan this way:

> Our motive was not territorial ambition or the desire of conquest. We went into the Midwest (later declared the Republic of Benin) purely in an effort to seize the serpent by the head; every other activity in that Republic was subordinated to that single aim. We were going to Lagos to seize the villain Gowon, and we took necessary military precautions.[3]

Despite the euphoric verbal heroics espoused by Ojukwu, John de St. Jorre, the well-regarded reporter for *The Observer*, provided a far more subdued picture of Biafran army readiness and organization:

> The Biafrans "stormed" through the Mid-West not in the usual massive impedimenta of modern warfare but in a bizarre collection of private cars, "mammy" wagons, cattle and vegetable trucks. The command

vehicle was a Peugeot 404 estate car. The whole operation was not carried out by an "army" or even a "brigade" . . . but by at most 1,000 men, the majority poorly trained and armed, and many wearing civilian clothes because they had not been issued with uniforms.[4]

In the days preceding the Biafran invasion I was informed by friends and relatives who lived in the Mid-West Region[5] that the air there was rife with rumors of an impending federal takeover to provide it with strategic and logistical access to Eastern Nigeria if war broke out. The leading political and traditional leaders of the Mid-West had made it clear to Gowon that they wanted no part of a civil war and that the region would be neutral in the event of any hostilities. There were several reasons for this position. Apart from a desire for peace during a precarious period, the leaders of that part of Nigeria recognized that their citizens were of a multiethnic background, including a sizable Igbo population.

The Biafrans utilized this knowledge in mapping out their strategy. The leaders of the offensive related their reasons for occupying the Mid-West as one "organized to prevent the Federal Government from 'forcing Mid Westerners to enlist to fight against their own people,' thus undermining the mediatory role which the Mid-West had been playing." Indeed, some scholars speculate that Governor David Ejoor, the military governor of the Mid-West, was informed of Ojukwu's intention to invade and that both men could have very well met to discuss the implications of such an action.[6]

Brigadier Victor Banjo was one of the masterminds[7] of this successful Biafran offensive. Ojukwu had released Banjo, a Nigerian soldier who had allegedly taken part in the January 15 coup d'état and was detained in Ikot Ekpene Prison. Banjo had been found guilty of treason by the Nigerian federal government despite his insistence of innocence. He decided to stay on Biafran soil after secession rather than return and face court-martial. Ojukwu got tactical, strategic, and political mileage from having

Banjo in Biafra, and he enjoyed the prospect of having a Nigerian soldier fight for him. Against protests in certain Biafran military quarters, Ojukwu brought Victor Banjo into the statehouse at Enugu as one of his close military confidants and advisers. Victor Banjo, it was widely known, was not in favor of Ojukwu's secessionist aspirations but favored a solution to Nigeria's problems that would result in the "deamalgamation" of the country back into Southern and Northern Nigeria.[8]

In the late evening of August 14, 1967, soon after the Biafrans invaded the Mid-Western Region, Brigadier Banjo spoke to Mid-Westerners and Nigerians over the airwaves from Benin. Hundreds of thousands of listeners across the nation tuned in, expecting a detailed explanation for the invasion and a description of the long-term plans of the Biafran army. Some of the questions running through my mind and the minds of many Nigerians across the nation included the following: Who exactly was behind this invasion? Was this a temporary occupation? What was the long-term plan? What would be the reaction of Gowon and the Nigerian federal forces?

Banjo's address was a disappointment. It sounded to me far more like a lament of the breakup of Nigeria than a speech coming from "a Biafran military leader" or an explanation for the invasion of Nigerian territory or Biafran secession.

Banjo dedicated the first half of his message to what sounded like an overview of Nigeria's political and military history and his own travails within that establishment. In the second half of the speech he finally got around to explaining to his listeners that the Biafran invasion was "not a conquest . . . or an invasion" but an exercise designed to "enable the people of the Mid-West to see the Nigerian problem in its proper perspective." Banjo appealed to all civil servants to return to work the very next day and assured them of their safety. In a veiled threat, he warned those who failed to comply that they would lose their jobs.[9]

Closely following Banjo's speech was the promulgation by the Biafrans of a new decree that established what would be known as the Republic of Benin (the area occupied by Biafran forces in the Mid-Western Region) and the appointment of Major Albert Nwazu Okonkwo as its military administrator. Okonkwo's administration, we were told, would supersede the previous government of the military governor, David Ejoor, who had been appointed by the Nigerian head of state.

Major Okonkwo found his brief, some might say draconian, rule—he imposed martial law, curfews, and limited accessibility—punctuated by insurrections and burdened by the assaults of organized underground resistance groups. Many Mid-Westerners passed along to me accounts of their conflicting feelings after the Biafran offensive: "We, on the one hand, were being told by the Biafran propaganda machinery that we were being liberated from tyranny, but on the other [we were] feeling like an occupied military zone under martial law."[10]

There was also growing discontent among the Biafran soldiers who were only there on military assignment but increasingly found themselves targets of local hostility. There were reports of Biafran troops seeking medical treatment for food poisoning suffered at the hands of cooks who had been recruited from the surrounding "occupied areas." The Biafran soldiers were under siege from several fronts.[11]

According to civil war lore, Ojukwu was livid upon learning about the contents of Banjo's speech to Mid-Westerners following Biafra's takeover because it did not "sufficiently demonstrate solidarity with his own secessionist aspirations to leave Nigeria."[12] Ojukwu apparently also had been told that Banjo was complicit in a plot that enabled David Ejoor—the erstwhile military governor of the Mid-Western Region—to escape from the clutches of the Biafran forces. This made it possible, the allegations continued, for Ejoor to meet with the federal government in Lagos and provide the Nigerian head of state with critical military and tactical information about the Biafran offensive. It was also alleged that Banjo failed on purpose to continue the surprise offensive as planned beyond

Ore in the Mid-West to Nigeria's administrative capital, Lagos, and largest commercial city, Ibadan, after direct contact with agents of the federal government and Yoruba leaders.[13] Banjo's detractors, who never trusted him in the first place, had by this time successfully labeled him a traitor and an enemy of the state of Biafra.

In 1982, Ojukwu provided a glimpse of his disappointment about the role that Banjo played in the Mid-West offensive: "The stop in Benin was the beginning of the error. . . . My plan for that operation was that by half past five in the morning, the Biafran troops would be in the peripheries of Lagos."[14]

A counterpoint can be obtained from the Nigerian general Olusegun Obasanjo's memoir *My Command: An Account of the Nigerian Civil War, 1967–1970.* In it Obasanjo creates some doubts as to whether or not Victor Banjo intentionally refused to proceed farther to Ibadan and Lagos as directed: "A renowned social critic . . . and [I] discussed Banjo's request for me to grant him unhindered access to Ibadan and Lagos at any price. Both the request and the price were turned down."

So did Banjo, without Ojukwu's consent, make a tactical decision not to proceed beyond Ore after the military intelligence available to him demonstrated that it could be a suicide mission? Was Victor Banjo a traitor or a misunderstood hero? I think posterity will debate this question for a long time, because Banjo was subsequently executed by Ojukwu and did not leave written documents to prove or disprove his innocence.[15]

Gowon Regroups

Following the Biafran invasion of the Mid-West, Gowon reorganized his war strategy. He placed some of his best military personnel in three key roles as part of his agenda to "crush the Biafrans." Mohammed Shuwa was commander in charge of the First Division of the federal army. His orders

were to advance from Northern Nigeria with his troops to take the Biafran towns of Nsukka and Ogoja.[1] Colonel Murtala Muhammed, in charge
of Division Two, had marching orders to retake Benin and the other parts
of the Mid-West occupied by the Biafran army, and then cross the River
Niger into Onitsha. Finally, Division Three of the Nigerian army, led by
Benjamin Adekunle (aka "the black scorpion"), would commandeer a
southern offensive.[2] Three months later the Nigerian forces, now more
organized and "armed to the teeth" with British weapons, had staged a
successful counteroffensive. The Biafrans were now in full retreat.[3]

The Nigerian army pushed back the Biafrans and arrived at the outskirts of "the Republic of Benin" in September 1967, led by Murtala
Muhammed. His Second Infantry Division mounted a resurgent attack
from two fronts—defending their advance and pushing forward in a classic "Greek army offensive."[4] The retreating Biafran forces, according to
several accounts, allegedly beat up a number of Mid-Westerners who
they believed had served as saboteurs. Nigerian radio reports claimed
that the Biafrans shot a number of innocent civilians as they fled the
advancing federal forces.[5] As disturbing as these allegations are, I have
found no credible corroboration of them.

The Asaba Massacre

The federal forces were soon able to snatch Benin from Biafran military
hands and advance quickly toward the River Niger, arriving in Asaba in
early October 1967. There are multiple versions of what transpired in
Asaba. The version I heard amounted to this: Murtala Muhammed—
chief commander (GOC) Division Two—and his lieutenants, including
Colonel Ibrahim Haruna, felt humiliated by the Biafran Mid-Western
offensive. Armed with direct orders to retake the occupied areas at all
costs, this division rounded up and shot as many defenseless Igbo men

and boys as they could find. Some reports place the death toll at five hundred, others as high as one thousand.[1]

The Asaba Massacre, as it would be known, was only one of many such postpogrom atrocities committed by Nigerian soldiers during the war. It became a particular abomination for Asaba residents, as many of those killed were titled Igbo chiefs and common folk alike, and their bodies were disposed of with reckless abandon in mass graves, without regard to the wishes of the families of the victims or the town's ancient traditions.[2]

His Holiness Pope Paul VI, having received no commitments from either the Nigerians or the Biafrans for a cease-fire, sent his emissary, the well-regarded Monsignor Georges Rocheau, to Nigeria on a fact-finding mission. The horrified Roman Catholic priest spoke to the French newspaper *Le Monde* following the visit, recounting what he witnessed:

> There has been genocide, for example on the occasion of the 1966 massacres. . . . Two areas have suffered badly [from the fighting]. Firstly the region between the towns of Benin and Asaba where only widows and orphans remain, Federal troops having for unknown reasons massacred all the men.[3]

General Gowon broke his silence thirty-five years later on this matter and apologized for this atrocity to the Igbos in Asaba:

> It came to me as a shock when I came to know about the unfortunate happenings that happened to the sons and daughters . . . of [Asaba] domain. I felt very touched and honestly I referred to [the killings] and ask for forgiveness being the one who was in charge at that time. Certainly, it is not something that I would have approved of in whatsoever. I was made ignorant of it, I think until it appeared in the papers. A young man wrote a book at that time.[4]

Testifying at the Justice Oputa Panel (a Nigerian version of South Africa's Truth and Reconciliation Commission), Major General Ibrahim Haruna, belligerent and unremorseful as ever, proclaimed:

> As the commanding officer and leader of the troops that massacred 500 men in Asaba, I have no apology for those massacred in Asaba, Owerri, and Ameke-Item. I acted as a soldier maintaining the peace and unity of Nigeria. . . . If General Yakubu Gowon apologized, he did it in his own capacity. As for me I have no apology.[5]

Murtala Muhammed advanced quickly following the abomination in Asaba to cross the Niger River Bridge to Onitsha. Muhammed's federal troops sustained many casualties in that guerrilla warfare, and from sniper attacks by Achuzia's Biafran troops, and they failed to take the market town in the first attempt.

Biafran Repercussions

The exhausted, fleeing Biafran soldiers crossed the River Niger and arrived in Enugu, Biafra's capital. Their actions had unanticipated consequences. Ojukwu, nursing the wounds of, as he saw it, a "self-inflicted defeat," summarily court-martialed the leaders of the exercise. The accused men—Brigadier Victor Banjo, Major Emmanuel Ifeajuna, Sam Agbamuche, and Major Phillip Alale—were found guilty of planning a coup d'état to overthrown Ojukwu's regime, a treasonable felony punishable by death. All four men were executed on September 25, 1967.[1]

It is important to point out that at the time Enugu had a conspiratorial atmosphere, and some in Ojukwu's inner circle added fuel to the fire. There was talk of alleged plots to overthrow the government. Rumors swirled that Major Ifeajuna, a mastermind of the January 15, 1966, coup, was spotted by Biafran intelligence in covert meetings with British secret service agents. Others alleged that the British had paid Victor Banjo a large commission—to the tune of several thousand pounds—to bungle the Mid-Western advance. Such was the climate of fear and paranoia.[2]

Blood, Blood, Everywhere

The Biafrans found themselves under heavy assault after the Mid-West offensive. Mohammed Shuwa's First Army Division, advancing with Theophilus Danjuma, quickly overran the university town of Nsukka, and then relentlessly bombarded Biafra's capital with heavy armaments. The military operation was aided by Egyptian mercenary pilots flying the Nigerian army's brand-new British, Czech L-29 Delphins, and Soviet MiG-17 and Ilyushin Beagle II-28 aircraft. Most of us in the civilian population had fled with family members into the hinterlands, ahead of the advancing Nigerian troops. By the second week of October 1967, overwhelmed by the Nigerian military pounding, the Biafran central government also receded southward, to Umuahia, where a new capital was set up.[1]

By now the world had started taking notice, and a number of international organizations were visiting Nigeria to try to broker a peace between the two warring parties. One of the first to intervene was the Organization of African Unity (OAU), which appointed Ghanaian lieutenant general Joseph Arthur Ankrah their emissary to Biafra. Ankrah had some experience with the conflict, having hosted the Aburi meeting in January. Many Biafrans, myself included, had mixed feelings about the OAU's choice, as Ankrah, widely regarded as "a Cold War pawn," was the man responsible for deposing one of the heroes of the African liberation struggle—Kwame Nkrumah. It was little surprise to those of us in

Biafra, therefore, to discover that under his guidance the OAU supported "a unified Nigeria" stance despite Biafra's protests.

The Calabar Massacre

The Nigerian forces overran Calabar in early 1968 without much resistance or investment. A seat of the ancient kingdom of the same name, Calabar is in the southeastern part of Biafra, on the banks of the majestic Calabar River. It had for decades been a melting pot of Easterners—Efik, Ibibio, Igbo, and others—that had produced a beautiful cultural mosaic of traditions and dialects.

In actions reminiscent of the Nazi policy of eradicating Jews throughout Europe just twenty years earlier, the Nigerian forces decided to purge the city of its Igbo inhabitants.[1] By the time the Nigerians were done they had "shot at least 1,000 and perhaps 2,000 Ibos [sic], most of them civilians."[2] There were other atrocities, throughout the region. "In Oji River," *The Times of London* reported on August 2, 1968, "the Nigerian forces opened fire and murdered fourteen nurses and the patients in the wards."[3] In Uyo and Okigwe more innocent lives were lost to the brutality and blood lust of the Nigerian soldiers.[4]

In April 1968, the Nigerians decided to mount a major strategic and tactical offensive designed to cut Biafra off from the seacoast. The over forty thousand troops of the Third Division, lead by army colonel Benjamin Adekunle, engaged in an amphibious, land, and air onslaught on the Niger River Delta city of Port Harcourt. After several weeks of sustained air, land, and sea pounding, a period reportedly characterized by military atrocities—rapes, looting, outright brigandry—Port Harcourt fell to the Nigerians on May 12, 1968.

The Third Division slowly marched north, crossing the Imo River, toward the market town of Aba. With heavy casualties along the way, Adekunle and his men shot gleefully through a fierce Biafran resistance and took Aba in August and Owerri in September. The Aba offensive was particularly gruesome:

> On entry into Aba, the Nigerian soldiers massacred more than 2000 civilians. Susan Masid of the **French Press Agency** reporting this horrifying incident had this to say: *"Young Ibos* [sic] *with terrifying eyes and trembling lips told journalists in Aba that in the villages Nigerian troops came from behind, shooting and firing everywhere, shooting everybody who was running, firing into the homes."* (Emphases in original.)[5]

Colonel Adekunle, no doubt a Nigerian war hero, had by now earned a reputation, at least in Biafran quarters, for cruelty and sadism. After a number of provocative public statements illustrating his zeal for warfare, coupled with verbal clashes with international journalists and observer teams, Adekunle became the subject of the local and international spotlight. I was told, away from the media glare, that his conduct became a source of embarrassment for Gowon's wartime cabinet.

Perhaps Adekunle's most heinous statement during the war was this: "[Biafran aid is] 'misguided humanitarian rubbish. . . . If children must die first, then that is too bad, just too bad.'"[6] That statement caused such an international uproar that the federal government of Nigeria found itself in the unenviable position of having to apologize for the actions not only of Adekunle but also of Haruna, leader of the Asaba Massacre infamy. Unbeknownst to Adekunle, a quiet retirement from the Nigerian army was in the offing.[7]

> I have often thought of the man who returns after an "operation"—this is what it is called, an "operation"—and has a wash and goes into the bar of his hotel and drinks whiskey. He has been on an "operation," and on the

other side you have maybe 120 people cut to pieces. A friend of mine had his three children—just like that, they went out to buy books—five minutes later, it was over—it does not take long—10 seconds. It is quite frightening.[8]

Meanwhile, on the northeastern front, Mohammed Shuwa's First Division easily overran Abakaliki and Afikpo.[9] Umuahia was the only major urban area in the secessionist republic that had not been overtaken by the Nigerians.

Gowon rapidly increased the size of his army to well over a quarter of a million men and women. His final offensive, which would be mounted on the three fronts that surrounded the Biafrans, was supposed to end the war swiftly, in three months. As he advanced for what he thought was to be a final push to claim a Biafran surrender in September 1968, he was met by fierce Biafran resistance—sniper fire and guerrilla warfare.[10] Several unanticipated events coalesced to form a perfect storm that bought the exhausted Biafran army much needed time to regroup, repair the much damaged Uli airstrip, and develop a defensive strategy. Antiwar sentiment worldwide was reaching a peak. Bombarded constantly with war imagery through their television sets and newspapers, particularly pictures of babies and women perishing and starving, several individuals and international human rights agencies started mounting demonstrations in world capitals—London, Washington, Lisbon—against the war.

Jean-Paul Sartre and François Mauriac in France[11] and John Lennon in London made public statements condemning the war. Dr. Martin Luther King Jr., long a champion of universal justice, had to suddenly cancel his planned trip to Nigeria over fears for his safety. Joan Baez and Jimi Hendrix were some of the famous musicians who took part in a Biafran relief concert in Manhattan, on August 29, 1968. Other British and American artists led peaceful protests of song to draw American public attention to the conflict. The newscasters in America were mesmerized by the story of a young college student, Bruce Mayrock, who set himself on fire to protest the killing of "innocent Biafran babies." Mayrock, sadly, later died in the hospital from his wounds. It was reported that he wanted to draw the attention of the media, delegates in session at the United Nations, and United States government officials to what he believed was genocide in Biafra.[12] Henry Kissinger, now under heavy pressure from civil society groups, found himself encouraging the Nixon administration to rethink their policy on the Nigeria-Biafra conflict.[13]

BIAFRA, 1969

First time Biafra
Was here, we're told, it was a fine
Figure massively hewn in hardwood.

Voracious white ants
Set upon it and ate
Through its huge emplaced feet
To the great heart abandoning
A furrowed, emptied scarecrow.

And sun-stricken waves came and beat crazily
About its feet eaten hollow
Till crashing facedown in a million fragments
It was floated gleefully away
To cold shores—cartographers alone
Marking the coastline
Of that forgotten massive stance.

In our time it came again
In pain and acrid smell
Of powder. And furious wreckers
Emboldened by half a millennium
Of conquest, battering
On new oil dividends, are now

At its black throat squeezing
Blood and lymph down to
Its hands and feet
Bloated by quashiokor.

Must Africa have
To come a third time?[1]

The Republic of Biafra

THE INTELLECTUAL FOUNDATION OF A NEW NATION

For most of us within Biafra our new nation was a dream that had become reality—a republic, in the strict definition of the word: "a state in which the supreme power rests in the body of citizens entitled to vote and is exercised by representatives chosen directly or indirectly by them."[1] We could forge a new nation that respected the freedoms that all of mankind cherished and were willing to fight hard to hold on to. Within Biafra the Biafran people would be free of persecution of all kinds.

It did not escape Biafra's founders that a great nation needed to be built on a strong intellectual foundation. Our modest attempt to put the beginnings of our thinking down on paper resulted in what would be known as the Ahiara Declaration.[2]

In the Harmattan Season of 1968, Ojukwu invited me to serve on a small political committee that the Ministry of Information was creating. The Ministry of Information was the only place that an author would be comfortable, he told me, because that was the venue of intellectual debate—where philosophy, cultural matters, literature, politics, and society with all its elements were discussed. The ministry had to play an important role in the new nation, he insisted, as Biafra tried to free itself from the faults it saw in Nigeria.

So I joined this group and set to work. The questions that we raised within the committee and later presented for broader discussion included: How would we win this war and begin the creation of a new nation with the qualities we seek? What did we want Biafra to look like?

What would be the core components of our new nation-state? What did we mean by citizenship and nationhood? What would be Biafra's relationship to other African countries? What kind of education would the general population need to aid Biafra's development? How would Biafra attain these lofty goals?

The Biafran leader was pleased with the committee's work and invited me to serve as the chairman of a larger committee that he wanted to set up within the state house. He called this new group the National Guidance Committee, and our business would be to write a kind of constitution for Biafra—a promulgation of the fundamental principles upon which the government and people of Biafra would operate. The final work would be a living document that could be modified over time and include at its core a set of philosophical rules that would serve as a guide for the people of Biafra. The Biafran nation, Ojukwu explained, had to have special attributes—the very principles that we approved of and were fighting for: unity, self-determination, social justice, etc. The final version of the document, we hoped, would also tell our story to the world—how Biafra had been pushed out of Nigeria by Nigerians and threatened with genocide. The only thing left for persecuted Easterners to do, we would stress, was to establish our own state and avert destruction. That, essentially, was the basis of the establishment of the Biafran nation.

Ojukwu then told me that he wanted the new committee to report directly to him, outside the control of the cabinet. I became immediately apprehensive. I was concerned that this arrangement could very easily become an area of conflict between the cabinet and this new committee that I was going to head. Who would be reporting to whom? And it seemed to me that Ojukwu wanted a hold on the organs of government— these two organs, plus the military—not so much separated but working at a pace and manner of his design. Nevertheless, I went ahead and chose a much larger committee of experts for the task at hand. I asked Ojukwu who he had in mind to be members of this larger committee. Several names were thrown about. Finally we arrived at quite an impressive group: Chieka Ifemesia, Ikenna Nzimiro, Justice A. N. Aniagolu, Dr. Ifegwu Eke, and Eyo Bassey Ndem.[3] But the group still lacked a scribe and secretary.

There was a healthy competition for the position between Professor Ben Obumselu, who was an Oxford graduate like Ojukwu, and Professor Emmanuel Obiechina, who held a PhD from Cambridge University. I remember telling Ojukwu that Obiechina was educated in Cambridge, and he said, in the tradition of classic Oxbridge rivalry, "Oh, he is from the other place," and we all laughed. In the end, Emmanuel Obiechina was appointed scribe and secretary.

The work of the National Guidance Committee eventually produced the treatise widely known as the Ahiara Declaration. It was called "Ahiara" because Ojukwu's headquarters at this time was a camouflaged colonial building in the village of Ahiara. Ojukwu was in hiding at that point of the hostilities. The retreats he had before, in Umuahia and Owerri, which became famously referred to as "Ojukwu bunkers," were no longer available to him, having been bombed by the Nigerian army.

The concept of the Ahiara Declaration was taken from a similar one issued by President Julius Nyerere in Tanzania, called the Arusha Declaration. The importance of Julius Nyerere in Africa at that time was immense. Nyerere particularly caught the attention of African scholars because he stood for the things we believed in—equality, self-determination, respect for human values. I particularly liked how he drew inspiration from traditional African values and philosophy. He was admired by all of us not just because of his reputation as an incorruptible visionary leader endowed with admirable ideological positions, but also because he had shown great solidarity for our cause. He was, after all, the first African head of state to recognize Biafra.

Though we shared an admiration for President Nyerere and the Arusha Declaration, members of the National Guidance Committee came to
work with diverse political beliefs, backgrounds, and influences; we did
not all come from the same ideological or political school of thought.
There were those on the committee who admired the American, British,
and French notions of democracy. There were those who harbored
socialist, even communist, views, who were influenced by the writings of
Marcus Garvey, Karl Marx, Vladimir Lenin, Fidel Castro, and the
Argentine physician and Marxist revolutionary Ernesto Che Guevera.
Others liked local intellectuals such as the centrist socialist Julius Nyerere, Patrice Lumumba, and Kwame Nkrumah. And still others like me
preferred democratic institutions not in the purely Western sense but in
a fusion of the good ideas of the West with the best that we had produced in our own ancient African civilizations.

In my case, I drew heavily on my background in literature, history,
and theology. I also tapped into what I call "the observation of my
reality"—an extension of the things taught in the formal education of
secondary school and university into the education from life I picked up
from our tradition. One influential group were the orators, a group that
fascinated me because they always seemed to be able to find the right
things to say to stop a crisis! I looked out for people like that, who
embodied a wholesome African wisdom—African common sense; they
were within our communities, and within the group that would be called
"the uneducated." But they were arbiters of the traditional values that
had sustained our societies from the beginning of time.

One man, an Ozo title holder whose eloquence I always remembered,
personified what I thought was the essence of what we were trying to
write and should try to communicate. I remember distinctly watching as
Okudo Onenyi, with his fellow Ozo title holders, dressed in their impressive traditional regalia, red caps and feathers, assembled for one of their
Ozo meetings. One of the things that struck me was the dignity of these

old men, who arrived at the site of the gathering carrying their little chairs that they would sit on.

At one particular meeting Okudo Onenyi was given a piece of chalk to mark his insignia on the mud floor or wall, as these men were wont to do. What surprised me was that Okudo took the piece of chalk and put down his initials. I did not realize that this man had gone to school, but he obviously had. My admiration for him rose, because he was one of those who was not easily persuaded to abandon his ancient traditions, like the rest, to join a new culture or religion, but he was willing to make a type of accommodation to his world's new dispensation. This man represented those who were still holding fort and not putting up a physical fight. So it was not enough in my view to state that we wanted to be radical and create a left-wing manifesto, but we also certainly did not want to be right wing. It was that ancient traditional virtue I wanted to channel into the Ahiara Declaration.

It took us several weeks to get the work we had done into one document. We worked day and night. Chieka Ifemesia, Emmanuel Obiechina, and I did the editing after the committee had spent days brooding over our situation and prospects. Chieka Ifemesia, an emeritus professor at the University of Nigeria, Nsukka, and a leading authority on Igbo history, would come to the table with much more than his own memories or abstract intellectual concepts, but with a great deal of relevant historical background and context. He was a solid historian—serious, studious. He came from my own village of Ikenga in Ogidi. At the time of the war he was regarded as a rising intellectual star and a person who many of us relied upon for intellectual and cultural stimulation and ideas. Emmanuel Obiechina pulled all the ideas together and transcribed the committee's work. My role was to keep some kind of control over the radical elements in the group who had more extreme left-wing thinking, for instance, the popular firebrand professor Ikenna Nzimiro.[4]

Nzimiro always had trouble with the establishment from his Nnamdi

Azikiwe youth wing "Zikist days." He did not like the direction Nigeria was going in, and he had no trouble expressing his dissenting views. He was perhaps the youngest representative on the local government council in those days, and he was very well-known everywhere for his radical positions. He was educated in Germany and England, and his escapades were legendary. His stories kept us all laughing for weeks.

Nzimiro disappeared in the middle of our writing the Ahiara Declaration, and we were all very concerned. One day we were informed that the police had locked him up. Apparently he had gotten into an argument with a police officer who did not care for his radical views. Insults were exchanged and Nzimiro was subsequently arrested. Emmanuel Obiechina told me what was going on. So we went to Ojukwu and informed him of what was happening to a member of our committee. Ojukwu called the chief of police, and we went to the police station to pick up our ultraradical colleague.

On June 1, 1969, very close to the end of the war, Ojukwu finally delivered this major speech, the Ahiara Declaration. It was an attempt to capture the meaning of the struggle for Biafran sovereignty. He provided a historical overview of the events that had led to the secession from Nigeria and the founding of the Republic of Biafra. The speech was as notable for its concentration on a number of issues that Biafra stood for—such as the rights to liberty, safety, excellence, and self-determination—as it was for the things the republic was against: genocide, racism, imperialism, and ethnic hatred, which were squarely condemned. The speech also decried the blockade of Biafra imposed by the federal government of Nigeria that was creating an avoidable humanitarian crisis, particularly among children, who were dying in the hundreds daily, and attacked the support of Nigeria by the major world powers.

The day this declaration was published and read by Ojukwu was a day of celebration in Biafra. My late brother Frank described the effect of this Ahiara Declaration this way: *"Odika si gbabia agbaba"* ("It was as if we should be dancing to what Ojukwu was saying"). People listened from wherever they were. It sounded right to them: freedom, quality, self-determination, excellence. Ojukwu read it beautifully that day. He had a gift for oratory.

The Biafran State

I would like to say something about the structure of the Biafran state. The Republic of Biafra took its name from the Bight of Biafra, the vast expanse of water covering the continental shelf into which the Niger River empties before flowing into the Gulf of Biafra. After Biafra's surrender that body of water was renamed the Gulf of Guinea. The origins of the word "Biafra" are difficult to trace, although historical records point to Portuguese writings from the sixteenth century that it may have been derived from.

The republic's capital was initially Enugu, a metropolis of over one hundred thousand at the time. It was also known as the coal city, a reference to the nearby Onyeama Coal Mines and other coal deposits that once served as the fuel that drove a large part of the Nigerian economy. Enugu was also the old administrative capital of the Eastern Region. A well-planned, sedate capital, it had a pleasant climate and the advantages of all the amenities of an important urban center without the pathologies of a large conurbation.

When Enugu fell to the Nigerian army on October 4, 1967, the administrative capital of Biafra was moved to Umuahia. Following the capture of Umuahia on April 22, 1969, Biafra's capital was moved once again, to Owerri, the last administrative seat before the end of the war in January 1970.[1]

The population of Biafra in June 1967 was just under fifteen million people, and it was home to a large number of ethnic groups in addition to the Igbo, who made up about 65 percent of the population. The other major groups were the Efik, Ibibio, Ijaw, and Ikwerre. Others included the Andoni, Agbo, Degema, Egbema, Eket, Ekoi, Ibeno, Ikom, Iyalla, Kana, Mbembe, Uyanga, and Yako.[2]

Biafra was divided initially into eleven administrative provinces with as many administrators. Later that number was expanded to twenty.[3]

Once secession was declared it became clear that the war effort required a great deal of military equipment—artillery, planes, boats, tanks, guns, grenades, mines, bombs, etc. Biafra needed a means to access foreign exchange and a legal tender for commerce. One of the first things the new government did was to establish the Bank of Biafra.

The Bank of Biafra was located in Enugu until the city fell in October 1967, and then it was moved several times to different locations all over Igbo land, with the seat of government. The bank's first governor was Dr. Sylvester Ugoh.[4]

The legal tender produced by the institution in January 1968 was designed by Simon Okeke and other talented local artists.[5] The first denominations were the five shilling and one pound notes. About a year later, the ten, five, and one pound as well as the ten and five shilling notes were issued. The currency was widely accepted in Biafra, although it was unavailable in large quantities, which quickly made it a prized possession. Despite its usefulness, it was not a recognized legal tender beyond Biafra's borders and could not be used for foreign exchange. This dilemma produced a number of challenges for the Biafran government, which, we were told, used private bank accounts of wealthy Biafrans to perform transactions abroad.

THE BIAFRAN FLAG

The flag of the Republic of Biafra was based on the Pan-Africanist teachings of Marcus Garvey and the Universal Negro Improvement Association and African Communities League (UNIA-ACL). Garvey was a towering and controversial figure, a major Pan-Africanist thinker and civil rights pioneer at the beginning of the twentieth century, and his philosophy, known as Garveyism, was widely admired by many Africans. It was Garvey's organization that first came up with the tricolored morphology of the Pan-African flag, with three horizontal bands, red, black, and green, to symbolize the common ancestry and political aspirations of all black people around the world. Kenya, St. Kitts and Nevis, and Malawi are just some of the many African and Caribbean nations that adopted variations of this flag.

The red in Garvey's conception highlighted the blood that links all people of African ancestry, as well as blood shed during slavery and liberation struggles around the globe. In the Biafran context it was used to represent blood shed during the pogroms and the quest for independence.

The black was seen as the affirmation of "an African nation State" by the UNIA-ACL. In Biafra, it was a symbolic ancestral connection to souls of years past. The green in both Garvey's and Biafra's concepts stood for Africa's abundant natural wealth and resources, and its radiant future. The Biafran flag also highlighted these aspirations with a rising golden sun and rays representing the eleven original provinces in the republic.[6]

THE BIAFRAN NATIONAL ANTHEM

The Nigeria-Biafra War led to an explosion of musical, lyrical, and poetic creativity and artistry. Biafra's founders tapped into this energy and commissioned a number of regimental drills, duty songs, and cadences[7] that they hoped would "spur armies to victory and excite the populace to political and economic vitality."[8]

The Biafran national anthem, "Land of the Rising Sun," was based on a powerful poem by Nigeria's first president, Nnamdi Azikiwe, called "Onitsha Ado N'Idu: Land of the Rising Sun."[9] Laced with irony, the poem contained several phrases that would become all too prophetic: "But if the price is death for all we hold dear, / Then let us die without a shred of fear. . . . / Spilling our blood we'll count a privilege; . . . / We shall remember those who died in mass; . . ."[10]

The anthem was set to the beautiful music of the Finnish composer Jean Sibelius[11]—*Finlandia* (Be Still My Soul)—a personal favorite of, and calculated choice by, Ojukwu, "in reference to the Nordic country's resistance to foreign domination."[12]

Later, after Azikiwe withdrew his support for the breakaway republic, we would learn that there was some controversy over the adaptation of Azikiwe's poetry. According to Zik, Ojukwu had used his work without permission, a charge the Biafran head of state vigorously denied.[13]

The Biafra National Anthem

LAND OF THE RISING SUN[14]

Land of the rising sun, we love and cherish, beloved homeland of our
    brave heroes; we must defend our lives or we shall perish,
We shall protect our hearth from all our foes; but if the price is
    death for all we hold dear,
Then let us die without a shred of fear.

Hail to Biafra, consecrated nation,
Oh fatherland, this is our solemn pledge: Defending thee shall be a
    dedication, spilling our blood we'll count a privilege;

The waving standard which emboldens the free shall always be our
   flag of liberty.

We shall emerge triumphant from this ordeal, and through the
   crucible unscathed we'll pass;
When we are poised the wounds of battle to heal, we shall remember
   those who died in mass;
Then shall our trumpets peal the glorious song of victory we scored
   o'er might and wrong.

Oh God, protect us from the hidden pitfall, Guide all our
   movements lest we go astray; Give us the strength to heed
   the humanist call:
"To give and not to count the cost" each day; Bless those who rule
   to serve with resoluteness, to make this clime a land of
   righteousness.[15]

THE MILITARY

Biafra had only two thousand troops at the beginning of the war. Most of
the soldiers were former Nigerian army soldiers—Easterners who were
based in Enugu and other former Nigerian military bases in the east.
General Philip Effiong, Biafra's chief of general staff, quickly recruited
an additional twenty thousand men and created a separate Biafran mili-
tia of civilian volunteers, who received on-the-spot training. The Biafrans were devoid of any heavy military equipment apart from that of the
former Nigerian battalion stationed in Enugu, Saracen armored cars, and
105 millimeter howitzers.[16] Federick Forsyth recalls in an excellent BBC
documentary, *Biafra: Fighting a War Without Guns*, that Biafran soldiers
marched into war one man behind the other because they had only one
rifle between them, and the thinking was that if one soldier was killed in

combat the other would pick up the only weapon available and continue fighting.[17]

The Biafrans were completely outgunned compared to the Nigerians. The Soviet Union and Britain not only supplied Nigeria with brand-new MIG-17 and II-28 Beagle (Ilyushin) jets but also with Soviet T-34 battle tanks, antiaircraft guns, AK-47 rifles, machine guns, grenades, mines, bombs, etc.[18]

In light of this imbalance of resources, international support for Biafra was crucial. Arguably the most notable of all the Europeans that came to the aid of Biafra was Carl Gustaf von Rosen. He was a Swedish nobleman and World War II veteran. Von Rosen became a legend in the 1930s when he volunteered to fly Red Cross relief supplies into Ethiopia and fight for Emperor Haile Selassie against the Italians.[19] He again came into the world's consciousness as the pilot of the much admired United Nations secretary general Dag Hammarskjöld, who was widely regarded as a "dove of peace." Hammarskjöld "mysteriously" died in an air crash while serving as the chief mediator of the Congo crisis of the 1960s, unfortunately at a time when his much trusted pilot, von Rosen, was ill.

It was von Rosen's Biafran involvement, however, that truly catapulted him to worldwide recognition. Von Rosen was outraged by the injustice of the war and Nigeria's imposition of an economic blockade on the Republic of Biafra, and he was moved to come to the aid of the suffering. It was in part because of this brave man's involvement that the world was motivated to pay attention to this conflict in a heretofore forgotten part of the world. Von Rosen bore witness to the atrocities and humanitarian emergency in Biafra, and his public statements and influence propelled a number of Western relief agencies to respond to the crisis.[20]

He led multiple relief flights with humanitarian aid into Uli airport— Biafra's chief airstrip. Fed up with Nigerian air force interference with

his peaceful missions, he entered the war heroes hall of fame after leading a five-plane assault on Nigerian aircraft in Port Harcourt, Benin
City, Ughelli, Enugu, and some other locations. He took the Nigerian air
force by total surprise and destroyed several Soviet-supplied aircraft in
the process.[21]

The Biafran air force was composed of a B-26, a B-25, and three heli-
copters[22] until Carl Gustaf von Rosen[23] came to the republic's assistance
in 1968. By year's end the government of Biafra had procured a moderate
amount of military ammunition from the neighboring former French
colonies of Ivory Coast and Gabon.

Indeed, Paris's ambassador to Gabon at the time of war, Maurice
Delauney, worked with Jacques Foccart's deputy, Jean Mauricheau-
Beaupré—described by French journalist Pierre Péan as the "chief con-
ductor of clandestine French support to the Biafran secessionists"—to
supply arms to Ojukwu's army.[24]

Uli airport was the major airport in Biafra for military and relief goods
at the height of the war, and it was described by various authorities as
one of the busiest airports in Africa, with more than 50 flights a night.[25]

Uli airport, originally part of a major highway, had been cut into the
countryside in the middle of a tropical rainforest and operated mainly
at night. I recall the airport's traffic control terminal, passenger facilities, and hangars were constructed in such a manner that the entire
runway and all of the planes on the ground could be heavily camouflaged with palm leaves and raffia fronds during the day, disguising it
from Nigerian army aircraft reconnaissance missions and radar.[26] At
night the airport became a beehive of activity. Incoming flights carrying
relief supplies, particularly from international locations such as São
Tomé, Abidjan in Ivory Coast, and Libreville, Gabon, were given the
airport's coordinates after appropriate background checks were done.
Pilots who were involved in the airlifts of relief supplies provided a compelling story:

In the middle of the vast expanse of tropical rainforest, we would be told to descend from our cruising altitude to about two thousand feet to avoid enemy fire, barely atop the forest in the pitch dark. All of a sudden, bright floodlights appeared from nowhere, illuminating the forest floor. Right before us was a breathtaking sight—an entire airport appearing from nowhere![27]

Ogbunigwe

The economic blockade enforced by Gowon led to great ingenuity and some unprecedented innovations. Biafran scientists from the research think tank RAP—the Biafran Research and Production unit—developed a great number of rockets, bombs, and telecommunications gadgets, and devised an ingenious indigenous strategy to refine petroleum.[28]

Still, some of these innovations deserve particular attention, though in doing so I would like to make it crystal clear that I abhor violence, and a discussion of weapons of war does not imply that I am a war enthusiast or condone violence.

Perhaps no more important instrument of war lay at the disposal of the Biafrans than the bomb called "Ogbunigwe." Gordian Ezekwe, Benjamin Chukwuka Nwosu, and the less well-known technician Willy Achukwe were among the group of originators of this notorious weapon. Ogbunigwe would later become widely adopted and manufactured by the RAP engineers. The bomb was a complex three-chamber apparatus that often included delayed action devices containing a propellant, an explosive substance—often gunpowder in an igniting base—and scraps of metal for maximal effect. Ogbunigwe bombs struck great terror in the hearts of many a Nigerian soldier, and were used to great effect by the Biafran army throughout the conflict.[29] The novelist Vincent Chukwue-meka Ike captures the hysteria and dread evoked by it in a passage in his important book *Sunset at Dawn: A Novel about Biafra*:

When the history of this war comes to be written, the *ogbunigwe* [*sic*] and the shore batteries will receive special mention as Biafra's greatest saviors. We've been able to wipe out more Nigerians with those devices than with any imported weapons. . . .

You must have heard that the Nigerians are now so mortally afraid of *ogbunigwe* [*sic*] that each advancing battalion is now preceded by a herd of cattle.[30]

BIAFRAN TANKS

The first Biafran "tanks" turned out to be steel-reinforced Range Rovers. By their third incarnation these armored fighting vehicles, or AFVs, had become quite sophisticated, with rocket launchers added.

Let me give one more dimension of what we were hoping to do in Biafra, and what this freedom and independence was supposed to be like. We were told, for instance, that technologically we would have to rely for a long, long time on the British and the West for everything. European oil companies insisted that oil-industry technology was so complex that we would never ever in the next five hundred years be able to figure it out. We knew that wasn't true. In fact, we learned to refine our own oil during the two and a half years of the struggle, because we were blockaded. We were able to demonstrate that it was possible for African people, entirely on their own, to refine oil.[31]

We were able to show that Africans could pilot their own planes. There is a story, perhaps apocryphal, that a Biafran plane landed in another African country, and the pilot and all of the crew came out, and there was not a white man among them. The people of this other country—which is a stooge of France—couldn't comprehend a plane being landed without any white people. They said, "Where is the pilot? Where are the white people?" They arrested the crew, presuming there had been a rebellion in the air!

There was enough talent, enough education in Nigeria for us to have been able to arrange our affairs more efficiently, more meticulously, even if not completely independently, than we were doing.[32] I tell these stories to illustrate the quality of the people available to Nigeria. One thinks back on this and is amazed. Nigeria had people of great quality, and what befell us—the corruption, the political ineptitude, the war—was a great disappointment and truly devastating to those of us who witnessed it.[33]

A TIGER JOINS THE ARMY

A great shot in the arm, and perhaps the single most effective tool for enlistment into the Biafran army, came in January 1968, when Richard Ihetu, also known as Dick Tiger, hung up his boxing gloves and enlisted in the army. Ihetu was a world-renowned boxer from Amaigbo in Imo state—"the land of the Igbos"—a town comprised of thirty-seven villages and steeped in ancient Igbo history.[34] Ojukwu made Dick Tiger a lieutenant in the army of Biafra as soon as he enlisted.[35]

Even though I was never a boxing fan, I remember how the whole of Nigeria was gripped by a feverish excitement at Dick Tiger's victories, first locally, as Nigeria's most celebrated boxing champion, then also later, after he emigrated to the United Kingdom and knocked over famous boxers across the British Empire, and ultimately won world championships both as a light-heavyweight and as a middleweight. We were all very impressed that this young man from a town near Aba in Imo state had traveled so far.[36] Dick Tiger's decision to enlist, and to return the MBE (Member of the British Empire) medal to Great Britain's government in protest of its support for Nigeria, caused a great stir internationally.[37]

Excitement at the news of Dick Tiger's arrival created a rippling sensation throughout Biafra. The government seized on this development and created jingles on the radio summoning young men to "follow the example of Dick Tiger and join the great Elephant (Enyi) of a new nation." But the realities of war—the death, the despair, the suffering— soon dampened any euphoria that we all had about having a champion fight for the cause.

FREEDOM FIGHTERS

Ojukwu created an organization called the Biafran Organization of Freedom Fighters (BOFF) as a unit that would improve the overall relationship between the Biafran army and the people it served and on whose behalf it fought. Colonel Ejike Obumneme Aghanya was appointed the chairperson. He had been president of the Nigerian Broadcasting Service Staff Union in Enugu when I was the controller of the Nigerian Broadcasting Service Eastern Region. Aghanya's BOFF staff included Dr. Ukwu I. Ukwu, Dr. Oyolu, and Major Okoye. Aghanya invited me to join the group and help develop an education strategy that would improve civilian-military relations.

Although this desire to bridge the civilian-military divide is nothing new, Ojukwu wanted the Biafran military to be different, to pay careful attention to the welfare of the people of Biafra. One interesting direction they took was to get young women into BOFF, and indirectly into the army.[38]

Ojukwu's Oxford education afforded him the luxury of having been exposed to both the great world philosophers and the revolutionaries of the day. He was heavily influenced by the writings of Fidel Castro, and he called the Biafran army the People's Army of Biafra. He also admired the way the Chinese army was structured, and it is relevant to note that BOFF arose at a time when China was making diplomatic inroads in Biafra. Ojukwu clearly was not a communist, but he borrowed some ideas from their revolutions.[39]

After I left the BOFF outfit I heard that it was engaged in the more militaristic and controversial aspects of war, such as enemy infiltration, guerrilla warfare, and propaganda.[40]

Traveling on Behalf of Biafra

In addition to working with BOFF, Ojukwu also asked me to serve the cause as an unofficial envoy of the people of Biafra. Being invited to serve by the leader of Biafra was both an important and satisfying opportunity, but it also came with great anxiety. What were we getting into? I thought. I never solicited the post, so being asked from the very top to come and help, especially from the angle of the intellectual, was very important to me. I wasn't absolutely sure how things would work out, but I thought I would do my best.

The first trip I undertook on behalf of the people of Biafra was at the direct request of General Ojukwu. He called me to his office soon after the conflict started and asked me to travel to Senegal to deliver a message to President Léopold Sédar Senghor. I was to be accompanied on this trip by a young academic, Sam Agbam, who spoke several European languages fluently. He was among the young intellectuals in the Biafran diplomatic service involved in one way or another in the framing of the "Biafran argument."

Sam and I set out for Senegal. During these "trips for the people" envoys were often put on a plane—a private plane . . . any plane, at midnight, from Uli airport, flying out of Biafra across the Sahara, occasionally to Europe or an African capital, from whence we would travel more freely to the destinations of our choice.

During this particular flight the pilot announced at about twenty thousand feet that the plane was experiencing "technical problems." It was marked by a great deal of turbulence and sudden losses of cabin pressure. We were all experiencing motion sickness, some were vomiting, and all were stricken by a sense of impending doom. The plane was diverted to an airport in the Sahara, where we disembarked, changed to a Senegalese airline, and flew to Dakar.

Sam Agbam "vanished" at some point during our travel; I was never told why he did not continue the journey. Soon thereafter he got in trouble with the Biafran government—accused of being part of a mutiny—and was executed with others for allegedly plotting a coup against Ojukwu, as discussed earlier.

After we lost each other I decided to take control of the journey, despite the language barrier. I arrived in the beautiful capital of the Republic of Senegal, Dakar, and checked myself into one of the city's many smart hotels.

I visited the presidential offices the day after my arrival and tried to get the letter from General Ojukwu in my possession to President Senghor. I couldn't get past the presidential aides. The officials there, all expatriate administrators, responded to my request with looks of incredulity. They could not even imagine anything like opening the door and showing me in to see the Senegalese president. They must have thought I was crazy!

There was one very tall man who spoke very good English, and he said to me that there was no way I could see the president.

"What do you want to see him for?" he asked.

I said that I would like to present my new novel, *A Man of the People*, to him. I also added that I knew that President Senghor was a great writer and poet, and I thought I should show my appreciation of his writing by presenting my humble effort at writing poetry. Clearly that was not what I wanted to do, but I was not about to disclose my true intentions to this uncooperative gentleman.

"Oh, that is easy enough: You give me the book and poems and I will take it to him, and I am sure he will be delighted," the official said.

I said that I would like to deliver it myself, that that was the reason I had come all this way. There was nothing more the official could tell me, and I was sent away.

The next day, and the next, I went back and repeated the process in an attempt to see Senghor. Either my tenacity was working or the staff was getting tired of seeing me every morning, because I got a new message five days into this ritual: "President Léopold Sédar Senghor will see you tomorrow." This message was brought in a black limousine. A member of the hotel staff ran up to my room, knocked on the door, and excitedly relayed that I had a message from the presidential palace. The esteem in which I was held in the eyes of the people and staff in the hotel, you can imagine, rose dramatically. After that my stay was very different. Soon after my arrival I had complained to the hotel front desk that the fan in my room was not working well, but nothing was done about it until the limousine visit from the presidential palace, soon after which I was informed that the fan had been attended to.

The next day I had my audience with President Léopold Sédar Senghor, a very extraordinary man. I was guided along a stone path in the gardens of the presidential palace and up the grand staircase to a secluded room. The first thing that struck me was the loneliness. We were standing in a room in this huge mansion, I in my Biafran attire, Senghor in his French suit, and he seemed all alone. He knew that I came from Biafra, in West Africa. I handed Senghor the letter that informed him of the real catastrophe building up in Biafra, and I told him that it was a message from the Biafran head of state, who had asked me to deliver the sealed envelope directly to him. Senghor regretted that I had spent several days in the country trying to reach him and apologized for the treatment I had received. Senghor was a profoundly adept diplomat, and he took on the business I brought: He glanced through the letter quickly, and then turned to me and said that he would deal with it overnight . . . as soon as possible.

Our conversation then turned to other things intellectual—writing, education, the great cultural issues of the day, including the movement he was spearheading called Négritude. La Négritude, as it was called, was already widely known in serious intellectual circles around the world: "The founders of la Négritude, *les trois pères* (the three fathers) [Léopold Sédar Senghor; Aimé Césaire, from Martinique; and Léon Gontran Damas, from Guyana] met while they were living in Paris in the early 1930s."[1]

It is important not to view Négritude in isolation but in the full context of the black consciousness movements of the first half of the twentieth century, a period that gave rise to a number of ideological and intellectual movements in America, the Caribbean, and Africa and a great deal of cross-fertilization and complexity.

Négritude in Africa can be seen as an extension of the earlier work of W. E. B. Du Bois, Booker T. Washington, Marcus Garvey, and C. L. R. James, among others; they all established black intellectual and political liberation struggles but from very different albeit equally important vantage points in America. In the African context it was a reaction to the colonial experience through literature and political thought. It had powerful political allies in Nnamdi Azikiwe in Nigeria, Kwame Nkrumah in Ghana, Jomo Kenyatta in Kenya, Julius Nyerere in Tanzania, Patrice Lumumba in Congo, and, later, Nelson Mandela, Steve Biko, and Walter Sisulu in South Africa. It is pertinent to note that the independence movement in Africa in turn had a profound impact on the civil rights movement in America.

I found what these intellectuals were trying to achieve—the reclamation of the power of self-definition to recast Africa's, and therefore their own, image through the written word—incredibly attractive and influential. Here were highly sophisticated individuals who believed in the need for blacks who had been victims of historical dispossession to appreciate and elevate their culture—literature, art, music, dance, etc. They encouraged Africans (in the word's broadest definition) to celebrate and espouse their culture as not only not inferior to European culture and civilization but equally acceptable even if fundamentally different.

Négritude also held that the rest of the world would benefit from such an intellectual black renaissance, which would at last produce an environment where race, a core fact of our existence, and the negative baggage linked to its definition and meaning, would be effectively deemphasized, liberating the world's people to work together unencumbered. It was very heavy stuff indeed![2] It is perhaps a great testament to the importance of this new thinking that it drew admirers as diverse and important as Frantz Fanon (who studied with Aimé Césaire), the great French writer Jean-Paul Sartre, and the Haitian writer Jacques Romain, as well as critics such as Wole Soyinka, who famously dismissed it.[3]

Senghor told me about the education minister who had been trained under him and had submitted a bill to Parliament to abolish the use of all French texts in all institutions of education in Senegal. Senghor smiled and told the young minister, "Thank you for your bill, but that would be too much Négritude." We both laughed, and then talked for about two hours—discussing his poetry and that of others from the black diaspora—Okigbo, Derek Walcott, Aimé Césaire, Langston Hughes, Countee Cullen, etc. He took me to one of the great windows of the presidential palace and showed me two hills; he observed that the mountaintops looked like "a lady lying down."

I also made an extensive trip to Scandinavia on behalf of the people of Biafra around this time. The Scandinavians had made great humanitarian gestures to alleviate the suffering in Biafra. I was also curious to visit the land of one of the most legendary of all the Europeans who came to our aid—the Swedish aristocrat Carl Gustaf von Rosen. On this trip I visited Sweden, Finland, and Norway.

I remember Norway vividly. Even though I visited during the winter, it appeared a lovely country— subdued, calm, and temperate. The people seemed very serious-minded, and businesslike, and very progressive in their thinking. My hosts took me almost immediately after I arrived to the Parliament. What struck me about this particular day was the importance the Norwegians place on time, even more than I had encountered in England. Here was a people that knew that time was critically important, and it was to be used judiciously. Another observation of significance had to do with the items on the program. It appeared to be like a service—a hymn or anthem was sung, followed by deliberations and readings—all in Norwegian, so I can't tell the reader exactly what was being said, but it sounded almost like a religious service. When they were done, I was ushered into this wonderfully built, ornate Parliament room, and a gentleman said to me: "Now Mr. Achebe, you can tell us what you came for." And I spent about twenty minutes telling my hosts about the humanitarian disaster that was Biafra. I received a warm round of applause and promises of continued humanitarian support.

The other thing that happened during my trip to Norway was, unfortunately for millions around the world, very sad. As I walked back to my hotel with my hosts, I was able to tell from the conspicuous news flashing on a huge screen that Robert Kennedy had been assassinated. I was able to figure out the devastating news from the flashing words, even without help from my hosts, and it struck me how bad news is so much more easily recognizable across languages than good.

My trip to Canada was very different from the others. I was invited to speak about the Biafran tragedy by the World Council of Churches and the Canadian Council of Churches. The World Council of Churches was one of the most magnanimous supporters and suppliers of humanitarian relief for the suffering and dying of Biafra, so I felt deeply obliged to attend their gathering. The general secretary of the WCC, Eugene Carson Blake, and the honorary president of the WCC, Willem Visser 't Hooft from The Netherlands, were very decent men. Blake, an American, was an ardent supporter of the American civil rights movement and a coauthor of the WCC's antiracism policies. Hooft helped set up the Ecumenical Church Loan Fund for the poor around the world.[4]

It is important to point out that the Protestants did not hold a monopoly on generosity during the war. Several Jewish groups and Roman Catholic orders also came to the aid of the destitute.

Reverend Father (Dr.) Georg Hüssler, former president of Caritas International, is particularly celebrated till this day by former Biafrans for his towering role in providing humanitarian and other aid during the conflict.

In any case, our hosts, the Canadian Council of Churches, organized a dinner in my honor and invited a number of very distinguished Canadians and religious leaders from around the world. When they brought out the first course—smoked salmon with steamed spinach—Eugene Carson Blake announced to the guests that we were about to eat a piece of Uli airport at night, which, many of them at the table were aware, was famously and effectively camouflaged with palm fronds and leaves to hide it from Nigerian air force reconnaissance missions. That statement was greeted with boisterous laughter. It occured to me once again how different Biafra had become from other places, where laughter was still available.

In May 1968, I was part of the Biafran delegation that attended the Kampala, Uganda, talks—one of the world's failed attempts (in this case, the British Commonwealth and the OAU) to forge a peace between Nigeria and Biafra. President Milton Obote of Uganda hosted the deliberations that also involved Commonwealth secretary Arnold Smith.[5] Sir Louis Mbanefo was the leader of that delegation, which also included Professor Hilary Okam, Francis Ellah, and a few others. It was at that meeting that I met Aminu Kano for the first time. As the Nigerian delegation, led by Anthony Enahoro, espoused their resolve to "crush Biafra" unless there was a complete surrender, Aminu Kano seemed very uneasy, often looking through the window. This was a man who was not pleased with either side or how the matter was being handled. That meeting made an indelible mark on me about Aminu Kano, about his character and his intellect.

In late 1968, I traveled to the United States with Gabriel Okara and Cyprian Ekwensi as part of an extensive university tour to bring the story of Biafra to the mainly progressive American intellectuals and writers. We visited scores of campuses, gave what seemed to be hundreds of interviews, and met with several very influential American leaders of thought.

During my visit we were educated about Igbo (Ebo) landing in St. Simons, Georgia. According to the local lore, "Ebo Landing" was the site where an ill-fated slave ship called *The Wanderer* had run aground. The valuable cargo—the captured Igbos—were taken onshore while the crew rescued what they could from the bowels of the ship. While the crew was distracted, the story continues, the Igbos made a suicide pact, deciding to walk into the ocean and drown themselves rather than allow the slave merchants to sell them into bondage. Locals swear that the shores of the tragedy are still haunted, and that on a clear moon-lit night a visitor who stands really still can hear the howls and agony of death.[6]

Refugee Mother and Child
(A Mother in a Refugee Camp)

No Madonna and Child could touch
Her tenderness for a son
She soon would have to forget. . . .
The air was heavy with odors of diarrhea,
Of unwashed children with washed-out ribs
And dried-up bottoms waddling in labored steps
Behind blown-empty bellies. Most mothers there
Had long ceased to care, but not this one;
She held a ghost-smile between her teeth,
And in her eyes the memory
Of a mother's pride. . . . She had bathed him
And rubbed him down with bare palms.
She took from the bundle of their possessions
A broken comb and combed
The rust-colored hair left on his skull
And then—humming in her eyes—began carefully to part it.
In their former life this was perhaps
A little daily act of no consequence
Before his breakfast and school; now she did it
Like putting flowers on a tiny grave.[1]

Life in Biafra

The Nigeria-Biafra conflict created a humanitarian emergency of epic proportions. Millions of civilians—grandparents, mothers, fathers, children, and soldiers alike—flooded the main highway arteries between towns and villages fleeing the chaos and conflict. They traveled by foot, by truck, by car, barefoot, with slippers, in wheelbarrows, many in worn-out shoes. Some had walked so long their soles were blistered and bleeding. As hunger and thirst grew, so did despair, confusion, and desperation. Most were heading in whatever direction the other was headed, propelled by the latest rumors of food and shelter spreading through the multitude like a virus. Refugees were on the move in no specific direction, anywhere, just away from the fighting. As they fled the war zones they became targets of the Nigerian air force. The refugees learned to travel nights and hide in the forests by day.

The international relief agencies started responding to the growing humanitarian challenge quite early in the conflict by establishing food distribution centers and refugee camps. There were many Biafran refugee camps dotting the landscape, from Enugu in the north to Owerri in the south, during the thirty-month conflict. Many held between a few hundred and a few thousand people. At the height of the war there were well over three thousand such centers and camps, a great number but woefully inadequate to the actual need.[1]

These camps were often hastily constructed tent villages set up beside bombed-out churches, in football or sports arenas, or in open fields in the forest. They uniformly lacked electricity, running water, or other comforts. Occasionally, the more established camps had sturdier shelters on the premises of abandoned schools or colleges, or built near freshwater streams or little rivers. Those were few and far between. Most had rows of mud huts and palm raffia roofs built hastily by the inhabitants themselves. They were occasionally fenced in by the international agencies, which placed guards on the camp perimeter to monitor movement in and out of the area. The relief agencies often hoisted their flags to indicate to the Nigerian officers that they were in neutral zones that should be protected from assault. That did not always keep the Nigerian troops from raiding these "safe havens," or even from bombing them.

Life in the camps varied in quality. Some of the better organized camps provided water, shelter, food, basic health care—mainly vaccinations for children against the most prevalent diseases, and treatment of common bacterial infections—and education. Other camps could only be described as deplorable, epidemic-ridden graveyards. In these camps the combination of poor sanitation, high population density, and shortages of supplies created a bitter cocktail of despair, giving rise to social pathologies and psychological traumas of all kinds—violence, extortion, and physical and sexual abuse.

My siblings and their families returned to my father's house in Ogidi from various parts of the country. My family did too: Christie and my children at the time, Chinelo and Ike, left Port Harcourt for my family's ancestral home.

My village is about six miles from Onitsha, the commercial hub of Eastern Nigeria and the location of the largest market in West Africa. Onitsha is also where the famous Niger Bridge is located, and so it serves as the entry point for all travelers entering the East from points west. The close proximity of Ogidi to Onitsha meant that we were in the eye of the storm, as it were, right at the border of the conflict. We were so close to the war zone we could hear the sounds of war—heavy artillery fire, bombs, and machine-gun fights.[2]

By the time I left Lagos to join my family in Ogidi, there were rumors that the Nigerian army was not that far behind. Casting my mind back, I am surprised at how little pandemonium there was during the early stages of the conflict. Families casually began to move deeper into the countryside to prepare for the inevitability of war.

Food was short, meat was very short, and drugs were short. Thousands—no, millions by then—had been uprooted from their homes and brought into safer areas, but where they really had no relatives, no property; many of them lived in school buildings and camps. The Committee for Biafran Refugees, understandably overwhelmed, did what it could. I found it really quite amazing how much people were ready to give.

Beyond the understandable trepidation associated with a looming war, one found a new spirit among the people, a spirit one did not know existed, a determination, in fact. The spirit was that of a people ready to put in their best and fight for their freedom. Biafran churches made links to the persecution of the early Christians, others on radio to the Inquisition and the persecution of the Jewish people. The prevalent mantra of the time was *"Ojukwu nye anyi egbe ka anyi nuo agha"*—"Ojukwu give us guns to fight a war." It was an energetic, infectious duty song, one sung to a well-known melody and used effectively to recruit young men into the People's Army (the army of the Republic of Biafra). But in the early stages of the war, when the Biafran army grew quite rapidly, sadly Ojukwu had no guns to give to those brave souls.

But the most vital feeling Biafrans had at that time was that they were finally in a safe place . . . at home. This was the first and most important thing, and one could see this sense of exhilaration in the effort that the people were putting into the war. Young girls, for example, had taken over the job of controlling traffic. They were really doing it by themselves—no one asked them to. That this kind of spirit existed made us feel tremendously hopeful. Clearly something had happened to the psyche of an entire people to bring this about.

Richard West, a British journalist, was so captivated by the meticulous nature with which Biafrans conducted the affairs of state that he wrote a widely cited article in which he lamented: "Biafra is more than a human tragedy. Its defeat, I believe, would mark the end of African independence. Biafra was the first place I had been to in Africa where the Africans themselves were truly in charge."[3]

Soon after I arrived in Ogidi we were told that Nigerian soldiers, led by Murtala Muhammed, were trying to cross the Niger Bridge from Asaba into Onitsha, and were being kept at bay by the Biafran colonel Achuzia (aka "Air Raid" Achuzia). Shuwa's troops were marching into Igbo land across the Benue River in the north at the same time. There was quite an overwhelming sense of anxiety in the air.

We had all gone to bed on one particular night—my family, Augustine and his family, and Frank and his family. We did not realize that Biafran soldiers had set up their armory outside my father's house, on the veranda, the porch, and outside in the yard. The house was in a choice location, atop a small hill, and was clearly chosen by the army as a perfect site from which to shell the advancing Nigerian army and to surprise them with sniper fire.

By this time in the war we—at least some of us—had gotten used to sleeping with the sound of shelling and explosions, and occasional howls of pain and what some villagers called "the stench of death." Others would recount that they did not sleep a wink through the war, an exaggeration of course, but a valid point nonetheless; sleeplessness was endemic. On this particular night we were oblivious to what was going on outside our father's house. While we were sleeping the Biafran army was turning our ancestral home into a military base of sorts. No one asked us for permission. They did not knock to ask or to inform. In hindsight, what happened next was enough to have caused sudden cardiac arrest in some people. We all were awakened violently from sleep by a loud ka-boom!, followed by the rattling of the house foundation and walls, indeed of the entire house. A number of people who were asleep fell off their beds, violently ushered back into reality by the vibrations, the shock, and the noise of the artillery fire outside. It was awful.

The men in the house went outside to find out what was going on. A colonel who was in charge of this exercise explained that they had decided to use our home as a tactical base because it provided them a logistical and strategic advantage as they shelled the encroaching federal troops. Surely it was time for us to leave.

The Abagana Ambush

On March 25, 1968, the Second Division of the Nigerian army finally broke through the Biafran resistance and entered Onitsha. (The federal troops had failed the first attempt to cross the Niger, suffering great casualties at the hands of Achuzia's guerrilla army; this was the second attempt.) Their plan following this development was to link up these federal troops with the forces of the First Division, led by Colonel Shuwa, that were penetrating the Igbo heartland from the north. The amalgamation of these two forces, the Nigerian army hoped, would then serve as a formidable force that would "smash the Biafrans."[1] Colonel Murtala Muhammed hastily deployed a convoy of ninety-six vehicles and four armored cars to facilitate this plan on March 31, 1968.

Biafran intelligence was swift to respond, and it informed Major Johnathan Uchendu, who formulated an elaborate plan. He arranged a seven-hundred-man-strong counterattack that essentially sealed off the Abagana Road. He commanded his troops to lie in ambush in the forest near Abagana, waiting patiently for the advancing Nigerians and their reinforcements. Major Uchendu's strategy proved to be highly successful. His troops destroyed Muhammed's entire convoy within one and a half hours. All told the Nigerians suffered about five hundred casualties. There was minimal loss of life on the Biafran side.

Very few federal soldiers survived this ambush, and those who did were found walking dazed and aimless in the bush. There were widespread reports of atrocities perpetrated by angry Igbo villagers who captured these wandering soldiers. One particularly harrowing report claimed that a mob of villagers cut their capture into pieces. I was an eyewitness to one such angry blood frenzy of retaliation after a particularly tall and lanky soldier—clearly a mercenary from Chad or Mali—wandered into an ambush of young men with machetes. His lifeless body was found mutilated on the roadside in a matter of seconds. "Gifts" of poisoned water–filled calabashes were left in strategic places throughout the deserted villages to "welcome" the thirsty federal troops.

My elder sister's family took refuge in Nnobi during all this commotion, the town where I was born. My father had settled there as a catechist and a teacher half a century earlier. The hosts of my sister and her family began to tell them that it was from my father that the people of that village learned to eat rice about fifty years before his children returned to this bucolic town as refugees. The host, a man of great consideration and taste, proclaimed that he was, therefore, going to cook rice for my sister's family to salute my father. There were attempts to humanize our existence despite the horrors that surrounded us all. Life went on as much as the people could manage it.

Through it all, there was a great deal of humor. I remember one occasion after an air raid—and these are really horrible things—somebody saw two vultures flying very high up, and he said, "That is a fighter and a bomber," and everybody burst into laughter. It was a very poor joke, I know, but laughter helped everyone there keep their sanity ... that is, if you wanted to survive.

I did not realize how I was being affected by living under those circumstances until I traveled out of Biafra on a mission to England. I heard planes taking off and landing at Heathrow Airport, and my first instinct was to duck under safe cover.[2]

AIR RAID

It comes so quickly
the bird of death
from evil forests of Soviet technology

A man crossing the road
to greet a friend
is much too slow.
His friend cut in halves
has other worries now
than a friendly handshake
at noon[1]

The Citadel Press

News filtered in that life approached some semblance of normalcy far away from the immediate arenas of war. A few weeks after my arrival in Ogidi I was informed that there was a job opening in Enugu, so I packed up my family at my father's house and headed farther east into Igbo land, and, we hoped, away from the war zone.

Christopher Okigbo left his work at Cambridge University Press in Ibadan, where he served as Cambridge's West Africa manager. He suddenly appeared in Enugu a few weeks after I arrived from Lagos. By the time we all arrived back in Eastern Nigeria, after escaping the massacres across the rest of the country, it became clear to me that it would be beneficial to the cause of Biafra if intellectuals worked together to support the war effort. Christopher came to me and requested that we establish a publishing house. It immediately seemed to me to be a very good idea, for we believed it was necessary at this time to publish books, especially children's books, that would have relevance to our society.

This was something we felt very strongly about. We felt we wanted to develop literature for children based on local thought, and we set up a firm called The Citadel Press. Biafra declared its independence while we were developing our plans, and we were more confident than ever that what we were doing was good for the cause. Christopher proceeded to get a plot of land in a key area of Enugu off one of the city's major thoroughfares—today's Michael Okpara Avenue.

It was a very strategic piece of land at the commercial nerve center of the future capital of Biafra, Enugu. The building that was erected had a few rooms—one for Christopher, one for me, one for our secretary, one area for printing and publishing machinery, and a smaller one was a toilet. Christopher made all the arrangements himself. That was his nature: He would get the work done before even broaching the subject, so that when you eventually agreed to his idea (something he was sure you would), he would then release a torrent of information, in this case about the office location, its design, and what the building would cost us.

The first book we worked on was called *How the Leopard Got Its Claws*. John Iroaganachi, a talented author, submitted a manuscript of a version of the African myth "How the Dog Became a Domesticated Animal," which Professor Ernest Emenyonu relates "abounds in various versions in many African cultures."[1] Christopher and I realized immediately that we wanted a different story, more or less, and decided to spend some time on it. Iroaganachi's story transformed into something entirely different as I worked on it, and began to take and find avenues and openings in a way that the original narrative hadn't. Christopher in particular was put off by the subservient character of the dog in the original version and was delighted to see the next incarnation of the story. To be certain that everyone was on the same page, Christopher asked Iroaganachi if he was ready to see his original story transformed. Iroaganachi had no problem with the changes we had suggested, and we settled on a joint authorship for our first book, between me, John Iroaganachi, and Okigbo, who wrote a powerful poem, "Lament of the Deer," on my invitation.

Christopher was seen less often as the war intensified. I kept on working at the office, and he came back whenever he had some time, and we discussed a number of matters.[2] The war clearly influenced the crafting of the new story. In the second version the leopard is the king of animals and is a peaceful and wise king. One day he is cast out by tyrants, led by the dog, into the cold, wet wilderness. The leopard seeks help from the blacksmith, who makes teeth and claws of steel for him, Thunder and Lightning, that grant him his roar and strength. Then he returns to his kingdom to retake his throne, punish the usurpers, and banish the dog to the services of man in perpetuity. In the end the new story not only turned the ancient African fable on its head but also clearly had manifestations of the Biafran story embedded in it.

The Ifeajuna Manuscript

Christopher and I encountered a wide variety of projects during our time at Citadel Press. Emmanuel Ifeajuna, one of the so-called five majors who executed the January 15, 1966, coup d'état, presented a manuscript to Christopher, and he excitedly brought it to me. I too was excited to receive it; I opened the package it came in and began to read it. It was the story of the military coup. I read the treatise through quickly and became more and more disappointed as I went along.

Ifeajuna's account showcased a writer trying to pass himself off as something that he wasn't. For one, the manuscript claimed that the entire coup d'état was his show, that he was the chief strategist, complete mastermind, and executer, not just one of several. He recognized the presence of his coconspirators but did not elevate their involvement to any level of importance.

The other problem I noted was the inconsistencies in the narrative. For instance, the group of coup plotters are said to have met in a chalet at a catering guest house in Enugu at night, and because what they were doing was very dangerous, there was no light in the room, and they all sat in pitch darkness. Despite the darkness, Ifeajuna, our narrator, goes on to say: "I stood up and addressed them while watching their faces and noting their reactions." The whole account was replete with exaggerations that did not ring true.

I also struggled with the fact that the writer seemed not to appreciate the seriousness of what he had done. Ifeajuna's manuscript passed off the assassination of the prime minister as light fare, as if it was all in good sport, almost as if he was saying to his readers "I did this and I was right. I am a hero."

When I saw Christopher Okigbo next I told him how impossible it was for me to believe this account—I wanted to get a real sense of what really happened on that fateful day in January 1966, not what Ifeajuna would want us to believe. Christopher, having read the manuscript as well said, "I thought it was lyrical." He then told me that he bumped into Nzeogwu shortly after receiving the manuscript, and Nzeogwu said to him: "I hear you and Achebe are planning to publish Emma's [Ifeajuna] lies." That comment from Nzeogwu further placed the manuscript in disrepute.

My own private conclusion was that Ifeajuna's manuscript was an important document, but it was not a responsible document. I believed Nzeogwu was right. But, unfortunately for all of us, the manuscript seems to have disappeared, which is not surprising considering what happened to all of the people involved in its story. Ifeajuna and Nzeogwu are both dead, robbing us all of the opportunity of reading two competing versions of what transpired. They are no longer here to help fill this void. This is what gives me my only regret: I could have published the manuscript and called it special publishing, as opposed to so-called regular or mainstream publishing, so that at least a version of what happened, however flawed, warts and all, would be available for debate.

Staying Alive

While I worked at the Citadel Press, Christie, with her characteristic ingenuity and flair for design, created a home for us in this new city. When we arrived in Enugu we quickly found accommodation on the outskirts of town. It was an apartment complex with two subunits. We took the flat upstairs and converted this empty space into a very livable, comfortable accommodation. She employed a number of workers, including painters, masons, carpenters, and electricians, over a short period of time in this miraculous feat of transformation. The other tenant of this building was a charming architect. He too went ahead, and architecturally altered the lower living quarters to meet his needs. We could leave to the eye of the beholder whether this pleasant artist's taste was eccentric or eclectic. But one thing was clear: His new design did not go down well with the landlord.

I put my family to bed one hot night toward the end of the renovation, and opened a window to let a gentle, cool breeze in. At about 2:00 A.M. Christie first heard the noise of an intruder. She alerted me, and I shouted at the top of my voice, "Where is my gun?" We saw the outline of a figure in the dark dash past us and jump through the open window. The intruder thankfully did not realize that I did not possess a gun and was adamantly against the use of firearms. The next day the workmen were one person short. When we asked where the missing man was we were told that he had gone to the hospital to nurse a broken leg.

I traveled abroad soon after the move to Enugu, on a mission for the people of Biafra. I asked my close friend Christopher Okigbo to take care of my family while I was away. Christie was pregnant, and I turned my young family over to Christopher for protection during this precarious time. In a quintessential Christopher Okigbo move, he promptly checked them into the catering guest house, a swank hotel chain of the day, first run smartly by the colonial British government and then quite well by the government of the first republic of Nigeria. This particular branch was now in the hands of the Biafrans and had, in the words of Christopher, clearly an unbiased judge, "returned to its former glory." In any case, Christopher had connections with the manager and introduced my wife and family as one of his own.

One day Christie asked Christopher to get her a number of things for lunch from a nearby restaurant and said that she would "pay for it all." She had a very powerful craving for fried plantains, beans, and a delicacy called *Isi Ewu*. Okigbo agreed to do so but instead telephoned the manager of the catering guest house, telling him that Christie Achebe, who was pregnant, needed the food items urgently, and that the food should be delivered to his room, and he would then make sure it got to her. After waiting two to three hours, Christie called Christopher about the food. Okigbo did not respond on the telephone but showed up in their room with the explanation that he had inadvertently eaten it, thinking it was a special lunch made for him. They could not believe it. On hearing this, my three-year-old son, Ike, who had uncharacteristically, for someone his age, been waiting patiently for lunch, launched at Okigbo, tackling him to the ground and punching him with everything he had. Okigbo howled and feigned pain, and then made sure he got my family a hearty dinner to eat.

I returned from my trip abroad to the news that my mother, who was quite frail, had suddenly become quite sick. Her able and diligent physician, Dr. Theophilus Mbanefo, had worked tirelessly to care for her, and now he thought it best for her entire family to come back briefly and pay their "last respects." I was very close to my mother, and I sent Christie and my family ahead of me while I worked through my private pain and wrapped up some business at the Citadel Press. My family subsequently left with our driver, Gabriel, for Ogidi to join the rest of my family at Mother's bedside.

Christopher and I were working in this office of ours that morning, the first day a military plane flew over Enugu. Our editorial chat was disturbed by the sudden drone of an enemy aircraft overhead, and the hectic and ineffectual small-arms fire that was supposed to scare it away, rather like a lot of flies worrying a bull. Not a very powerful bull, admittedly, at that point in the conflict. In fact, air raids were crude jokes that could almost be laughed off. People used to say that the safest thing was to go out into the open and keep an eye on the bomb as it was pushed out of the invading propeller aircraft. We heard the sounds of more bombs exploding in the distance, and Christopher, who already seemed familiar with planes and military hardware, shouted, "Under the table!" Most of the other Biafrans were going about their business as usual, unperturbed by this menace flying above their heads. As Christopher and I listened uneasily, an explosion went off in the distance somewhere, and the attack was soon over. We completed our discussion and departed. But that explosion that sounded so distant from the Citadel offices was to bring him back for a silent farewell on that eventful day.[1]

After the plane disappeared into the distance, Christopher said he had to leave, and I went to check on something that was already in the press—the first booklet that we were publishing for children. As I sat there working that day I heard the sound of an aircraft above, followed by bedlam in the distance. I shrugged this particular *katakata*, or chaos, off as another bombing raid from the Nigerians and got on with my chores. I set out to visit a business colleague and decided to stop at the house for a minute before proceeding to my original destination. At the house I saw a huge crowd and realized that it was my apartment complex that had been bombed![2]

I pushed my way through the assembly to the edge of a huge crater in the ground beside the building, about a hundred feet from my children's swing set. Luckily Christie and the children had left in the nick of time. Had there been anyone in the house they would not have survived.[3]

Okigbo was standing among the crowd. I can still see him clearly in his white gown and cream trousers among the vast crowd milling around my bombed apartment, the first spectacle of its kind in the Biafran capital in the second month of the war. I doubt that we exchanged more than a sentence or two. There were scores of sympathizers pressing forward to commiserate with me or praise God that my life or that the lives of my wife and children had been spared. So I hardly caught more than a glimpse of him in that crowd, and then he was gone like a meteor, forever. That elusive impression is the one that lingers out of so many. As a matter of fact, he and I had talked for two solid hours that very morning. But in retrospect that earlier meeting seems to belong to another time.[4]

I set off after that brief encounter with Christopher, homeless, to see my mother. My entire family was present in Ogidi, huddled, with long faces, grieving. Women could be heard sobbing in the distance. Some, like my brother Augustine, had just come in from Yaba, Lagos. Others, like Frank, our eldest brother, had arrived from Port Harcourt, where he worked for the Post and Telecommunications Corporation (P&T). I was informed soon after I got there that Mother had asked to see us all. We trooped into her bedroom one at a time and got to spend some private time with her. Soon after that, she passed away. Our people report that her spirit called my family away from Enugu to save their lives. I will not challenge their ancient wisdom.

Death of the Poet: "Daddy, Don't Let Him Die!"

I was driving from Enugu to Ogidi one afternoon, where I lived following the bombing, with my car radio tuned to Lagos. Like all people caught in a modern war, we had soon become radio addicts. We wanted to hear the latest from the fronts; we wanted to hear what victories Nigeria was claiming next, not just from NBC Lagos, but even more ambitiously, from Radio Kaduna. This station, also known as Radio Nigeria, was notorious as the mouthpiece of the Nigerian federal government; it only reported Nigerian military victories and successes, and those of us caught in a conflict wanted to hear balanced, unbiased news. We needed to hear what the wider world had to say to all that—the BBC, the Voice of America, the French Radio, Cameroon Radio, Radio Ghana, Radio Anywhere.

The Biafran forces had just suffered a major setback in the northern sector of the war with the loss of the university town of Nsukka. They had suffered an even greater morale-shattering blow with the death of that daring and enigmatic hero who had risen from anonymity to legendary heights in the short space of eighteen months: Major Chukwuma Kaduna Nzeogwu. Christopher Okigbo had begun to talk more and more about Nzeogwu before his enlistment, but I had not listened very closely; the military did not fascinate me as it did him. In hindsight, I wish I had listened—listened for all our sakes.

I was only half listening to the radio now when suddenly Christopher Okigbo's name stabbed my slack consciousness into panic life. "Rebel troops wiped out by gallant Federal forces," the announcement proclaimed. Among the rebel officers killed: Major Christopher Okigbo.[1]

It's rather different when a soldier is killed in battle—they get the body. I don't know what happens, but if they can identify him, and if they think they can make capital out of it, they immediately announce it. The killing of officers is something of which they are very proud. Christopher was a major.[2]

I pulled up at the roadside. The open parkland around Nachi stretched away in all directions. Other cars came and passed. Had no one else heard the terrible news?

When I finally got myself home and told my family, my three-year-old son, Ike, screamed: "Daddy, don't let him die!" Ike and Christopher had been special pals. When Christopher came to the house the boy would climb on his knees, seize hold of his fingers, and strive with all his power to break them while Christopher would moan in pretended agony. "Children are wicked little devils," he would say to us over the little fellow's head, and let out more cries of feigned pain.[3]

Christopher fell in August 1967, in Ekwegbe, close to Nsukka, where his poetry had come to sudden flower seven short years earlier. News of his death sent ripples of shock in all directions. Okigbo's exit was totally in character. Given the man and the circumstance it was impossible for everyone to react to the terrible loss in the same way. The varied responses, I think, would have pleased Okigbo enormously, for he enjoyed getting to his destination through different routes.[4]

I remember visiting Okpara Avenue, the site of the Citadel Press, soon after the war, and I was appalled at the scale of destruction that had befallen that small building. It is important to mention that a number of buildings in the vicinity had been unscathed by the conflict, but this one was pummeled into the ground; chips of the concrete blocks scattered everywhere had been pulverized as if with a jackhammer. It was the work of someone or some people with an ax to grind. It appeared as if there was an angry mission sent to silence the Citadel—for having the audacity to publish *How the Leopard Got Its Claws*—a book that challenged the very essence of the Nigerian federation's philosophy, depicting the return of the spurned former ruler to vanquish and retake his throne from the wretched and conniving usurper. Having had a few too many homes and offices bombed, I walked away from the site and from publishing forever.

A few months later my friends Arthur Nwankwo and Samuel Ifejika decided to establish a publishing company that they called Nwamife Books. One of the new company's first publications was a compendium of stories that chronicled the harrowing war years. I submitted a contribution to that important anthology, and then took the opportunity to persuade them to publish *How the Leopard Got Its Claws*. They agreed. The talented Scandinavian Per Christiansen illustrated for the work, and effectively united the prose and poetry in a visual consonance. I was grateful to see the manuscript Christopher and I had worked so hard on back in print.

Mango Seedling

Through glass windowpane
Up a modern office block
I saw, two floors below, on wide-jutting
concrete canopy a mango seedling newly sprouted
Purple, two-leafed, standing on its burst
Black yolk. It waved brightly to sun and wind
Between rains—daily regaling itself
On seed yams, prodigally.
For how long?
How long the happy waving
From precipice of rainswept sarcophagus?
How long the feast on remnant flour
At pot bottom?

Perhaps like the widow
Of infinite faith it stood in wait
For the holy man of the forest, shaggy-haired
Powered for eternal replenishment.
Or else it hoped for Old Tortoise's miraculous feast
On one ever recurring dot of cocoyam
Set in a large bowl of green vegetables—
This day beyond fable, beyond faith?
Then I saw it
Poised in courageous impartiality
Between the primordial quarrel of Earth

And Sky striving bravely to sink roots
Into objectivity, midair in stone.

I thought the rain, prime mover
To this enterprise, someday would rise in power
And deliver its ward in delirious waterfall
Toward earth below. But every rainy day
Little playful floods assembled on the slab,
Danced, parted round its feet,
United again, and passed.
It went from purple to sickly green
Before it died.

Today I see it still—
Dry, wire-thin in sun and dust of the dry months—
Headstone on tiny debris of passionate courage.[1]

Refugees

Enugu fell to the Nigerian army a few months after Christopher fell in battle. I fled to Umuahia with my family to stay with my sister-in-law, Elizabeth Okoli, who had moved there from Aba. Lizzy was a nurse working in Umuahia-area hospitals tending to the war wounded. Her story is quite remarkable: Lizzy was educated at Queen's College, Lagos, and in England, and was known in those days as the "Queen of Sheba," because of her grace and beauty. She was well regarded for her clinical skills and her intellect and would become the chief nursing officer of Anambra state in a new incarnation following the civil war. Elizabeth was a bit of an enigma and an eccentric, and a former Mrs. Odumegwu Ojukwu to boot, but she never wanted to talk about that! My brother Augustine and his family were also in Umuahia. Shortly after our arrival, as I have mentioned, I was sent abroad as an envoy for the people of Biafra. Christie reports that Umuahia was subsequently strafed very close to where my family was staying.

After the bombing that barely missed Lizzy's residence, my family moved to Ezinifite, a town north of Umuahia in the Aguata local government area of present-day Anambra state. I returned from my short trip abroad and rejoined my family there. It was there that we visited a family who in the past had sent one of their sons to live with and be educated by my father.

Now we were refugees, and this family who had received the magnanimity of my parents opened their homes and their resources to us—the three Achebe families—Augustine's, John's, and mine—and we moved into the quarters offered to us. It was a large estate. The head of the household lived in the largest of about four houses. The sons, who were also married, had homes built within the family compound. The sons gave each Achebe guest and their families a room and a parlor.

Finding food in Ezinifite was a difficult proposition. The women had to wake up very early in the morning—about 4:00 A.M.—to attend the daily markets to procure food. When the Nigerians found out where the open markets were and started bombing them, the women moved their commercial activities into dense forests. Christie remembers one of the early morning markets she went to—the villagers from the surrounding towns and hamlets would congregate in these markets to sell their fresh vegetables, fruit and chicken, and other household wares. If one had the money—one could use the Nigerian pound and the Biafran pound interchangeably—there were a variety of expensive, locally grown legumes, pawpaw, mangoes, bananas, and plantains, and other vegetables and fruits to purchase. The traders coveted the Nigerian pound, because it was particularly valuable in the black market and for purchasing and smuggling goods and food across the border. The Nigerians bombed the market a day after Christie visited the market. She remembers vividly:

> The bombardment from the Nigerian Air Force on this day was particularly heavy, as if the pilots had been upset at not discovering the market sooner. Most of the bombs fell before dawn. In the morning we discovered the most harrowing of sights. One image still haunts me till today: that of a pregnant woman split in two by the Nigerian blitz. That was a horrendous experience for most of us, and we were all very frightened after that.[1]

The Nigerian air force intensified its bombing exercises soon after this incident. Word had reached the Biafran authorities that the Nigerians had classified information about the location of civilian "hideout shelters." Our hosts were understandably concerned for our overall safety and built makeshift bunkers throughout their compound. The bunkers were built of mud-and-clay bricks and clearly were not structurally capable of withstanding a shelling, but we were grateful nonetheless, because they were large, comfortable spaces underground, away from the houses that would be obvious targets of the Nigerian air force. Whenever we heard the siren we all rushed to the bunkers for safety and waited out the air strikes.

The Biafran government had issued a public safety warning to all citizens to abstain from wearing clothes of light colors like white or cream or sharp colors such as orange, purple, or red that could be easily spotted by the Nigerian air force. The Nigerian pilots approaching their chosen targets would often switch off the engines of the planes, then fly very low—treetop level—before they would begin the bombing onslaught. One could see that the plane crew was pushing out these bombs with their hands, tossing them out from an open aircraft door or shaft! Occasionally when the Nigerians used their aircraft guns to shoot at civilian or military installations, we noticed that some of the bullet cases were from large hunting ammo usually reserved for wild game.[2]

On this particular day we did not hear the siren or the planes; no one knew that the Nigerians were in the air. When we noticed a plane zooming in for the kill we rushed into the bunkers and looked around to account for everyone, counting all the children. To our horror we realized that our third child, Chidi, was not there.

We looked out and saw the toddler in his white diaper taking his time, walking from the gate of the compound toward one of the houses. People tried to prevent Christie from leaving the bunker to rescue the infant for fear that her heroism might reveal the site of the bunker.

One said: "Leave him, he is innocent, nothing will happen to him." Clearly unconvinced and ignoring their advice, Christie dashed out from the bunker, grabbed the baby, and arrived inside seemingly in time to avoid notice.

During our stay we had a number of confrontations not just with the Nigerian army but with nature. As we ran from one zone of attack to another we often ended up seeking shelter in mud huts deep in the hinter-land. One particular episode comes to mind: Christie had hung up a brown and black dress on a palm frond door that opened into the room shielded by a thatch roof in a mud building we were staying in. Exquisitely put together, these homes are ideal for the wet, damp weather of the trop-ics and provide cool solace from the often uncompromising elements.

The one downside of this ancient architecture is the fact that mud buildings serve as an elaborate ecosystem of insects, arachnids, rodents, amphibians, and reptiles—in other words, an entomologist's and a zoolo-gist's dream! So on this day, as Christie put on her dress, she received a sting that produced excruciating pain. We rushed to her side and discov-ered that a centipede had engaged her skin in a tenacious battle. The vil-lagers quickly relieved her of the vermin with a hot object warmed in a coal fire. Though we were reassured that this was not a species that was poisonous, we slept in our car that night. We would have other narrow escapes with scorpions, serpents, and blood-sucking larvae, and became very vigilant.

My nephew, Uche Achebe, had left to join the army from our Ezinifite base around this time. Uche, a bright lad, later became a surgeon and was at one point the medical director of Nigeria's National Orthopaedic Hospital in Enugu. In any case, things were not working out very well for him in the army during this period. Uche is a practical, rational person by temperament, and he noted that the Nigerian army was quickly approaching, and there were so many bombings that cost the lives of scores of Biafrans on a daily basis. He lamented the fact that the Biafrans were not well equipped and appeared to be in perpetual retreat. Com-pounding this desperate situation, he observed, was the fact that the Biafran people were becoming disenchanted.

Unfortunately, Uche made his observations known to one of his fel-low army officers, saying something to the effect of: "If we are not able to do this, why don't we give up?" He was subsequently reported and arrested for treason. In the end, after some intervention from several sources, he managed to escape court-martial.

Irony plays a wicked game with life. The Nigerian army took over Ezinifite very soon after the prophetic statements of my nephew, and we fled once again, this time to the beautiful lakeside town of Oguta. We had a fairly quiet spell in Oguta, because the Nigerians had been repulsed prior to our arrival. The locals credited this victory to Ohamiri, the goddess of Lake Oguta, who protected the Oguta people.

From time to time, one could hear the artillery shelling as the federal government troops tried on multiple attempts to obliterate the Uli airport, which was near Oguta. The federal troops at that point had not discovered that there were two airports—Uli was the earlier one, which was very close to Oguta and the nerve center of Biafran relief efforts. A second, smaller airport, less well-known, was in Nnokwa and was also used for military missions.

Nnokwa is a little-known ancient village that played a vital role in Igbo cosmology and in the development of its civilization. The townsfolk were particularly noted for their role in the transmission of the knowledge of Nsibidi, an ancient writing first invented by the Ejagham (Ekoi) people of southeastern Nigeria, and then adopted and used widely by their close neighbors—the Igbo, Efik, Anang, and Ibibio. The very existence of this alphabet, dating back to the 1700s without any Latin or Arabic antecedent, is a rebuke to all those who have claimed over the centuries that Africa has no history, no writing, and no civilization! But we always knew of the beauty of our culture, and one can understand why Nnokwa was a place to be protected by the Biafrans at all costs.

In Oguta, we moved into my friend Ikenna Nzimiro's uncle's house— a huge mansion. Some joked that it was as large as Buckingham Palace. One could see that the mansion was virtually empty, as those who lived there, including the staff, had all fled. The "mother of the house," if you like, Nzimiro's elderly auntie, stayed behind with one or two of her attendants; she seemed ill and did not appear very often. Nzimiro's uncle had died several years before the conflict. With her blessing we were given luxurious quarters and had quite a comfortable stay.

It was during our sojourn in Oguta that Christie started a school to keep the children of our hosts and the Achebe children engaged in their studies. Christie had books that she had bought from shops, and she used these to teach the children, with Chinelo, our first child and daughter. Each child started from the last class they were in before the war broke out, and then graduated after they completed the lesson plans. Despite the chaos and madness all around, some privileged children, at least, still went to school.

From Oguta we would be driven out to the Shell compound, aka Shell Camp, in Owerri after the city had been recaptured by the Biafrans. In the colonial era Shell Camp was the residential quarters of some colonial officers and Shell senior officials, before Royal Dutch/Shell BP moved their permanent quarters to Port Harcourt in present-day Rivers state, in the Niger River Delta area. Shell Camp in those days was a fairly lovely part of town, a neatly manicured estate with well-maintained bungalows and lawns, telecommunications facilities, good roads, and a reliable water supply.

Christie was expecting a baby and was ill during this time. She was moved to a Roman Catholic hospital of high repute in the region, admitted by the physician on staff, and cared for by the nursing sisters, a number of whom were from Europe. We heard during her hospital stay that the Nigerians had finally broken through the blockade mounted by the Biafran soldiers, rearmed, and launched a second offensive, pushing closer to Owerri. It clearly had become quite serious when we noticed Biafran soldiers coming into the hospital to warn the clinical staff to leave and evacuate all the patients. Christie was summarily discharged.

When we returned to Shell Camp we saw that the area had been infiltrated by the Nigerian army, some wearing mufti, who watched us closely. We noticed that the entire estate was almost deserted. The main roads were jammed with civilians trying to escape before the Nigerian troops arrived. Some of the federal forces who had already entered Owerri would snicker at the civilians; some would wave cynically. It was eerie and frightening.

We picked up the few belongings we had in the house and jumped back into the car. During the war years one never really unpacked; one always had the belongings in the trunk of the car and took only the absolute necessities into the temporary shelter that you found yourself in. We decided to get off the major thoroughfares, so we meandered through the rural areas, villages, and hamlets and arrived in the village of Okporo. This pleasant community holds a special place in Biafran lore, because it was the site of a special hospital for children run by Caritas, and it was one of the sites chosen to gather sick babies for the famous airlift of Biafran babies to Gabon and Ivory Coast organized by international relief agencies.

I recall visiting a clinic that had been hastily set up by one of the many foreign nongovernmental organizations (NGO) during this time. They had chosen an abandoned secondary school complex and set up shop in what must have been the cafeteria. There were bullet holes in the limestone and concrete walls and pieces of glass shattered on the floor, suggesting a recent gun battle. The patients were strewn on the shiny red laterite floor on bamboo and raffia mats—the adults in one section and the children in the other. It was raining on that day, and the holes in the corrugated iron roofs provided a steady stream of water that dripped directly on some patients (who appeared not to care) and collected in puddles throughout the building. The visitor was greeted by the strong smell of vomit, diarrhea, and other bodily fluids that are kept private in sunnier times. In the distance one could hear the screams of pain from what appeared to be a makeshift operating room, where surgeons performed procedures with woefully limited anaesthesia.

There was a child in a corner who was being fed a white meal—the relief meals were almost always white, I thought—and it was a concoction that meant the difference between an early grave or another day to see the sun. On this day, at least, this reed-thin child, with a skull capped with wiry rust-colored tufts of hair and a body centered on a protuberant stomach, provided a toothy smile. I spent a short while smiling back at her, and she reached out to touch my hand. Her touch was as light as feathers.

Dr. Aaron Ifekwunigwe, now a professor emeritus of pediatrics at the University of California, was the director of health services for Biafra at the time of the war. He performed extensive and important clinical research and treatment during this time. He studied the impact of starvation on the Biafran population. One of his most compelling research projects, in March 1968, found during this early period of starvation that 89 percent of those affected were children under five years of age. The remaining 11 percent were age five to fifteen.[3, 4]

> [On] an early fact-finding mission in 1968, conducted by ICRC [International Committee of the Red Cross], Doctor Edwin Spirgi found that at least 300,000 children were suffering from kwashiorkor . . . and three million children were near death.[5]

There was another epidemic that was not talked about much, a silent scourge—the explosion of mental illness: major depression, psychosis, schizophrenia, manic-depression, personality disorders, grief response, post-traumatic stress disorder, anxiety disorders, etc.—on a scale none of us had ever witnessed. One of the saddest images of the war was not just the dead and the physically wounded but also the mentally scarred, the so-called mad men and women who had been psychologically devastated by the anguish and myriad pressures of war. They could often be seen walking seemingly aimlessly on the roads in tattered clothes, in conversation with themselves.

WE LAUGHED AT HIM

We laughed at him our
hungry-eyed fool-man with itching
fingers that would see farther
than all. We called him
visionary missionary revolutionary
and, you know, all the other
naries that plague the peace, but
nothing would deter him.

With his own nails he cut
his eyes, scraped the crust
over them peeled off his priceless
patina of rest and the dormant
fury of his dammed pond
broke into a cataract
of blood tumbling down
his face and chest. . . . We
laughed at his screams the fool-man
who would see what eyes
are forbidden, the hungry-eyed
man, the look-look man, the
itching man bent to drag
into daylight fearful signs
hidden away from our safety
at the creation of the world.

He was always against
blindness, you know, our quiet
sober blindness, our lazy—he called
it—blindness. And for
his pains? A turbulent, torrential
cascading blindness behind
a Congo river of blood. He sat
backstage then behind his flaming red
curtain and groaned in
the pain his fingers unlocked, in the
rainstorm of blows loosed on his head
by the wild avenging demons he
drummed free from the silence of their
drum-house, his prize for big-eyed greed.
We sought by laughter to drown
his anguish until one day
at height of noon his screams
turned suddenly to hymns
of ecstasy. We knew then his pain
had risen to the brain
and we took pity on him
the poor fool-man as he held
converse with himself. "My Lord,"
we heard him say to the curtain
of his blood, "I come to touch
the hem of your crimson robe!"
He went stark mad thereafter
raving about new sights he
claimed to see, poor fellow; sights
you and I know are as impossible for this world

to show as for a hen to urinate—if one
may borrow one of his many crazy vulgarisms—
he raved about trees topped with
green and birds flying—yes actually
flying through the air—about
the Sun and the Moon and stars
and about lizards crawling on all
fours. . . . But nobody worries much
about him today: he has paid
his price and we don't even
bother to laugh any more.[1]

The Media War

The Nigeria-Biafra War was arguably the first fully televised conflict in history. It was the first time scenes and pictures—blood, guts, severed limbs—from the war front flooded into homes around the world through television sets, radios, newsprint, in real time. It probably gave television evening news its first chance to come into its own and invade without mercy the sanctity of people's living rooms with horrifying scenes of children immiserated by modern war.

One of the silver linings of the conflict (if one can even call it that) was the international media's presence throughout the war. The sheer amount of media attention on the conflict led to an outpouring of international public outrage at the war's brutality. There were also calls from various international agencies for action to address the humanitarian disaster overwhelming the children of Biafra.[1]

Said Baroness Asquith in the British House of Lords, "[Thanks to the miracle of television we see history happening before our eyes. We see no Igbo propaganda; we see the facts."[2] Following the blockade imposed by the Nigerian government, "Biafra" became synonymous with the tear-tugging imagery of starving babies with blown-out bellies, skulls with no subcutaneous fat harboring pale, sunken eyes in sockets that betrayed their suffering.[3]

Someone speaking in London in the House of Commons, or the House of Lords, would talk about history happening all around them, but for those of us on the ground in Biafra, where this tragedy continued to unfold, we used a different language . . . the language and memory of death and despair, suffering and bitterness.

The agony was everywhere. The economic blockade put in place by Nigeria's federal government resulted in shortages of every imaginable necessity, from food and clean water to blankets and medicines. The rations had gone from one meal a day to one meal every other day—to nothing at all. Widespread starvation and disease of every kind soon set in. The suffering of the children was the most heart wrenching.

Narrow Escapes

At another stop, in the town of Okporo, we met a very pleasant gentleman who took my entire family in. He offered Christie and me the only finished room in the mud house he was still building. The rest of the floors were yet to be plastered. He moved out his belongings from the finished room and moved our things into it. We argued with him, but he would not hear it, and insisted that we stay in his most comfortable room. We more or less settled in.

One was not sure where the war was headed, so we decided to stay in Okporo for as long as our hosts would have us. There was a great deal of confusion about the status of the republic. This was at the tail end of the conflict. At that point in the hostilities, both sides were really exhausted. One noticed it in the shuffling gait of the soldiers, in the less than chipper drill-song choruses, in the number of stories of army desertions.

The news about surrender was already in the air. Tragically, there were many false rumors that the war had ended. Some people who had survived the war lost their lives that week because they had heard that people were being asked to come back to Enugu, that everything was over and returning to normal. Some of them were killed by Nigerian troops on the way.

The federal troops soon arrived in Okporo and broke our idyllic village existence. With their arrival came the horrendous stories of nurses and local women being raped and violated in unthinkable ways.[1]

One day the Nigerian soldiers came to the compound, and we hid our daughter, Chinelo, who was eight. I was in the kitchen making bread in the earth (laterite) oven that we had designed. I watched the soldiers from the kitchen window for a while as they pranced around the compound and demanded that its owner hand over a large black-and-white-spotted goat that was tied to the fence, in a corner near a building that served as the storage area. The animal was oblivious of the soldiers' menacing presence and busy chewing cud, its jaw swaying from side to side in between nibbles of long strands of elephant grass.[2]

The goat had sentimental importance to the wife of the owner of the residence, we learned from her pleas. It had been a gift from her father, so she refused to hand over the animal to the soldiers. I talked to the soldiers for a while, overwhelmed by the strong smell of Kai Kai, a local gin, on their breath, and in Igbo persuaded the wife of our host to give the soldiers the animal or be willing to lose her life and ours in the process.

A small crowd had gathered to watch this spectacle. The soldiers at this point were showing off, pointing their rifles in our faces. As they marched off they instructed the animal's owner to take care of the goat for them in their absence, because they were still on duty. If the goat was not there when they came back, they warned, "you will all be responsible."

As soon as the soldiers left the wife of our host, in a state of panic, untied the goat from the fence with the intention of hiding it in a dry well nearby. I called out to her to leave the goat alone.

"Let them take it," I said, "and leave you alone." Fortunately for everyone the soldiers never returned for the war plunder.

I had the privilege of having an official car that had been assigned to me by the government of Biafra, which came with a driver. The driver was one of those hyperreligious individuals who wore only white (a sign of purity, apparently) and preached endlessly to his company, condemning everyone and everything "to the damnation that awaitest thee if you don't repent!" He was a truly curious character but an excellent driver nonetheless.

One morning, as we woke to the greeting of the cock crow in the distance, I walked out to the brisk damp dawn, stretched, and smiled as I glanced around—the villages in Nigeria always had an organic, wholesome, earthy smell to them—and then it struck me: I noticed that the government vehicle had disappeared. Someone in the yard confirmed that the government driver had packed the entire car in the wee hours of the morning and fled with our belongings.

We had traveled up to that point in a two-car convoy—I drove my own car, a Jaguar, and the official car was driven by the chauffeur. Luckily, we still had the Jaguar, and we decided to leave Okporo with our own driver, who we knew was much more trustworthy. We took the other driver's disappearance as some sort of omen, thanked our hosts for their wonderful hospitality, and departed in the early afternoon with the intention of traveling back to Ogidi, my ancestral home. We headed north toward Onitsha, six miles from Ogidi. It was getting quite dark by the time we got to the outskirts of Oba, a few miles from Otu-Onitsha.

Refined petroleum was available but not always readily accessible, and petrol depots were obvious targets of the federal troops. The driver reported that we had an empty gas tank and we were desperately in need of filling up the tank if we were to make the rest of the trip without incident. Almost immediately we heard the vehicle wobble and then just stop. A deep darkness had enveloped us—there was no moonlight, so it seemed even darker—and our circumstances made the darkness seem even more ominous. We knew that one never ventured into canteens or restaurants for fear of meeting one's death at the hands of drunken soldiers. We decided that we would spend the night in the car.

In the middle of the night some young men started walking around the car—circling menacingly. They had come out of a restaurant, where they had been drinking, staggering clumsily and laughing and speaking at the top of their voices. We were very frightened. The driver and I got out of the car and started pushing the vehicle, for quite some time, until we encountered some Biafran soldiers in a jeep. The captain recognized me and advised us not to travel any farther this particular night, and he got his men to help us push the car the rest of the way to a petrol depot, where we filled our gas tank, parked the car at the corner, and passed the night there. The next morning we set out very early, gradually, moving in occasional spurts and starts, since the fuel in the car's tank clearly was adulterated. Not for the last time, we were happy to be unscathed.

Vultures

In the grayness
and drizzle of one despondent
dawn unstirred by harbingers
of sunbreak a vulture
perching high on broken
bones of a dead tree
nestled close to his
mate his smooth
bashed-in head, a pebble
on a stem rooted in
a dump of gross
feathers, inclined affectionately
to hers. Yesterday they picked
the eyes of a swollen
corpse in a water-logged
trench and ate the
things in its bowel. Full
gorged they chose their roost
keeping the hollowed remnant
in easy range of cold
telescopic eyes. . . .

Strange
indeed how love in other
ways so particular
will pick a corner

in that charnel house
tidy it and coil up there, perhaps
even fall asleep—her face
turned to the wall!
... Thus the Commandant at Belsen
Camp going home for
the day with fumes of
human roast clinging
rebelliously to his hairy
nostrils will stop
at the wayside sweetshop
and pick up a chocolate
for his tender offspring
waiting at home for Daddy's
return ...
Praise bounteous
providence if you will
that grants even an ogre
a tiny glowworm
tenderness encapsulated
in icy caverns of a cruel
heart or else despair
for in the very germ
of that kindred love is
lodged the perpetuity
of evil.[1]

PART 3

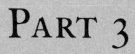

The Fight to the Finish

By the rainy season of 1968, Gowon's three-pronged attack had surrounded millions of civilians who were harbored in a narrow corridor around Umuahia. He was counting on a strategy of decisive force to which the Biafrans responded with a classic guerrilla war strategy out of Che Guevara's playbook.

The Biafrans surprised the Nigerians with their perseverance. Overwhelmingly outgunned, Philip Effiong's army was able to withstand the attack by breaking conflict zones into classic smaller wars, where the few arms he had would prove more effective. This strategy required "no front lines, a reliance on small unit operations and great individual discipline."[1]

The Economic Blockade and Starvation

The Biafrans paid a great humanitarian price by ceding a great deal of territory to the Nigerians and employing this war strategy. The famine worsened as the war raged, as the traditional Igbo society of farmers could not plant their crops. Gowon had succeeded in cutting Biafra off from the sea, robbing its inhabitants of shipping ports to receive military and humanitarian supplies. The afflictions marasmus and kwashiorkor began to spread farther, with the absence of protein in the diet, and they were compouded by outbreaks of other disease epidemics and diarrhea. The landscape was filled by an increasing number of those avian prognosticators of death as the famine worsened and the death toll mounted: *udene*, the vultures. By the beginning of the dry season of 1968, Biafran civilians and soldiers alike were starving. Bodies lay rotting under the hot sun by the roadside, and the flapping wings of scavengers could be seen circling, waiting, watching patiently nearby. Some estimates are that over a thousand Biafrans a day were perishing by this time, and at the height of Gowon's economic blockade and "starve them into submission" policy, upward of fifty thousand Biafran civilians, most of them babies, children, and women, were dying every single month.

Ojukwu seized upon this humanitarian emergency and channeled the Biafran propaganda machinery to broadcast and showcase the suffering to the world. In one speech he accused Gowon of a "calculated war of destruction and genocide."[1] Known in some circles as the "Biafran babies" speech, it was hugely effective and touched the hearts of many around the world. This move was brilliant in a couple of respects. First, it deflected from himself or his war cabinet any sentiments of culpability and outrage that might have been welling up in the hearts and minds of Biafrans, and second, it was yet another opportunity to cast his arch nemesis, Gowon, in a negative light.[2]

Ojukwu dispatched several of his ambassadors to world capitals, hoping to build on the momentum from his broadcast. His envoys received little new support or pledges. Frustrated by the obstacles he found in coaxing a more pro-Biafra policy from the United States, Sir Louis Mbanefo famously rebuked the Americans, saying:

We are especially resentful of the ambivalent pretenses the United States makes, that it is trying to help us. . . . If we are condemned to die, all right, we will die. But at least let the world, and the United States, be honest about it.[3]

Meanwhile, on the other side of the planet, Nigerian and Biafran envoys were meeting with His Imperial Majesty Emperor Haile Selassie of Ethiopia to sort out the modality of air and land transport for relief supplies to Biafra.[4] The diplomatic battles had reached a fever pitch by the middle of 1968. Gowon, under immense international pressure and bristling from the whirlwind of publicity about Biafra, decided to open up land routes for a "supervised transport" of relief. To the consternation of Gowon, Ojukwu opted out of land routes in favor of increased airlifts of food from São Tomé by international relief agencies. Ojukwu, like many Biafrans, was concerned about the prospect that the Nigerians would poison the food supplies.[5]

The Silence of the United Nations

Biafrans had their own reasons to lament the death of the widely respected secretary general of the United Nations, Dag Hammarskjöld, who was killed in an air crash in September 1961. The Burmese diplomat U Thant, selected to replace him, would lead the UN from 1961 to 1971. Unlike Dag Hammarskjöld, who was an expert at conflict resolution, and a humanist, U Thant was a decidedly different kind of man.[1]

A noninterventionist who deferred to local bodies such as the Organization of African Unity for policy advice and guidance, U Thant provided the OAU a great deal of latitude in decision making and implementation. An argument could be made for this stance, at least at the beginning of the conflict, but as the humanitarian catastrophe worsened, leading ultimately to the starvation and death of millions, even the most committed anarchist would have expected greater United Nations involvement. That did not happen, and I and several others believe that had the United Nations been more involved, there would not have been as many atrocities, as much starvation, as much death.

In October 1969, when Ojukwu reached out desperately to the United Nations to "mediate a cease-fire as a prelude to peace negotiations,"[2] his pleas were met with a deafening silence. U Thant turned to the Nigerians for direction. Gowon insisted on Biafra's surrender, and he observed that "rebel leaders had made it clear that this is a fight to the finish and that no concession will ever satisfy them."[3]

This was a calculated strategy from the Nigerians, who now had the international cloak of the United Nations under which to commit a series of human rights violations. Failing to end the protracted Biafran guerrilla offensive, the Nigerian army openly attacked civilians in an ill-advised, cruel, and desperate attempt to incite internal opposition to the war and build momentum toward a quick surrender.[4]

The vacuum in moral and humanitarian leadership from the United Nations meant that the Nigerian federal government could operate with reckless abandon, without appropriate monitoring from international agencies. There would be precious little proof of the wartime atrocities had it not been for private nongovernmental agencies and individuals. In February 1969 alone nearly eight hundred civilians were massacred by targeted Nigerian air force strikes on open markets near Owerri—Umuohiagu and Ozu-abam. The Nigerian air force pilots were particularly noteworthy for not respecting Geneva Convention resolutions describing civilian safe havens, such as hospitals, refugee and food distribution camps, and centers of religious worship.

In an article called "Who Cares About Biafra Anyway?" that was published in the *Harvard Crimson*, Jeffrey D. Blum described the horrors witnessed by Harvard University School of Public Health professor Jean Mayer:

> Distribution centers and refugee camps are bombed and strafed if any large numbers of people are visible in the daylight. Red Cross insignias are singled out for special attention by Nigerian bombers. Mayer saw one European engaged in working on the Biafran side of the war front carrying 117 dying children in his truck to a hospital in a single night.[5]

These air strikes backfired for Nigeria, further eroding international support for their war effort. Ojukwu seized on this opportunity, releasing a statement to the international press following an address to the consultative assembly in Umuahia. He lambasted the federal troops for having "begun a last desperate effort in the form of a land army pogrom." Ojukwu categorically denied any attempts by the Biafrans to surrender and reported that there would be an increased emphasis on the cultivation of staple crops to meet the mounting food needs of the starving Biafrans.

Many of us wondered where and how exactly this "cultivation" would take place, given the fact that the land mass controlled by Biafra was at this point of the conflict a fraction of its original size. Ojukwu clearly intended to try to feed the starving masses. It was important to him for Biafrans to see him making an effort even if he failed at achieving his lofty goals. Many listening on the Biafran side were willing to receive this food for thought even if there was no food for their stomachs. Ojukwu also warned the government of Harold Wilson of Great Britain that the British will "forfeit all holdings in Eastern Nigeria" if it continued to provide military and logistical aid to the Nigerians.[6]

Wilson's government was feeling the heat of the glaring lights of international media scrutiny. On one of my trips to London, on August, 12, 1968, I was an eyewitness to one of the debates on the Biafran issue in the House of Commons, and I came away with this impression: If government was largely unmoved by the tragedy, ordinary people were outraged. I witnessed from the visitors' gallery what was described as "unprecedented rowdiness" during a private members' motion on Biafra. Harold Wilson, villain of the peace, sat cool as a cucumber, leaving his foreign secretary, Michael Stewart, to sweat it out. It was hardly surprising that many remarkable people would want to visit the scene of such human tragedy.[7]

Harold Wilson was concerned that the growing opposition to his Nigeria policy might cause him to lose the next general election. He tried to assuage domestic and international opinion by planning an elaborate trip to Nigeria. Baroness Castle famously and aptly described Lord Wilson as "indulging in his near fatal weakness for gestures as a substitute for action."[8] By the time Harold Wilson arrived at the theater that he had set on fire on March, 29, 1969, he chose to do so in an "11,000 tonne amphibious assault ship called *Fearless* with an extra platoon of marines aboard."[9]

Claiming to have arrived to negotiate a peace between the warring parties, Lord Wilson met only with Gowon, extending a Trojan invitation to Ojukwu—to meet outside Nigeria, on Nigerian ground, or on the British ship *Fearless* anchored in the Lagos Lagoon. As a meeting in Biafra was not one of the choices, all the options were unsatisfactory to the Biafrans, who turned down the purely political invitation.[10]

Like the cruel deception of locusts that appear from a distance as a welcome visit of dark clouds gorged with rain, Lord Wilson failed to deliver on any resolution to help end the Nigeria-Biafra conflict and left the land stripped bare of what many felt was the last substantive hope of peace.

Azikiwe Withdraws
Support for Biafra

Beyond the military histrionics, there were a number of important attempts at peace made by several local and international statesmen, including Nnamdi Azikiwe, Nigeria's first president, who called on the United Nations to help end the conflict in Nigeria. In a speech at Oxford University on February 16, 1969, the former president and a one-time emissary of Biafra outlined a fourteen-point peace plan to be implemented by a proposed "UN peace keeping force made up of international and local peace keeping forces" that would stay on the ground for at least a year during the implementation of both a cease-fire and peaceful resolution of ethnic, economic, and political tensions. Azikiwe's proposals also called on Nigeria and Biafra to sign a modus vivendi "to be enforced by the Security Council of the United Nations."[1]

Azikiwe's lecture could not have come at a more critical time. I remember many of us in Biafra were hoping that his intervention would bring about a breakthrough in the stalemate. That hope was crushed when, following his triumphant lecture at Oxford, his strategy, which was submitted to both United Nations officials and the federal government of Nigeria, was soundly rejected as "unworkable."

It is instructive to note that many of Azikiwe's strategies and suggestions—international conflict resolution with United Nations peacekeeping forces, the use of international observer teams and military personnel to complement existing resources on the ground, etc.—have become standard United Nations practices today. Nevertheless, exactly six months later Nnamdi Azikiwe decided to discontinue any public support for the secessionist aspirations of Biafra and turned in his diplomatic credentials.

There has been a great deal of speculation as to why Azikiwe withdrew his support for Biafra. He was in a tough position and made a very
difficult decision after his counsel went mostly ignored by Ojukwu. The
late Dr. Okechukwu Ikejiani provides for posterity a rare insight into
Azikiwe's thinking, apprehension, and intellectual struggle:

> His [Azikiwe's] feeling was that when a leader of a nation wants to go to
> war, he should consult people. Primarily Ojukwu should have consulted
> Zik. Secondly, he should have consulted [Michael] Okpara [premier of
> eastern Nigeria]. Thirdly, he should have consulted other leaders. The
> only people that Ojukwu consulted were [Louis] Mbanefo and [Francis]
> Ibiam. I have Ibiam's letter here. It was a great mistake. I told Ojukwu
> [to] invite these people [and inform them]. He told me they would com-
> promise. That's what he said. He didn't invite them, never asked them
> questions. That's not how to lead. That's what led us into trouble. There
> are many areas we would have compromised. Ojukwu did not compro-
> mise. That's one of the mistakes we made in the war. . . . It wasn't that
> Zik opposed the war. Anybody with an intellect, with a sense would con-
> sider carefully the implications of a war. War is destructive. There's no
> country that went to war that didn't suffer, not one. When we went to
> war, we destroyed everything we had. That's true.[2]

One must also remember that Azikiwe had spent his entire life first
fighting for Nigerian independence under the One Nigeria mantra. In a
curious twist of irony he found the same position manipulated by the
British he had helped oust from his homeland. To add insult to injury,
Azikiwe watched helplessly as the words he helped invent were then
used by the Nigerian army—made up of some of the very same people
who from the get-go had rejected the concept of a unified Northern
and Southern Nigeria. Azikiwe supporters allege that the refusal by
Ojukwu to consider many peaceful strategies to end the conflict, coupled

with the prospects of annihilation of his people, was, I was told, just too much for the "great Zik of Africa" to bear.

The Recapture of Owerri

The psychologically devastated Biafrans were wrestling with two dire prospects in the latter part of the Harmattan Season of 1969: mass starvation or death by organized "ethnic cleansing" at the hands of Gowon's military. A third possibility, surrender, was not in the cards. By this time there were close to one hundred thousand men, women, and children, mainly children, perishing every six weeks. The Biafrans would get an emotional reprieve at the news of the recapture of Owerri, one of Biafra's largest cities, from the Nigerian troops.[1]

Gowon was furious to learn that Owerri had fallen back into the hands of the army he had sworn to defeat in three months. He instituted a major reorganization of his army's leadership. The Nigerian Third Battalion was now to be commanded by Olusegun Obasanjo, the Second Division switched commanders from Haruna to Lieutenant Colonel Gibson Sanda Jalo, and the First Battalion was now led by Brigadier Iliya Bisalla, in place of Shuwa.

The next several weeks saw an energized Biafran army engage the federal troops with heightened vigor. They were able to keep the Nigerian army at bay on several fronts—across the Imo River; through Uzuakoli to the seat of power in Umuahia and around the perimeter of Owerri, Nekede; and on the road to Aba. Colonel Joseph Achuzia, who had been placed in charge of the Biafran offensive by Ojukwu, even contemplated a major military push to Port Harcourt. The lack of ammunition or military supplies made this lofty goal a suicide mission, and even the radical Joseph "Air Raid" Achuzia knew his limitations.[2]

Achuzia was one of the most complicated, some say eccentric characters of the war. He was well-known throughout the East as a "no-nonsense, disciplined, tactical and strategic military genius," and was highly
respected, if not feared by the Nigerian federal forces for his mastery of
guerrilla warfare and for giving them a "run for their money" on the battlefield. Military experts report that Achuzia remained Ojukwu's "ace
commander" throughout the conflict, and he was often called upon to
solve problems or build upon military theater advantages. His detractors,
who refer to him as "a war zealot," provide the counterpoint that no
action on the battlefield should be elevated to the level of "genius," and
that Achuzia's desire for military discipline often, allegedly, meant shoot-
ing a number of Biafran soldiers in order to get the others to fall in line.[3]
Achuzia survived the conflict and was appointed the secretary general of
the influential pan-Igbo group Ohaneze NdiIgbo in later years.

Biafra Takes an Oil Rig: "The Kwale Incident"

In the middle of the rainy season of 1969, Biafran military intelligence
allegedly obtained information that foreign oilmen, particularly staff
from the Italian government's oil conglomerate, Eni,[1] were aiding the
Nigerian army. The foreign workers were allegedly providing sensitive
military information to the federal forces—about Biafran troop positions, strategic military maneuvers, and training.

This information was quickly made available to the Biafran command, which swiftly sent soldiers on a stealth dawn operation during
which they invaded Eni's combine in Kwale, in the Niger River Delta's oil
reserve known as Okpai oil field. By the end of the "exercise" eleven
workers had been killed—ten of the dead were Italian and one was from

Jordan. The Biafrans took eighteen Eni employees hostage. Fourteen were Italian, three were German, and one was Lebanese. What happened next would stir international outrage of epic proportions and threaten the fragile emotional and moral support that the Biafrans had developed during the course of the war.

The men were quickly detained on Biafran soil, tried, and found guilty of supporting the enemy—the federal troops of Nigeria—to wage a war of genocide. Predictably, there was a spontaneous outcry and appeals for clemency from disparate groups and countries. The Vatican and the embassies of Italy, Germany, Portugal, and Biafra's African supporters—Ivory Coast and Gabon—were at the vanguard of those asking for the release of the prisoners.[2]

Biafra's local and international supporters were dismayed. One observer commented at the time: "This indeed was not what the cause was about.... [W]e were engaged in a fight for self-determination.... [T]his was an unnecessary and costly distraction."[3] Biafran officials were adamant, even obstinate; the enclave's minister for information, Ifegwu Eke, had this to say about the incident: "Oilmen are more dangerous than mercenaries.... These are the people responsible for our suffering." Ojukwu's own radio pronouncements about the incident were equally irascible:

> Oscillating amid impassioned outrage and constrained eloquence, the Biafran leader exclaimed: "For 18 white men, Europe is aroused. What have they said about our millions? Eighteen white men assisting in the crime of genocide. What do they say about our murdered innocents? How many black dead make one missing white? Mathematicians, please answer me. Is it infinity?"[4]

After Ojukwu received a private letter from the pope in June 1969, personally pleading for the release of the oilmen, many in Ojukwu's inner circle were concerned about an international backlash. If the situation was not resolved swiftly, they feared, it could precipitate an instant sinking of Biafra's international reputation and a permanent loss of Vatican, Italian, indeed international humanitarian support. Eventually, in late June 1969, the eighteen detained men were released and flown out of Biafra in the custody of diplomats from the Ivory Coast and Gabon.

Some scholars believe that Ojukwu's calculation was that a combination of Biafran military resistance and the disruption of oil operations in the region would reduce oil revenue flowing to Nigeria's supporters and into the Nigerian treasury, crippling their war machinery and bringing about an accelerated negotiation to end the war.[5] Others are less charitable and feel that the whole affair was a blunder for the record books; they ascribe Ojukwu's decision to free the men as informed as much by the pope's letter as by the prospect of Italian "armed intervention to free their citizens"[6]—and his own rapid tumble from power in such a scenario.

Be that as it may, the fact that seemed to have completely escaped the Biafran leaders was this: As a people proclaiming victimization at the hands of Nigeria, and rightfully so, we could not be seen as victimizers in any situation or setting, in order to continue receiving the widespread moral and humanitarian support we needed to survive. This failure to recognize this fundamental principle, I believe, contributed immensely to the downturn in Biafra's fortunes. I personally believe that this fiasco was the clearest evidence of the mental fatigue of the Biafran military leadership.

The summer of 1969 would prove a busy one on the diplomatic front. Pope Paul VI, buoyed by the success of his emissaries in diffusing the Kwale incident, focused his energies next on procuring a lasting peace between the warring parties. During an official trip to Uganda the pontiff met the Biafran and Nigerian emissaries separately in lengthy talks, during which he expressed his desire that a peaceful resolution be found.[7]

The pontiff addressed the Ugandan Parliament on August 10,

following an exhausting ceremony during which he consecrated twelve new African bishops, and repeated the Vatican's desire to mediate a lasting peace between Nigeria and Biafra:

[I]n a region of Africa dear to us ... there still rages an agonizing conflict. . . . We have not only sought to secure goods and medical assistance, impartially and by every means available, but have also tried to apply the remedy of a certain initial reconciliation. Up to now we have not succeeded and this gives us heartfelt pain. But we are resolved to continue our modest but affectionate and fair efforts of persuasion to help heal this fatal dissension.[8]

In America, the Nixon administration increased diplomatic pressure on the Gowon administration to open up avenues for international relief agencies at about the same time, following months of impasse over the logistics of supply routes. Many congressmembers, government officials, indeed lay citizens were increasingly exasperated by the endless streaming television imagery of dying Biafran babies, and by the blockade imposed by the Gowon government. Biafra had in Senator Edward M. Kennedy a humane and sympathetic ear. Kennedy called for early and sustained U.S. humanitarian intervention throughout the bloody conflict.[9] Strom Thurmond, a senator from South Carolina, also became particularly vocal about America's intention to continue providing relief supplies to the needy irrespective of the Nigerian federal government's obstinate blockade measures.[10]

Thurmond, an unlikely supporter of the breakaway Republic of Biafra, was a former "'Dixiecrat'"[11]—a member of the conservative base of the "old Democratic party of the 1950s and early 1960s" that fled to the safety of the Republican Party following the reverberations of the civil rights period. He also had a not too flattering reputation for commandeering the filibuster of the Civil Rights Act of 1957. He was,

however, a well-respected and high-profile congressman and a particularly effective legislator—all the characteristics that the desperate Biafrans needed.[12]

Biafran diplomats began to see some of the repercussions of the
Kwale incident by the end of 1969, and the erosion of the goodwill that
had been built up so successfully over the previous twenty-seven months.
Neutral countries like Canada, hitherto officially silent, more or less,
while engaged in spirited humanitarian support of the suffering, openly
criticized the Ojukwu administration as one "that was more interested in
getting arms than food or medical supplies and had made up reasons for
rejecting [humanitarian aid]."[13] For the Biafrans, particularly those of us
who had made trips to Canada to secure their humanitarian support, this
rhetoric was particularly devastating.

1970 and The Fall

In Biafra, the Harmattan Season leading into 1970 was particularly harsh.
I remember vividly the suffering of the people; everything seemed particularly bleak. The dry, sandy air seemed to be an additional torment,
delighting in covering the body with layers of the Sahara Desert's fine
dust, blown in from hundreds of miles away. This made it impossible for
bare, weeping, vulnerable skin lesions to heal. It was particularly hard on
the children. Looking around one could see a proud, devastated people.

The Nigerians at this point were also worried about the physical and
psychological impact that this war was having on their troops. The federal government, it was well-known, increased the recruitment of a great
number of mercenaries from the neighboring countries of Chad and
Niger, and from far away Mali, to supplement their numbers. The federal
ranks were also plagued by widespread dissatisfaction with the war
effort, the escalating number of casualties, and the lack of a clear vision

for ending the conflict. To make matters worse for Gowon, the general population had grown impatient with what now appeared to be an endless conflict that had entered its thirtieth month.

Gowon was clearly in a bind. He responded to this predicament by sending off secret memos to relay the details of his final offensive, a scorched-earth policy to crush the Biafran resistance once and for all. By the middle of January 1970, the Nigerian troops had regained the upper hand decisively. Biafra, for all terms and purposes was crushed emotionally, psychologically, financially, and militarily, and it came crashing down soon after the new year began.

After failing many times over the thirty-month period, Gowon finally had Biafra surrounded on three fronts. In mid-January 1970, after Owerri had been recaptured by the federal troops and Uli airport was under heavy air and land assault by federal troops led by Olusegun Obasanjo, I knew the end for Biafra was near. That feeling was confirmed for millions of others in Biafra when Ojukwu went on the radio and announced that he was "leaving the People's Republic of Biafra to explore alternative options for peace." We all learned later that he had traveled to Ivory Coast, one of Biafra's early African supporters, where his longtime friend president Félix Houphouët-Boigny, with French backing, had offered him asylum. Nigeria mounted attempts to repatriate Ojukwu for at least five years following the war in order to try him for war crimes, but they failed mainly because the French made access to him impossible.

After that announcement there was sheer pandemonium throughout Biafra. Millions of Biafrans could be seen scrambling to get away from the Nigerian military forces, which at this point seemed to be advancing from every direction. Many of the classic *Time* and *Life* photos of this era were taken during this time of great panic, despair, and anxiety.

There have been several debates over the decades since about why Ojukwu, the resistance leader of a people so wronged, left (some say fled) Biafra at this critical juncture, declaring in his classic style: "Whilst I

live, Biafra lives."[1] His detractors, many of whom are still alive, still
believe that this particular act was one of great cowardice, and that true
heroes go down with the cause.

I think Ojukwu's departure, like many things that he did before, during, and after the war, was a complicated matter. It was clear to the Biafran leader that the end was near, that his troops had been defeated, at
least militarily, and that the mostly Igbo Easterners on whose behalf he
had waged this war were broken in every respect and were standing at
the precipice of annihilation. By taking himself out of the equation, so to
speak, Ojukwu robbed his old nemesis Gowon of the war booty he
sought the most—his head. Therefore, the protracted internal rivalry
between the two men that I have referred to had no resolution, and he
had robbed Gowon of closure and complete satisfaction in victory.
Indeed, many psychologists believe that Gowon may not have been as
conciliatory as he ended up being had Ojukwu stayed behind.

Gowon does not stray far from my conclusions on this subject:

What you should remember about the time—and, at least, give us some
credit for it—is that we did not take what would be considered normal
action under such circumstances. In such an instance, all the senior officials involved—politicians as well as in the military—would have
been strung up for their part in the war. This is what happened at the end
of the Second World War in Germany; it happened in Japan at the end of
the campaign in that part of the world. This is the civilized world's way
of doing things. But we did not do even that. We did set up committees
to look into cases such as where rebel officers had been members of the
Nigerian Armed Forces, and their loyalty was supposed to be to the Federal Government. When the war ended, we reabsorbed practically everyone who was in the Army. But there were officers at a certain senior level
[who] we insisted had to accept responsibility for their role in the

secession. It was the only thing to do. Probably I could have given pardon; however, I was not the one who gave pardon to Ojukwu. . . .

[I]n the case of Ojukwu, he had committed treason against the country! No matter how you see it, as far as the Nigerian context was concerned, he was the guilty party. In other areas, he would have been eliminated, and I thank God that He never put him in my hands. Otherwise I would have found it very difficult to save his life, even though I would try my best to save his life, because he was an old colleague, an old friend. But the public pressure would have made it impossible. So that was what happened in the case of people like Effiong. A few of the senior ones [who] were directly involved, we felt they should go. I think Effiong was dismissed. All that happened to the others was that they lost the few years of seniority gained during the period of the civil war.[2]

In Ojukwu's absence, Sir Louis Mbanefo, the chief justice, and General Philip Effiong, the defeated republic's leading military officer, met with a small group of Biafran government officials and made the fateful decision to surrender to the federal government of Nigeria. Effiong went on Biafran radio to announce the capitulation, and he spoke to the fear-stricken populace, urging calm and encouraging the troops to lay down their weapons. He announced that he was currently negotiating an armistice with the federal government of Nigeria, and that General Ojukwu had left the nation. This drew a very clear line between what was going on in the country and what was about to happen—which was the fall of Biafra.

Before that the defeat was already quite apparent. There were a few people who refused to recognize it and planned to continue to fight. I did not feel that continuing the conflict was an option at all. I felt that the best way to deal with this tremendous disaster was to not prolong the agony but to bring it to a close.

In the end, Biafra collapsed. We simply had to turn around and find a way to keep those people still there alive. It was a desperate situation, with so many children in need, kwashiorkor rampant, and thousands perishing every week. The notoriously incompetent Nigerian government was not responding to those in need quickly enough. With ill-advised bravado Gowon was busy banning relief agencies that had helped Biafra.[3] It was in this environment of desperation that some people said, Let's go into the forest and continue the struggle. That would have been suicidal, and I don't think anybody should commit suicide.

We had spent nearly three years fighting, fighting for a cause, fighting to the finish . . . for freedom. But all that had collapsed, and Biafra with it. A very bitter experience had led to it in the first place. And the big powers prolonged it.

You see we, the little people of the world, are ever expendable. The big powers can play their games even if millions perish in the process. And perish they did. In the end millions (some state upward of three million, mostly children) had died, mainly from starvation due to the federal government of Nigeria's blockade policies.[4]

General Gowon made a national broadcast on the eve of the official surrender to announce the end of the thirty-month war that he said had claimed over one hundred thousand military service men and women and over three million Biafrans. His "no victor, no vanquished" speech[5] as it has come to be known, strove to strike a conciliatory tone, calling for the full reintegration of Igbos into the fabric of Nigerian life. There was great celebration throughout Nigeria and Biafra at the news of the end of the hostilities.

A day later, on January 15, 1970, the Biafran delegation, which was led by Major General Philip Effiong and included Sir Louis Mbanefo,

M. T. Mbu, Colonel David Ogunewe, and other Biafran military officers, formally surrendered at Dodan Barracks to the troops of the Federal Republic of Nigeria. Among the Nigerian delegation were: General Yakubu Gowon; the deputy chairman of the Supreme Military Council, Obafemi Awolowo; leaders of the various branches of the armed forces, including Brigadier Hassan Katsina, chief of staff; H. E. A. Ejueyitchie, the secretary to the federal military government; Anthony Enahoro, the commissioner for information; Taslim Elias, the attorney general; and the twelve military governors of the federation.

At the end of the thirty-month war Biafra was a vast smoldering rubble. The head count at the end of the war was perhaps three million dead, which was approximately 20 percent of the entire population. This high proportion was mostly children. The cost in human lives made it one of the bloodiest civil wars in human history.[6]

The sequelae of wars often begin with an armistice. The suffering and humanitarian disaster left in the wake of war's destruction goes on long after the weapons are silenced—for months and years. Entire towns and villages, schools and farms in Biafra were destroyed. Roads and the rural areas were littered with landmines that continued to maim and kill unsuspecting pedestrians well after the hostilities ended. Many people had lost all that they owned. Loved ones in the thousands were reported missing by families. There were stories of scores of suicides. This was not just a case of Ani, or the land and its protector, the land goddess, "bleeding," as my people would describe catastrophic events of this nature. It was worse: a case of Ani nearly "exsanguinating to death."

My generation had great expectations for our young nation. After the war everything we had known before about Nigeria, all the optimism, had to be rethought. The worst had happened, and we were now forced into reorganizing our thinking, expectations, and hopes. We (the former Biafrans) had to carry on in spite of the great disaster that was military defeat and learn very quickly to live with such a loss. We would have to adjust to the realities and consequences of a Nigeria that did not appeal to us any longer. Nigeria had not succeeded in crushing the spirit of the Igbo people, but it had left us indigent, stripped bare, and stranded in the wilderness.

The Question of Genocide

I will begin by stating that I am not a sociologist, a political scientist, a human rights lawyer, or a government official. My aim is not to provide all the answers but to raise questions, and perhaps to cause a few head-aches in the process. Almost thirty years before Rwanda, before Darfur, over two million people—mothers, children, babies, civilians—lost their lives as a result of the blatantly callous and unnecessary policies enacted by the leaders of the federal government of Nigeria.[1]

As a writer I believe that it is fundamentally important, indeed essen-tial to our humanity, to ask the hard questions, in order to better under-stand ourselves and our neighbors. Where there is justification for further investigation, then I believe justice should be served.

In the case of the Nigeria-Biafra War there is precious little relevant literature that helps answer these questions: Did the federal government of Nigeria engage in the genocide of its Igbo citizens through their puni-tive policies, the most notorious being "starvation as a legitimate weapon of war"? Is the information blockade around the war a case of calculated historical suppression? Why has the war not been discussed, or taught to the young, over forty years after its end? Are we perpetually doomed to repeat the mistakes of the past because we are too stubborn to learn from them?

We need not get into the prickly thicket of diagnosing the reasons for the federal government's attempts to fool the world about what happened in Biafra. However, it may be helpful to start by defining the term genocide. Robert S. Leventhal provides this description:

> The term genocide derives from the Latin (*genos* = race, tribe; *cide* = killing) and means literally the killing or murder of an entire tribe or people. The Oxford English Dictionary defines genocide as "the deliberate and systematic extermination of an ethnic or national group. . . ." By "genocide" we mean the destruction of a nation or an ethnic group. The UN General Assembly adopted this term and defined it in 1946 as " . . . a denial of the right of existence of entire human groups."[2]

The Arguments

Throughout the conflict the Biafrans consistently charged that the Nigerians had a design to exterminate the Igbo people from the face of the earth. This calculation, the Biafrans insisted, was predicated on a holy jihad proclaimed by mainly Islamic extremists in the Nigerian army and supported by the policies of economic blockade that prevented shipments of humanitarian aid, food, and supplies to the needy in Biafra.[1]

The argument extended by Harold Wilson's government in defense of the federal government of Nigeria is important to highlight:

> The charges of Jihad have also been denied by British officials who assert that more than half the members of the Federal Government are Christian, while only 1,000 of the 60–70,000 Federal soldiers are Muslim Hausas from the North. (House of Commons Debate, cited earlier.)[2]

Herbert Ekwe-Ekwe, professor of history and politics and an expert on genocide, reminds us that supporters of the Biafran position point not only to the histrionic pronouncements of the leaders of the Nigerian army—often dismissed as typical outrageous wartime rhetoric—but to an actual series of atrocities, real crimes against humanity, that occurred on the battlefield and as a result of the policies of the federal government of Nigeria.

> The International Committee in the Investigation of Crimes of Geno-
> cide carried out exhaustive investigation of the evidence, interviewing
> 1082 people representing all the actors in the dispute (the two sides of the
> civil war and international collaborators). After a thorough painstaking
> research, the Commission concludes, through its Investigator (Dr. Men-
> sah of Ghana): "Finally I am of the opinion that in many of the cases
> cited to me hatred of the Biafrans (*mainly Igbos*) and *a wish to extermi-
> nate them was a foremost motivational factor*." [Emphasis in original.][3]

In his well-researched book *The Brutality of Nations*, Dan Jacobs uncovers a provocative paragraph from an editorial in the *Washington Post* of July 2, 1969:

> One word now describes the policy of the Nigerian military government
> towards secessionist Biafra: genocide. It is ugly and extreme but it is the
> only word which fits Nigeria's decision to stop the International Com-
> mittee of the Red Cross, and other relief agencies, from flying food to
> Biafra.[4]

Jacobs also reveals the lamentations of Pope Paul VI over the Nigeria-Biafra War:

> The war seems to be reaching its conclusion, with the terror of possible
> reprisals and massacres against defenseless people worn out by depriva-
> tions, by hunger and by the loss of all they possess. The news this

morning is very alarming. . . . One fear torments public opinion. The fear that the victory of arms may carry with it the killing of numberless people. There are those who actually fear a kind of genocide.[5]

The distinguished American historian, social critic, and political insider Arthur M. Schlesinger provides this contribution on the dire situation in Biafra:

The terrible tragedy of the people of Biafra has now assumed catastrophic dimensions. Starvation is daily claiming the lives of an estimated 6,000 Igbo tribesmen, most of them children. If adequate food is not delivered to the people in the immediate future hundreds of thousands of human beings will die of hunger.[6]

In what is likely to be the most compelling statement of the era from an American president, Schlesinger provides this powerful extract from Richard Nixon's campaign speech on September 10, 1968:

Until now efforts to relieve the Biafran people have been thwarted by the desire of the central government of Nigeria to pursue total and unconditional victory and by the fear of the Ibo [*sic*] people that surrender means wholesale atrocities and genocide. But genocide is what is taking place right now—and starvation is the grim reaper. This is not the time to stand on ceremony, or to 'go through channels' or to observe the diplomatic niceties. The destruction of an entire people is an immoral objective even in the most moral of wars. It can never be justified; it can never be condoned.[7]

Two distinguished Canadian diplomats, Mr. Andrew Brevin and Mr. David MacDonald (members of the Canadian Parliament), "reported that genocide is in fact taking place [and] one of them stated that 'anybody who says there is no evidence of genocide is either in the pay of Britain or being a deliberate fool,'" following a visit to the war-torn region.[8] *New York Times* journalist Lloyd Garrison, who covered the conflict, submitted harrowing accounts of genocidal activity on the part of the Nigerian troops: "The record shows that in Federal advances . . . thousands of Igbo male civilians were sought out and slaughtered."[9]

Supporters of the Nigerian federal government position maintain that a war was being waged and the premise of all wars is for one side to emerge as the victor. Overly ambitious actors may have "taken actions unbecoming of international conventions of human rights, but these things happen everywhere." This same group often cites findings from groups (sanctioned by the Nigerian federal government) that sent observers to the country during the crisis that there "was no clear intent on behalf of the Nigerian troops to wipe out the Igbo people, . . . pointing out that over 30,000 Igbos still lived in Lagos, and half a million in the Mid-West."[10]

The British government, wary of the morally bankrupt position that Harold Wilson had toed from the onset of the conflict, sought to explain away their reckless military adventure in Africa. There were real excesses to account for: If the diabolical disregard for human life seen during the war was not due to the Northern military elite's jihadist or genocidal obsession, then why were there more small arms used on Biafran soil than during the entire five-year period of World War II?[11] Why were there one hundred thousand casualties on the much larger Nigerian side compared with more than two million—mainly children—Biafrans killed? The government of Harold Wilson proffered what it called a "legitimate strategy" excuse in which it postulates that the indisputable excesses seen during the war were due to the Nigerian military's "excellence"—clearly making it the strongest candidate for an all-time foot-in-the-mouth prize.[12]

The Case Against
the Nigerian Government

It is important to point out that most Nigerians were against the war and abhorred the senseless violence that ensued as a result of the conflict. Gowon's wartime cabinet, it should also be remembered, was full of intellectuals like Obafemi Awolowo and Anthony Enahoro and super-permanent secretaries like Allison Akene Ayida among others who came up with a boatload of infamous and regrettable policies. A statement credited to Chief Obafemi Awolowo and echoed by his cohorts is the most callous and unfortunate:

> All is fair in war, and starvation is one of the weapons of war. I don't see why we should feed our enemies fat in order for them to fight harder.[1]

It is my impression that Chief Obafemi Awolowo was driven by an overriding ambition for power, for himself in particular and for the advancement of his Yoruba people in general. And let it be said that there is, on the surface, at least, nothing wrong with those aspirations. However, Awolowo saw the dominant Igbos at the time as the obstacles to that goal, and when the opportunity arose—the Nigeria-Biafra War—his ambition drove him into a frenzy to go to every length to achieve his dreams. In the Biafran case it meant hatching up a diabolical policy to reduce the numbers of his enemies significantly through starvation—eliminating over two million people, mainly members of future generations.

If Gowon was the "Nigerian Abraham Lincoln,"[2] as Lord Wilson would have us believe, why did he not put a stop to such an evil policy, or at least temper it, particularly when there was international outcry? Setting aside for the moment the fact that Gowon as head of state bears the final responsibility of his subordinates, and that Awolowo has been much maligned by many an intellectual for this unfortunate policy and his statements, why, I wonder, would other "thinkers," such as Ayida and Enahoro, not question such a policy but advance it?[3]

The federal government's actions soon after the war could be seen not as conciliatory but as outright hostile.[4] After the conflict ended

> the same hard-liners in the Federal government of Nigeria cast Igbos in the role of treasonable felons and wreckers of the nation and got the regime to adopt a banking policy which nullified any bank account which had been operated during the war by the Biafrans. A flat sum of twenty pounds was approved for each Igbo depositor of the Nigerian currency, regardless of the amount of deposit.[5]

If there was ever a measure put in place to stunt, or even obliterate, the economy of a people, this was it.

After that outrageous charade, the leaders of the federal government of Nigeria sought to devastate the resilient and emerging Eastern commercial sector even further by banning the importation of secondhand clothing and stockfish—two trade items that they knew the burgeoning market towns of Onitsha, Aba, and Nnewi needed to reemerge. Their fear was that these communities, fully reconstituted, would then serve as the economic engines for the reconstruction of the entire Eastern Region.

The Enterprises Promotion Decree of 1974, also known as the Indigenization Decree, was ostensibly pushed through by the leaders of the federal government in order to force foreign holders of majority shares of companies operating in Nigeria to hand over the preponderance of stocks, bonds, and shares to local Nigerian business interests. The move was sold to the public as some sort of "pro-African liberation strategy" to empower Nigerian businesses and shareholders.

The chicanery of the entire scheme of course was quite evident.

Having stripped a third of the Nigerian population of the means to acquire capital, the leaders of the government of Nigeria knew that the former Biafrans, by and large, would not have the financial muscle to participate in this plot.[6] The end result, they hoped, would be a permanent shifting of the balance of economic power away from the East to other constituencies.[7] Consequently, very few Igbos participated, and many of the jobs and positions in most of the sectors of the economy previously occupied by Easterners went to those from other parts of the country.

Ironically, and to the consternation of Lord Wilson and the British cabinet in England, the Enterprises Promotion Decree of 1974 also meant that the British/Dutch conglomerate Royal Dutch/Shell BP and other holdings valued at $720 million at the time, would have to share ownership of oil investments with the federal government—the very development Wilson was trying to avoid by backing Gowon in the first place.[8]

For those who would defend Gowon's cabinet, suggesting that at times of war measures of all kinds are taken to ensure victory, I will counter by stating that the Geneva Conventions were instituted after the Holocaust to make sure that human rights are still protected in times of conflict.

There are many international observers who believe that Gowon's actions after the war were magnanimous and laudable.[9] There are tons of treatises that talk about how the Igbo were wonderfully integrated into Nigeria. Well, I have news for them: The Igbo were not and continue not to be reintegrated into Nigeria, one of the main reasons for the country's continued backwardness, in my estimation.[10]

Borrowing a large leaf from the American Marshal Plan that followed World War II and resulted in the reconstruction of Europe, the federal government of Nigeria launched an elaborate scheme highlighted by three Rs—for Reconstruction, Rehabilitation, and Reconciliation. The only difference is that, unlike the Americans who actually carried out all three prongs of the strategy, Nigeria's federal government did not. The administrator of East Central state, Mr. Ukpabi Asika, announced that

Eastern Nigeria required close to half a billion pounds to complete the reconstruction effort. None of us recall that he received anything close to a fraction of the request.

What has consistently escaped most Nigerians in this entire travesty is the fact that mediocrity destroys the very fabric of a country as surely as a war—ushering in all sorts of banality, ineptitude, corruption, and debauchery. Nations enshrine mediocrity as their modus operandi, and create the fertile ground for the rise of tyrants and other base elements of the society, by silently assenting to the dismantling of systems of excellence because they do not immediately benefit one specific ethnic, racial, political, or special-interest group. That, in my humble opinion, is precisely where Nigeria finds itself today!

Gowon Responds

To get General Gowon's point of view on a number of the same questions that I have raised in this section of this book, I asked the eminent journalist and writer Pini Jason to interview the former Nigerian head of state. A portion of the interview is reproduced here:

> PINI JASON: The Igbo still believe that they are being punished because of the civil war. The Indigenization Decree is an [action], they point out, that was taken when the group was economically weakened and thus, as it were, kept them out of playing a role in the economy. They still feel they are being punished because of the civil war.
>
> GOWON: It is a pity that they think this way. The Indigenization Decree—I think it was 1972 or '73—that decree was really to ensure the participation of every part of the country, unlike the privatization policy now in place. Businesses are indigenized within one's

own area—in the North, in the East, in the West, etc. And who are the beneficiaries in those areas? It is mostly the people native to the particular area. And I am sure that by 1972, many Igbo had recovered sufficiently enough to participate, not only in their own area, but also in Lagos. You tell me, who owns most of Lagos?

PINI JASON (CUTTING IN): Two years with twenty pounds; the Igbo were still trying to find their feet! They were in no position to buy into any company!

GOWON: No. Remember, what was being indigenized before it was speeded up were some of the small Lebanese businesses, like textile stores, in which, in any case, the Igbo were very well established, yesterday, today, and even tomorrow. Probably in Lagos, they were not able to buy into as many such businesses as they would have desired. Otherwise, certainly I know that by 1972 there was sufficient recovery enabling the Igbo to participate. Now the incident of twenty pounds that you refer to was enforced immediately at the end of the war. Because your economic gurus will tell you that because of your economic value, you cannot exchange the Biafran note; what is it called?

PINI JASON: The Biafran pound.

GOWON: Is it the Biafran pound? But now, I am told that it is selling like hotcake! I am told that it is being used especially in the West Coast! So I said, Well, you see the ingenuity of the Igbo man? [*General laughter*] People say it is even more valuable than the naira!

PINI JASON: Maybe as a collector's item!

GOWON: But there it is! No. I think the policy of twenty pounds was never an attempt to impoverish the Igbo people. The government was very generous in giving funds to Ukpabi Asika so that the government of the East could circulate money and get businesses off the ground, as well as [to] embark on various rehabilitations and reconstructions that were taking place. Probably the exchange rate in Nigerian currency for the Biafran pound seemed not to be on equitable terms. If we said they could exchange at par . . .

PINI JASON (CUTTING IN): I would have been a millionaire!

GOWON: You're telling me! [*General laughter*] And probably bought off the rest of the country! That was not the policy of indigenization. It was meant to help. For example, the government was able to provide Asika with funds so that people could get Nigerian currency even as a loan. It was probably some of the bigger businesses indigenized later that you are talking about, but that occurred only after my overthrow. The government of Obasanjo, I think between 1975 and '79, speeded up taking over some of the big businesses, especially in Lagos, which was to the advantage of his people, because they were the ones on the spot, and a lot of their people were in the banks and knew how to use the banks to give loans to their own people to buy some of these things. But this was not the case in other parts of the country. So when it comes to that, you can rest assured that it was not only the Igbo that felt left out; other parts of the country that were not as well positioned as the people from the West felt the same way.

PINI JASON: Another issue was that of abandoned property, especially in Rivers state, and the context in which your government allowed some property belonging to the Igbo to be taken over. The case was made by the new Rivers state government that its people were like tenants in their own state. After you left office it became clear that several individuals actively exploited the issue, buying up former Igbo-owned property and using these properties as collaterals for business ventures, often obtaining loans from banks controlled by certain people with anti-Igbo sentiments. Many blamed [this] series of developments around abandoned property on you. What is your reaction?

GOWON: There was no doubt that it was a very knotty issue. I think there should have been justice and fair play. And as far as I was concerned, although pressure was being brought by the governor and the government of Rivers state at the time, my position was, if any property was to be taken for the use of the government, it had to pay proper compensation. And true enough, I think at the time, there were many Igbo who wanted to sell their property. Therefore, there was hardly any problem from that point of view. But I know that later the Rivers state indigenes themselves became fully involved, and virtually pressurized the subsequent government.

I think, honestly, that a lot of the damage was not done during our time. At least, we were keeping it under control, and working hard to ensure that there was justice. Since it was one Nigeria, we must allow people who wanted to come back to at least come back to their business and properties. But I know that quite a lot of this did not happen subsequently, and it left a very bad feeling that, as you said, the Igbo were being penalized because of the war. I am not sure of what really happened at that time, since I was away from the country. But I know that my effort was not to deprive people of their property. Those who wanted to sell did so at the market price at the time. But those properties the government wanted for their use, it was to pay the economic rate at the time. Of course, policies changed thereafter.[1]

PART 4

Nigeria's Painful Transitions:
A Reappraisal

The post Nigeria-Biafra civil war era saw a "unified" Nigeria saddled with a greater and more insidious reality. We were plagued by a home-grown enemy: the political ineptitude, mediocrity, indiscipline, ethnic bigotry, and corruption of the ruling class. Compounding the situation was the fact that Nigeria was now awash in oil-boom petrodollars, and to make matters even worse, the country's young, affable, military head of state, General Yakubu Gowon, ever so cocksure following his victory, proclaimed to the entire planet that Nigeria had more money than it knew what to do with. A new era of great decadence and decline was born. It continues to this day.

At this point, the intellectuals, particularly the writers, were faced with a conundrum. We could no longer pass off this present problem simply to our complicated past and the cold war raging in the background, however significant these factors were. We could not absolve ourselves from the need to take hold of the events of the day and say, Okay, we have had a difficult past. . . . From today, this is the program we have; let's look at what we have not done. Of course, putting it this dramatically makes the matter appear simple.

However, it became crystal clear that we needed to fight this new enemy with everything at our disposal. Most important, Nigeria needed to identify the right leader with the right kind of character, education, and background. Someone who would understand what was at stake— where Africa had been, and where it needed to go. For the second time in our short history we had to face the disturbing fact that Nigeria needed to liberate itself anew, this time not from a foreign power but from our own corrupt, inept brothers and sisters!

After waiting around a while and determining that no messiah was about to come down and save the day, some of us joined the political process. I joined the left-of-center Peoples Redemption Party and was appointed its deputy national president. The goal of being an active participant in Nigerian politics would be to elevate the national discourse to a level that stirred up the pot, if you like, and got Nigerians to begin to ask critical questions about their future, such as: How can the country conduct free and fair elections? How can we elect the right kind of leaders and ensure that they will keep to the tenure that was agreed upon? How do we ensure that our leaders don't double their tenure, or even change it into a dynasty to hand over to their sons?

My sojourn in politics was marked by disappointment, frustration, and the realization that despite the fact that there were a few upright political figures like Mallam Aminu Kano, the vast majority of the characters I encountered in the political circles were there for their own selfish advancement. Having grand ideas was fine, but their execution required a strong leader. And clearly, Nigeria's principal problem was identifying and putting in place that elusive leader.

That road to a remedy of Nigeria's political problems will not come easily. The key, as I see it, lies in the manner in which the leadership of the country is selected. When I refer to leadership I am really talking about leaders at every level of government and sphere of society, from the local government council and governors right up to the presidency. What I am calling for is for Nigeria to develop a version of campaign election and campaign finance reform, so that the country can transform its political system from the grassroots level right through to the national party structures at the federal level.

Nigerians will have to find a way to do away with the present system of godfatherism—an archaic, corrupt practice in which individuals with lots of money and time to spare (many of them half-baked, poorly educated thugs) sponsor their chosen candidates and push them right through to the desired political position, bribing, threatening, and, on occasion, murdering any opposition in the process. We will have to make sure that the electoral body overseeing elections is run by widely respected and competent officials chosen by a nonpartisan group free of governmental influence or interference. Finally, we have to find a way to open up the political process to every Nigerian citizen. Today we have a system where only those individuals with the means of capital and who can both pay the exorbitant application fee and fund a political campaign can vie for the presidency. It would not surprise any close observer to discover that in this inane system, the same unsavory characters who have destroyed the country and looted the treasury and the nation blind are the ones able to run for the presidency!

The question of choice in selecting a leader in Nigeria is often an academic exercise, due to the election rigging, violence, and intimidation of the general public, particularly by those in power, but also by those with the means—the rich and influential. There is also the unpleasant factor of the violence associated with partisan politics that is often designed to keep balanced, well-educated, fair-minded Nigerians away. So it can be said that the masses—the followership we are concerned about—don't really have a choice of leadership, because there's not a true democratic process.[1]

It may appear impossible now to rectify, because we've allowed this situation of confusion to go on since our independence. It has been growing steadily worse . . . and it accelerated particularly under the military, when there was a near total denial of the democratic rights of the people. The general knowledge that a people have, for example, inalienable rights is simply something advanced societies take for granted, because they have fostered stable democracies now for some time. I am asked, "Why don't the people fight back?" Well, once a people have been dispossessed and subjugated by dictatorships for such a long time as in Nigeria's case, the oppressive process also effectively strips away from the minds of the people the knowledge that they have rights. Restoring flawed democratic systems will not make the country a success overnight.

The Igbo are a very democratic people. The Igbo people expressed a strong antimonarchy sentiment—*Ezebuilo*—which literally means, a king is an enemy. Their culture illustrates a clear-cut opposition to kings, because, I think, the Igbo people had seen what the uncontrolled power of kings could do. There is no doubt that in their history they experienced the high-handedness of kings, so they decided that a king cannot be a trusted friend of the people without checks and balances. And they tried to construct all kinds of arrangements to whittle down the menace of those with the will to power, because such people are there in large numbers in every society. So the Igbo created all kinds of titles that cost much to acquire. Aspirants to titles, in the end, become impoverished in the process and end up with very little. So that individual begins again, and by the time his life is over, he has a lot of prestige but very little power.

Democracy is the very antithesis of military or absolutist rule. And democracy is not a fancy word; it is something that is full of meaning, even in our ancient African cultures. Dictatorships by their very nature concentrate power and the resources of the state in the hands of a very few people (or, as we have seen in Africa, in one person's hands). Dictators hang on to power by resorting to tactics designed to keep the mass of the people silent and docile. Dictatorships that have used violence, murder, and bribery, and psychological, financial, and social intimidation to force the opposition into perpetual retreat are many and widespread.[2]

This is not a time to bemoan all the challenges ahead. It is a time to work at developing, nurturing, sustaining, and protecting democracy and democratic institutions. Winston Churchill perceptively said, "Democracy is the worst form of government, except for all those other forms that have been tried from time to time."[3] We have to go by that wisdom. Therein lies an opportunity for Great Britain, America, and the West to be involved positively in African affairs, this time not by imposing themselves or their self-selected rulers on a desperate continent but by aiding African nations in their struggles to become viable democracies.

We also realize that we must learn patience and not expect instant miracles. Building a nation is not something a people does in one regime, or even in a few years; it's a very long process. The Chinese had their chance to emerge as the leading nation in the world in the Middle Ages but were consumed by inter-ethnic political posturing and wars and had to wait another five hundred years for another chance!

Another crucial ingredient in sustaining a democracy is the ability to stage free and fair elections. The last general election in Nigeria was not perfect, but overall it was an improvement over past travesties that were passed off as elections in Nigeria. The Independent National Electoral Commission (INEC), Chairman (and professor) Attahiru Muhammadu Jega, and his team should be allowed to build upon the gains of that exercise for the good of the nation.

I think it is important to discuss some real events that occurred during Nigeria's Fourth Republic (circa 2004), during which the very opposite of the democratic ideal was at work. Anambra state, the past home of several venerated Nigerians, such as Nnamdi Azikiwe, the Okigbo brothers—Pius and Christopher—Kenneth Dike, and others—was literally and figuratively on fire. There was a succession of events during a tussle for political power that resulted in renegades arresting a sitting governor and buildings being looted and government property ransacked and burned to the ground by hoodlums—those infamous rent-a-crowd hooligans at the beck and call of corrupt politicians with plenty of money and very low IQs.

What seemed almost incredible to me was that it was clear from all accounts that the presidency was behind the chaos in the state—was encouraging the destabilization of the government of Anambra state as well as encouraging a small group of people whose sole interest seemed to be in getting their hands on the financial allocation made to the state. In other words, to use the money that was intended for work on the state for their own private ends—and that these were friends of the president.

For any clear-headed observer such a scenario would be unimaginable—that the head of state, or his government or his office, should be encouraging crime in one of the federation's constituent states, encouraging anarchy in a part of the country, Nigeria. That state, of course, as you might know, is also my home state. It's also part of Igbo land, which has had a peculiar history in Nigeria, some of which involves this particular former president of Nigeria—his attitude to this part of Nigeria, which he and some like him consider responsible for the troubles of the Nigerian civil war. And so it just seemed to me totally irresponsible for leadership to be involved, to be promoting chaos instead of preventing it. It was in a sense the very end of government itself, where government leaps beyond the precipice, dismisses itself, and joins ranks with crime.[4]

I decided that I wasn't going to be part of any of this. Elie Wiesel reminds us, "There may be times when we are powerless to prevent injustice, but there must never be a time when we fail to protest."[5] I had very little at my disposal to protest with, so the strongest statement I could make was to turn down the honor of commander of the federal republic, which I was awarded.

Corruption and Indiscipline

Corruption in Nigeria has grown because it is highly encouraged. In *The Trouble with Nigeria* I suggest, "Nigerians are corrupt because the system they live under today makes corruption easy and profitable. They will cease to be corrupt when corruption is made difficult and unattractive." Twenty-eight years after that slim book was published, I can state categorically that the problem of corruption and indiscipline is probably worse today than it's ever been, because of the massive way in which the Nigerian leadership is using the nation's wealth to corrupt, really to destroy, the country, so no improvement or change can happen. Recently, out of despair, I stated, "Corruption in Nigeria has passed the alarming and entered the fatal stage, and Nigeria will die if we continue to pretend that she is only slightly indisposed."

The World Bank recently released numbers indicating that about $400 billion has been pilfered from Nigeria's treasury since independence. One needs to stop for a moment to wrap one's mind around that incredible figure. This amount—$400 billion—is approximately the gross domestic products of Norway and of Sweden. In other words, Nigeria's corrupt ruling class stole the equivalent of the entire economy of a European country in four decades! This theft of national funds is one of the factors essentially making it impossible for Nigeria to succeed. Nigerians alone are not responsible. We all know that this corrupt cabal of

Nigerians in power has friends abroad who not only help it move the billions abroad and help them hide the money, but also shield the perpetrators from prosecution![3]

State Failure and
the Rise of Terrorism

In 2011, Nigeria was ranked number fourteen in the Failed States Index,[1] just below other "havens of stability"—Afghanistan, Somalia, and Iraq! State failure has many definitions, so I will bother the reader with only two short descriptions relevant to the Nigerian situation:

> [A failed state] is one that is unable to perform its duties on several levels: when violence cascades into an all-out internal war, when standards of living massively deteriorate, when the infrastructure of ordinary life decays, and when the greed of rulers overwhelms their responsibilities to better their people and their surroundings.[2]
>
> [Failed States are seen in] instances in which central state authority collapses for several years.[3]

Economic deprivation and corruption produce and exacerbate financial and social inequities in a population, which in turn fuel political instability. Within this environment, extremists of all kinds— particularly religious zealots and other political mischief makers—find a foothold to recruit supporters and sympathizers to help them launch terrorist attacks and wreak havoc in the lives of ordinary citizens.[4]

Over eight hundred deaths, mainly in Northern Nigeria, have been attributed to the militant Islamist sect Boko Haram[5] since its formation in 2002. The group's ultimate goal, we are told, is to "overthrow the

Nigerian government and create an Islamic state."[6] In many respects, Nigeria's federal government has always tolerated terrorism. For over half a century the federal government has turned a blind eye to waves of ferocious and savage massacres of its citizens—mainly Christian Southerners; mostly Igbos or indigenes of the Middle Belt; and others—with impunity.

Even in cases where their hands were found dripping in blood, the perpetrators have many a time evaded capture and punishment. Nigeria has been doomed to witness endless cycles of inter-ethnic, inter-religious violence because the Nigerian government has failed woefully to enforce laws protecting its citizens from wanton violence, particularly attacks against nonindigenes living in disparate parts of the country. The notoriously (some say conveniently so) incompetent Nigerian federal government, and some religious and political leaders, have been at least enablers of these evil acts. I have stated elsewhere that this mindless carnage will end only with the dismantling of the present corrupt political system and banishment of the cult of mediocrity that runs it, hopefully through a peaceful, democratic process.

State Resuscitation and Recovery

Many pundits see a direct link between crude oil and the corruption in Nigeria, that putting in place an elaborate system preventing politicians or civilians from having access to petrodollars is probably a major part of a series of fixes needed to reduce large-scale corruption. For most people the solution is straightforward: If you commit a crime, you should be brought to book. Hold people responsible for misconduct and punish them if they are guilty. In a country such as Nigeria, where there are no easy fixes, one must examine the issue of accountability, which has to be a strong component of the fight against corruption.

Every Nigerian knows that there should be accountability, that people should be accountable. But if the president—the person running the whole show—has all of the power and resources of the country in his control, and he is also the one who selects who should be probed or not, clearly we will have an uneven system in which those who are favored by the emperor have free rein to loot the treasury with reckless abandon, while those who are disliked or tell the emperor that he is not wearing any clothes get marched swiftly to the guillotine!

Nigeria's story has not been, entirely, one long, unrelieved history of despair. Fifty years after independence Nigerians have begun to ask themselves the hard questions: How can the state of anarchy be reversed? What are the measures that can be taken to prevent corrupt candidates from recycling themselves into positions of leadership? Young Nigerians have often come to me desperately seeking solutions to several conundrums: How do we begin to solve these problems in Nigeria, where the structures are present but there is no accountability?

Other pressing questions include: How does Nigeria bring all the human and material resources it has to bear on its development? How do we clean up the Niger Delta? What do we need to do to bring an end to organized ethnic bigotry? How can we place the necessary checks and balances in place that will reduce the decadence, corruption, and debauchery of the past several decades? How can we ensure even and sustained development? And so forth. . . . And that would be a big debate to keep Nigeria busy for a long time.

The Sovereign National Conference that was held a couple of years ago was a good idea. I believe the concept was right—a platform to discuss Nigeria's problems and challenges and pave a path forward— however, the execution was not. Debate about a nation's future should not turn into an excuse for politicians to drink or feast on meals in Abuja. It should continue for decades, in small forums, in schools, offices, on the radio, on TV, in markets, in our newspapers, and on the streets, until we get things right. Most advanced nations in the world constantly appraise and reappraise their countries' paths and destinies.

I foresee the Nigerian solution will come in stages. First we have to nurture and strengthen our democratic institutions—and strive for the freest and fairest elections possible. That will place the true candidates of the people in office. Under the rubric of a democracy, a free press can thrive and a strong justice system can flourish. The checks and balances we have spoken about and the laws needed to curb corruption will then naturally find a footing. A new patriotic consciousness has to be developed, not one based simply on the well-worn notion of the unity of Nigeria or faith in Nigeria often touted by our corrupt leaders, but one based on an awareness of the responsibility of leaders to the led—on the sacredness of their anointment to lead—and disseminated by civil society, schools, and intellectuals. It is from this kind of environment that a leader, humbled by the trust placed upon him by the people, will emerge, willing to use the power given to him for the good of the people.

After a War

After a war life catches
desperately at passing
hints of normalcy like
vines entwining a hollow
twig; its famished roots
close on rubble and every
piece of broken glass.

Irritations we used
to curse return to joyous
tables like prodigals home
from the city. . . . The meter man
serving my maiden bill brought
a friendly face to my circle
of sullen strangers and me
smiling gratefully
to the door.

After a war
we clutch at watery
scum pulsating on listless
eddies of our spent
deluge. . . . Convalescent
dancers rising too soon
to rejoin their circle dance
our powerless feet intent

as before but no longer
adept contrive only
half-remembered
eccentric steps.

After years
of pressing death
and dizzy last-hour reprieves
we're glad to dump our fears
and our perilous gains together
in one shallow grave and flee
the same rueful way we came
straight home to haunted revelry.[1]

POSTSCRIPT:
THE EXAMPLE OF
NELSON MANDELA

Not too long ago my attention was caught by a radio news item about Africa. As I had come to expect, it was not good news, and it was not presented with, nor did it deserve, respect. It was something of a joke. This was the announcement of the death of President Eyadema of Togo, whom it described as the longest-serving president in Africa (or maybe the world—I forget which). Then it gave another detail: Eyadema had died from a heart attack even as he was about to be flown to Europe for treatment. And it concluded with the information that Eyadema's son would succeed him as the next president of Togo!

If Eyadema stayed that long because he was so good, why was there no hospital in Togo to attend to his condition? Did Eyadema, who had given nothing but bad news to Togo since the 1960s, imagine that the solution to problems created largely by him would be solved by a dynasty of Eyademas? Which reminded me of another First Son: the son of the president of Equatorial Guinea, who was seen around the world on television as he shopped extravagantly in Paris for expensive clothes. Unfortunately, he seemed no less a bum in the suits he was trying on than out of them.[1]

This event brought me once again face-to-face with Africa's leadership charade. What do African leaders envision for their countries and their people? I wondered yet again. Have they not heard that where there is no vision the people perish? Does the judgment of history on their rule mean anything to them? Do they remember how a man called Mandela, who had spent twenty-seven years in prison for South Africa, gave up the presidency of that country—a position that he so richly deserved—after only four years and made way for another and younger patriot? Why do African leaders choose bad models like Malawian president Kamuzu Banda instead of good ones like Mandela? Have they considered how Zimbabwean president Robert Mugabe has ruined the cause of land distribution by demagoguery and a thirty-year tenancy in power?

Which makes me wonder whether any of these life presidents consider how Mandela became the beacon of justice and hope on the continent, indeed for the world. For those who do not know, Mandela did not have an easy life. He fought alongside African heroes such as Steve Biko, Walter Sisulu, and Oliver Tambo, among other brave activists, for the liberation of his people from one of the most racist systems the world has ever known. For his efforts, he was sent to prison.

Most men would have been broken, or consumed by bitterness. But not Mandela. This giant among men walked free that fateful day, on February 11, 1990, after nearly three decades of imprisonment on Robben Island, hands held high, fist in the air. His release was beamed across the planet. The world was pleased, but nowhere as ecstatic as his African brethren around the globe, who saw in Mandela the personification of their highest aspirations and the embodiment of the kind of leadership Africa needs desperately.

Mandela has delivered magnificently on those dreams. And it is to this great man, lovingly known as Madiba—father of the nation of South Africa, antiapartheid leader, lawyer, writer, intellectual, humanitarian—that present and future African leaders must all go for sustenance and inspiration.

APPENDIX

Brigadier Banjo's Broadcast to Mid-West[1]

NOTE: "BRIGADIER" BANJO WAS THE
COMMANDER OF THE BIAFRAN INVASION

Benin, August 14, 1967, at 20:00 GMT.

Fellow Nigerians and Biafrans, I am sure I do not need to introduce myself either to you nor perhaps to many people outside our country. You have already had ample opportunity to hear of my name in January 1966 when this political crisis started in our country. Unfortunately at that time I also only heard about the circumstances under which my name was being publicized at a time when I was in no position to do anything about it. I was then accused of having attempted the life of the late Supreme Commander, Maj.-Gen. J. T. U. Aguiyi-Ironsi, and that for the attempt I have been arrested and detained.

Fellow Nigerians, nothing could be further from the truth. The mutiny in the Army which started the revolution in January 1966 was as much of a surprise to myself as it was to some of my colleagues. I spent all of my time [words indistinct] of the events in ascertaining the true state of affairs in the country. My colleague, then Lt.-Col. Yakubu Gowon, was the first officer who gave me precise information about the state of affairs. It then appeared to me that sufficient had taken place to ensure the removal of several Governments of the Federation and that the sum total of the trend of events could be regarded as the beginning of a national revolution. I then considered it my duty to ensure that no further military action took place which might have the effect of totally destroying the stability of the nation.

I felt that the young officers who had started the action were only anxious to destroy what had become a most corrupt and discredited Government. As such, I spent a considerable time in an effort to urge the late Major General to assume responsibility for the State with the support of the Army from national collapse. It was then my view that any attempt to use the Nigerian Army for any military action within Nigeria would only have the effect of breaking the Army into its tribal components of which the Northern component would represent the lion's share. This Northern component, effectively under the control of the Northern feudalists, would then inevitably be employed to impose on the rest of Nigeria the most repressive feudal domination. I was one of the senior officers of the Nigerian Army who took the decision to accept responsibility for Nigeria. In fact, on that occasion I was the chief spokesman for that decision. I therefore considered it my duty to remain with the General as closely as possible rather than accept the office of the Military Governor of the West which he then proposed to me and which I declined in favor of the late Lt.-Col. Adekunle Fajuyi. On the day after the General had assumed full responsibility for the State I was arrested by a few of my colleagues while waiting to see the General. I was never given a reason for my arrest, nor given an opportunity to defend myself against any charges that could be raised. I went to prison for 14 months under a false accusation, the details of which I only found out from the press and radio after I got to prison. I have since had the opportunity of speaking to the so-called actors in that drama of my arrest, and I now appreciate that the action was an act of hatred motivated primarily by fear and suspicion. I spent a considerable part of my time in prison sending warnings to the late Major-General and my colleagues about the policies that would appear to represent a continuation of the policies of the Balewa Government, which could have the effect of encouraging counterattempts, which might not only destroy the Nigerian Army but would also, by the extent of the bloodshed and the tribal selectiveness of the [word indistinct], destroy the Nigerian nation as well.

The inevitable has now happened, which would seem to confirm that my fears were well-founded. There is now an army at the disposal of the feudal North, an army that has lost all the traditions, discipline, and standards of a responsible army. There is now a Government of the Federation that is sustained by violence and is therefore tied to the ambitions of the Northern Feudalists. There has been a considerable amount of bloodshed, chaos, and tribal bitterness among such people. Such tribal rivalry, as used to be exploited by our previous political parties for the harnessing of the opinion of the North and its people, is now translating itself into a most extreme form of brutality and of despicable savagery.

Finally, the dismemberment of our nation has commenced in the breakaway of Biafra. In August 1966, I wrote to my colleagues from prison to inform them that I did not consider that we, military leaders of this country, had the right to carry out such action as the proclamation of the dismemberment of presiding over the dismemberment of Nigeria. I still do not think that we have the right to destroy a nation that was handed over to us to save at a moment of crisis. The 29th July 1966 Federal Military Government came into being as a result of a mutiny in which the primary action was directed at the elimination of a particular ethnic group and the supremacy of another ethnic group in Nigeria. This has had the effect of destroying the basic mutual trust and confidence among the people of Nigeria and has created the decentralization of the Nigerian people into tribal groups. This action, more than any other event that has occurred throughout the history of Nigeria, has had the greatest effect on the dismemberment of Nigeria. The Federal Military

Government cannot claim to represent the Government of the people of Nigeria and to fight for the unity of Nigeria while constantly rejecting fundamental human rights for all people forming parts of Nigeria. The Federal Military Government cannot claim to be seeking a peaceful solution to the problems of achieving Nigerian unity while at the same time contemptuously ignoring the wishes of the people of the Mid-West and the West in their previous demands for the removal of the unruly troops of the North from their territories in order to allow the unfettered discussion of the present political crisis.

The Federal Military Government cannot claim to be genuinely interested in the progress and welfare of the Nigerian people while at the same time inflicting the bloodiest warfare on the people of Nigeria and employing unscrupulous foreign mercenaries in a total war that really destroys hundreds of our people and the economy of our nation. . . .

The people of Biafra have a right to fight a Government that has constantly treated its people to the most savage forms of brutality and persists in denying these people its fundamental human rights while claiming to represent other interests. It is my view that the people of Biafra were prepared to remain part of the nation into which they have for so many years invested their resources of manpower and material and with which they had the closest social ties. Provided the people of Biafra could live within such a nation under a Government that truly represents all sections of its people and truly tries to pursue such measures as are designed to promote the welfare of all Nigerians irrespective of tribe or religion [*sic*] [sentence as broadcast]. It is the remnants of the old Nigerian Army that broke away in July that now threatens the Nigerian nation. This Northern army is now under the power and control of a group of Northern feudalists who have as their aim the total conquest of Nigeria. The Federal Military Government, having been brought to power and control by that army, is playing to that end. Hence policies are inevitably directed toward achieving the objectives of the Northern feudalists who control that army. . . .

It is my idea that the peaceful settlement of the Nigerian problem will be readily achieved when that fragment of the Nigerian Army now at the disposal of the Northern feudalists has been completely disarmed. Toward this end, the Liberation Army is irrevocably committed. It is not at all an invasion, and it is not intended to promote the domination of any group of the Nigerian people by any other group through the presence of the Liberation Army. I wish to stress once again what I said during the press conference and previously on the radio, that the movement of this Army into the Mid-West is not a conquest. It is also not an invasion. It is to enable the people of the Mid-West to see the Nigerian problem in its proper perspective. I firmly believe that the people of the Mid-West would prefer to be able to declare their stand in the conflict that has arisen in Nigeria free from any [pressure] either from the North or from anywhere. I believe that the people of the Mid-West would like to be given an opportunity to state their case, free from the coercive influences due to the presence of Northern troops. It is my view that the political future of Nigeria rests with all the people of Nigeria. It has become a matter of great concern to me, however, to be informed that certain ethnic groups are jubilating as a result of the presence of the Liberation Army in this Region. As a consequence, I also understand that certain other ethnic groups are feeling depressed and frustrated. I wish to assure all ethnic groups in the Mid-West that the achievement of the Liberation Army does not give any ethnic group an advantage over any other. I wish also to appeal to all ethnic groups to exercise restraint and humility and not to indulge in acts which may result in confusion, bringing distress to a large number of our people. Any misbehavior on the part of any group of persons will give rise to a chain of unpleasant reactions. . . .

I am informed that since the Liberation Army came into the Mid-West a number of civil servants have become so frightened that they have either refused to come to their places of work or reported only for a few hours and then left before the closing time. I wish to take this opportunity to appeal to all civil servants to return to work not later than 15th August 1967, and to assure them of their safety. Those, however, who fail to report on this day will be in danger of permanently losing their jobs. . . .

While on the question of cooperation among the various ethnic groups in the Mid-West, I would like to stress that all tribal meetings should stop, as such meetings are not conducive to peace and mutual understanding. In order to foster cooperation among the people of the Mid-West, I propose within the next few days to invite a cross section of the people of the Mid-West to a meeting to explain to them the present situation and objectives of the Liberation Army, and I believe this will go a long way to giving them the true picture of the situation and instill confidence in the future of the Mid-West. I understand that anxiety is being expressed in some quarters about the safety of the Military Governor of the Mid-West, Brig. David Ejoor. I wish to inform you that I have personally held discussions with Brig. Ejoor and to assure you that he is in good health and is not under detention. . . .

I have, therefore, today promulgated a decree setting up an interim administration in Mid-Western Nigeria. This decree has suspended the operation in Mid-Western Nigeria of the Constitution of the Federation of Nigeria, the Constitution of Mid-Western Nigeria, and other constitutional provisions applicable in Mid-Western Nigeria, except those constitutional provisions absolutely necessary for the efficient functioning of the machinery of State. All legislative and executive powers have been vested in me during the period of interim administration. In order to assist me in the task of administering Mid-Western Nigeria during the interim period I propose to appoint a military administrator and an administrative council. I have also established a Mid-Western Nigerian Army and a Mid-Western Nigerian Police Force, which will for the moment remain independent of the Nigerian Army, the Nigerian Police Force, the Biafran Army, or the Biafran Police Force. The Mid-Western

Nigerian Army shall, however, during this interim period be part of the Liberation Army. All courts in Mid-Western Nigeria shall continue to function as usual and it may be necessary to establish a court of appeal until it becomes possible to resume [words indistinct] the Supreme Court of Nigeria. As soon as it is practicable I propose to hand over the administration of Mid-Western Nigeria in order to proceed to the war front and to complete the liberation of Nigeria.

Good Night.

NOTES

Introduction

1. Author conversation with Robert Farris Thompson, Yale University, April 2010.
2. See "Nigeria: Lugard and Indirect Rule" (June 1991); www.country-data.com/cgi-bin/query/r-9347.html; also www.encyclopedia.com/topic/Indirect_rule.aspx.
3. The effects of that imposition are still felt today.
4. Berth Lindfors, ed., "Interview with Charles H. Rowell," *Conversations with Chinua Achebe* (Jackson, MS: University Press of Mississippi, 1997), p. 181.

Part 1

Pioneers of a New Frontier

1. Henry Venn and his colleagues at the Church Mission Society of England had launched a number of successful expeditions throughout Nigeria. The expeditions were led by an Englishman, Henry Townsend, and a remarkable man of Yoruba descent, from Freetown, Sierra Leone, Samuel Adjai Crowther. Later Crowther would not only be consecrated bishop of the Niger Territories in 1864, but he would have a profound influence on the development of the early Christian church throughout Nigeria. See also: Elizabeth Isichei: *A History of Christianity in Africa: From Antiquity* (London: Society for Promoting Christian Knowledge, 1995), chapt. 5; Toyin Falola and Mathew M. Heaton, *A History of Nigeria* (Cambridge, England: Cambridge University Press, 2008), pp. 61–85.

The Magical Years

1. The Igbo people of Eastern Nigeria.

A Primary Exposure

1. Translation (roughly): "There will be no fooling around in Okongwu's school." Information provided by the Okongwu family. Interview with Nmutaka Okongwu, January 2011.
2. Well-known folklore about Okongwu.
3. His son Sonny Chu Okongwu would become Nigeria's finance minister from 1986 to 1990.
4. Well-known folklore about Okongwu.

Leaving Home

1. Chike Momah related this story to me a few years later.
2. Herbert M. Cole's *Mbari, Art and Life Among the Owerri Igbo* is an excellent resource (Bloomington: Indian University Press, 1982).

The Formative Years at Umuahia and Ibadan

THE UMUAHIA EXPERIENCE

1. Achebe Foundation interviews. Number 33: Professor Bede N. Okigbo in conversation with Professor Ossie Enekwe, Uduma Kalu, and Alvan Ewuzie. August 7, 2006.
2. Master Agambi was the other student who got a major scholarship. Agambi's alma mater, Government College, Ibadan, has produced a significant number of prominent Nigerians, such as the T. M. Aluko; Dr. T. S. B. Aribisala, Cyprian Ekwensi, Anthony Enahoro, Wole Soyinka, Christopher Kolade, the late Dr. Akinola Aguda, Chief Olu Ibukun, the late ambassador Leslie Harriman, and Victor Olunloyo. Information from Government College, Ibadan, Old Boys Association (GCIOBA).

THE IBADAN EXPERIENCE

3. When I returned to Nigeria after five years of self-imposed exile in the United States, following the Nigeria-Biafra War, I was attracted to the University of Nigeria, Nsukka, in part because Ezeilo was the university president!

Discovering *Things Fall Apart*

1. Notes from discussion with Professor Jerome Brooks at Bard College (a version of which was later published as "The Art of Fiction" in the *Paris Review*, no. 139 [Winter 1994]).

2. Ezenwa-Ohaeto, *Chinua Achebe: A Biography* (Bloomington: Indiana University Press, 1997), p. 62.
3. I was told the story by the late Alan Hill.
4. Katie Bacon, "Atlantic Unbound: An African voice, Chinua Achebe," *The Atlantic*, August, 2, 2000.

The March to Independence

1. I have written extensively about the influence of Azikiwe on my life (see Zik's kitchen in *The Education of a British-Protected Child*) and that of colonial and postcolonial Nigeria.
2. Eminent sons and daughters such as Dr. Akanu Ibiam, a Hope Waddell Training School and Kings College, Lagos, graduate who went on to the University of St. Andrews in Scotland and qualified as a medical doctor in 1935. Another major figure of the time and Azikiwe contemporary was the educator Alvan Ikoku, who was a deeply religious and studious man, and another Hope Waddell alumnus. Ikoku would provide a steady source of advice for Azikiwe during periods of political tumult.

   Azikiwe also worked closely with a number of associates and lifelong friends, one of whom was Adeniran Ogunsanya (Ogunsanya was the son of the Odofin of Ikorodu). Ogunsanya, later the first attorney general and commissioner for justice in Lagos state, was a graduate of Madariola Private School in Ikorodu, one of the earliest preparatory schools in Nigeria. That school boasted among its alumni Yoruba titans such as Professor Bolaji Idowu and the vivacious Theophilus Owolabi Shobowale (T. O. S.) Benson, another early Azikiwe associate. Benson later became the first deputy mayor of the city of Lagos and Nigeria's first federal minister of information, culture, and broadcasting.

   There were others still, such as Eyo Ita from Calabar, a Columbia University graduate, who would become a deputy national president of the National Council of Nigeria and the Cameroons (NCNC) in the 1950s and the leader of the Eastern government in 1951. Mbonu Ojike, who was also educated in the United States, A. A. Nwafor Orizu, who would become Nigeria's first president of the Senate, Michael Okpara, the premier of Eastern Nigeria, the entertaining and vivacious K. O. Mbadiwe, and the indescribable and stunning Margaret Ekpo were all early Azikiwe associates. Alongside these eminent achievers could be found the stalwarts of the Zikist Movement, a youth branch of the NCNC.

   Sources: Helen Chapin Metz, ed., *Nigeria: A Country Study* (Washington, DC: Government Printing Office for the Library of Congress, 1991); K. A. B. Jones-Quartey, *A Life of Azikiwe* (London: Penguin African Series, 1965); Nnamdi Azikiwe, *My Odyssey* (London: C. Hurst & Co. Publishers, 1971); Falola and Heaton, *A History of Nigeria*; Chudi Uwazurike, Nwagwu, Cletus N., *The Man Called Zik of New Africa: Portrait of Nigeria's Pan-African Statesman* (New York: Triatlantic Books, 1996).

3. It is important to note that Nigeria by the 1940s had an educated class of people in the large urban centers of Lagos, Ibadan, Ogbomosho, Onitsha, Port Harcourt, and Enugu, and in a few places in Northern Nigeria, such as Kano and Kaduna. Some families could boast of two generations of college-educated members. There was to be a certain amount of tension between these competing camps, if you like, as time went on. Azikiwe was a gifted and savvy politician and well aware of this possible friction, and he made great gestures to reach out to many of the prominent individuals of the day. Many of his acquaintances were nonpoliticians.

Nigeria was particularly fortunate to have a very strong legal system. Some of the legal luminaries included Azikiwe's contemporary Sir Adetokunbo Ademola, who by the late 1950s had become the chief justice of the federation of Nigeria. Ademola was a Cambridge University law graduate and the son of Sir Ladapo Ademola, the Alake (paramount ruler) of Egbaland, in the Western Region of Nigeria. Other major names of the time included Justice C. D. Onyeama, the first Nigerian justice at the International Court of Justice at The Hague, and Sir Louis Mbanefo. Mbanefo would rise to become a Supreme Court justice in 1952 and, after the Nigerian-Biafra War broke out, would serve as the chief justice of Biafra and ambassador plenipotentiary. Sir Louis would also play an important role in peace talks and, with Major General Philip Effiong, make the final decision to end the war in 1970, after General Odumegwu Ojukwu had fled the nation for Ivory Coast.

Sources: Author's recollections of the time and Metz, ed., *Nigeria*; Jones-Quartey, *A Life of Azikiwe*; Azikiwe, *My Odyssey*; Falola and Heaton, *A History of Nigeria*; Uwazurike and Nwagwu, *The Man Called Zik of New Africa*.

4. Chief Anthony Enahoro recalls of this period: "In those days, a nationalist newspaper was a monitor of wrongdoings by the colonial government of the day, and the newspaper was an advocate and promoter of the termination of colonial rule. Our newspapers were advocates of democracy and social advancement." Interview Number 21 by Pini Jason, January 2006 © Achebe Foundation.

The Cradle of Nigerian Nationalism

1. Metz, *Nigeria*.
2. Richard L. Sklar, *Nigerian Political Parties: Power in an Emerging African Nation* (Trenton, NJ: Africa World Press, 2004); Metz, *Nigeria*.
3. Ibid.
4. Ibid. Falola and Heaton, *A History of Nigeria*; *Nigeria Youth League Movement: A Resumé of Programme* (Service Press, 1940); Richard L. Sklar and Whitaker Jr., C. S., "Nigeria," in James S. Coleman and Carl G. Rosberg, eds., *Political Parties and National Integration in Tropical Africa* (Berkeley: African Studies Center/University of California Press, 1964), p. 597; Jones-Quartey, *A Life of Azikiwe*; Azikiwe, *My Odyssey*.

The NPTA (Nigerian Produce Traders' Association) was an advocacy group based in Western Nigeria that had been especially effective in protecting and improving the commercial interests of small traders and cocoa farmers in the Western Region.

5. Metz, *Nigeria*; Sklar, *Nigerian Political Parties*; Obafemi Awolowo, *Awo: The Autobiography of Chief Obafemi Awolowo* (Cambridge, England: Cambridge University Press, 1960); Falola and Heaton, *A History of Nigeria*; Sklar and Whitaker Jr., "Nigeria," in Coleman Jr. and Rosberg, *Political Parties and National Integration in Tropical Africa*.

6. An honorific title that means "war leader or head of the bodyguards," depending on the Hausa expert one encounters.

7. Sklar, *Nigerian Political Parties*; Metz, *Nigeria*; Falola and Heaton, *A History of Nigeria*; *Nigeria Youth League Movement*; Sklar and Whitaker Jr., "Nigeria"; Jones-Quartey, *A Life of Azikiwe*; Azikiwe, *My Odyssey*.

8. Ibid.

9. Ibid.

10. Ibid.

Post-Independence Nigeria

1. When Osei Boateng of the *New African*, in a November 2008 cover story titled "Nigeria: Squalid End to Empire," meticulously outlined how colonial "Britain rigged Nigeria's independence elections *so that its compliant friends in the North would win power, dominate the country, and serve British interests after independence*" (emphasis added) it only confirmed what most of us already suspected:

> "As long as the Federal Government [of Nigeria] remains dependent, our strategic requirements are constitutionally secure," one of the documents says. "In the Westminster model, Parliament is the matrix of the Executive. When this model is exported to dependent territories, we are forced in the transitional stages to modify it in the interests of strong and stable government. This we do by *rigging the parliament through official majorities, a restricted franchise and so forth*," another document reveals. "In the last resort, we must make sure that the government of Nigeria is strong, even if possibly undemocratic or unjust," says yet another document.

It is to the credit of British intellectuals and institutions that the documents showcasing this electoral swindle are now available. Series A, Volume 4 of the British Documents on the End of Empire Project (BDEEP), published by the Institute of Commonwealth Studies, University of London, provides a bounty of startling revelations.

Sources: Robin Ramsay, *Politics & Paranoia* (Geat Britain: Picnic Publishing, 2008), p. 258; Johannes Harnischfeger, *Democratization and Islamic Law: The Sharia Conflict in Nigeria* (Frankfurt: Campus Verlag, 2008), p. 63, fn. 90.

The Decline

1. Chinua Achebe, "The Duty and Involvement of the African Writer." Excerpted from Wilfred Cartey and Kilson, Martin, *The Africa Reader* (New York: Random House, 1970).

The Role of the Writer in Africa

1. "The Beginnings of African Literature," http://www.unc.edu/-hhalpin/ThingsFall Apart/literature.html.
2. Bacon, "Atlantic Unbound"; Achebe, "The Duty and Involvement of the African Writer"; Achebe, "Chinua Achebe on Biafra," *Transition*, no. 36 (1968), pp. 31–38. Published by Indiana University Press on behalf of the W. E. B. Du Bois Institute, www .jstor.org/stable/2934672; Lindfors, *Conversations with Chinua Achebe*. Achebe Foundation Archives © 2004–2011.
3. Ode Ogede, *Achebe and the Politics of Representation* (Trenton, NJ: African World Press, 2001).
4. Bacon, "Atlantic unbound"; Achebe, "The Duty and Involvement of the African Writer"; Achebe, "Chinua Achebe on Biafra," *Transition*; Lindfors, *Conversations with Chinua Achebe*. Achebe Foundation Archives © 2004–2011.
5. Ali Mazrui, *The Trial of Christopher Okigbo*, African Writers Series (London: Heinemann, 1971). Achebe Foundation Archives © 2004–2011.
6. Ibid.
7. Bacon, "Atlantic Unbound"; Achebe, "The Duty and Involvement of the African Writer"; Achebe, "Chinua Achebe on Biafra," *Transition*; Lindfors, *Conversations with Chinua Achebe*. Achebe Foundation Archives © 2004–2011.
8. Ibid. See also the preface I wrote for Richard Dowden's book *Africa: Altered States, Ordinary Miracles* (London: Portobello Books, 2008).
9. Ibid.
10. Adapted and updated from the following: Bradford Morrow, "Chinua Achebe, An Interview," *Conjunctions* 17 (Fall 1991); Achebe, "Chinua Achebe on Biafra," *Transition*; Lindfors, *Conversations with Chinua Achebe*.
11. Ibid.
12. From the preface I wrote for Richard Dowden's book *Africa: Altered States, Ordinary Miracles*.

1966

1. Chinua Achebe, *Collected Poems* (New York: Anchor Books, 2004).

January 15, 1966, Coup

1. An honorific title whose original meaning was likely "war leader" or "captain of the bodyguards," depending on the Hausa language expert one talks to.

The Dark Days

1. It is important to mention that Dr. Ogan was educated in Great Britain and was the first board-certified obstetrician-gynecologist not just in Nigeria, but if I am not mistaken, in all of West Africa! Dr. Ogan is a remarkable man who came from an extraordinary family of achievers in Item, Imo state; his younger brother Agu Ogan, a future professor of biochemistry and rector of Federal Polytechnic, Owerri, also became a close friend. Dr. Okoronkwo Ogan served his nation admirably and, with so many others, he served Biafra with equal distinction when the time came, in his case as a wartime surgeon at several places, including St. Elizabeth's Hospital, Umuahia. I remember being told by him how he was often overwhelmed by the sheer number of war wounded brought to his surgical service. These were Biafran army casualties, killed and maimed at the hands of Egyptian mercenary pilots flying for the Nigerian air force because the Nigerians, not surprisingly, did not have enough well-trained pilots!
2. Ikejiani was well-known for his attempts to end nepotism and clannishness in the Coal Corporation, fully integrating the organization that he ran with qualified Nigerians from all over the nation. His efforts drew great ire in many quarters.
3. Author's recollections. Also Ezenwa-Ohaeto, *Chinua Achebe: A Biography*.
4. Ibid.
5. Chinua Achebe, "Chinua Achebe on Biafra." *Transition*.
6. Robin Luckham, *The Nigerian Military: A Sociological Analysis of Authority and Revolt, 1960–1967*. African Studies Series, vol. 4 (Cambridge, England: Cambridge University Press Archive, 1971), p. 17.
7. Chinua Achebe, *The Trouble with Nigeria* (Enugu, Nigeria: Fourth Dimension Publishers, 1983), p. 43.

BENIN ROAD

1. Chinua Achebe, *Collected Poems* (New York: Anchor Books, 2004).

A History of Ethnic Tension and Resentment

1. Achebe *The Trouble with Nigeria*, p. 46.
2. Ibid. Paul Anber, "Modernisation and Political Disintegration: Nigeria and the Ibos," *Journal of Modern African Studies* 5, no. 2 (September 1967), pp. 163–79. Anber's work provides a snapshot of the threat that Igbo educational, economic, and political success posed to other ethnic groups in Nigeria's perpetual internal struggles for political and economic dominance. His work also provides useful background information on the ethnic rivalry that existed in Nigeria right up to independence and beyond. Robert M. Wren, *J. P. Clark* (Farmington Hills, MI: Twayne Publishers, 1984).
3. Anber. "Modernisation and Political Disintegration," pp. 163–79.
4. Achebe, *The Trouble with Nigeria*, p. 46.
5. Anber, "Modernisation and Political Disintegration," pp. 163–79.
6. Ibid. Anber's own observations of this shortcoming are instructive:

> Like most parvenus, many Igbos also became arrogant and self-righteous in their new status, thus arousing the resentment of other ethnic groups, the Northerners in particular, whom the Igbos generally regarded contemptuously as backward and inferior. Caught in the "revolution of rising expectations," confronted with a political system in which the numerically superior Northerners were destined to maintain dominance, cognisant of the corruption in government circles and the obstacles to effective constitutional change, the Igbos also quickly became aware of the contradiction between their aspirations and the actualities of their condition. Their elevated status, educationally and economically, contrasted with their subordinate status politically.

7. Ibid. See also Achebe, *The Trouble with Nigeria*, pp. 48–49.
8. Anber, "Modernisation and Political Disintegration," pp. 163–79.
9. Crawford Young, *The Politics of Cultural Pluralism* (Madison: University of Wisconsin Press, 1979), p. 467.
10. Ibid.
11. Anber, "Modernisation and Political Disintegration," pp. 163–79.
12. Ibid. See also Achebe, *The Trouble with Nigeria*, p. 25.
13. Young, *The Politics of Cultural Pluralism*, p. 467.
14. Achebe, *The Trouble with Nigeria*, p. 25.
15. Falola and Heaton, *A History of Nigeria*, with special attention to timeline and notable people in Nigerian history; Luckham, *The Nigerian Military*; Achebe, *The Trouble with Nigeria*.

The Army

1. Information passed on to me directly from Christopher Okigbo and other personal sources; Alexandar Madiebo, *The Nigerian Revolution and the Biafran War* (Enugu, Nigeria: Fourth Dimension Publishers, 1980), p. 14; Adewale Ademoyega, *Why We Struck: The Story of the First Nigerian Coup* (Ibadan, Nigeria: Evans Brothers, 1981).

2. Ademoyega, *Why We Struck*; Luckham, *The Nigerian Military*.

3. Alex Madiebo, Robin Luckham, Dr. Nowa Omoigui, and other authorities on this subject suggest that over two scores of military officers and civilians were killed during that bloody coup. These include: "Chief F. S. Okotie-Eboh, Finance Minister of the Federation; Brigadier Zakari Mai-Malari, Commander of the 2nd Brigade Nigerian Army; and Colonel K. Mohammed, Chief of Staff, Nigerian Army. Other casualties of this coup were Lieutenant-Colonel A. C. Unegbe, Quartermaster General; Lieutenant-Colonel J. T. Pam, Adjutant General, Nigerian Army; Lieutenant-Colonel A. Largema, Commanding Officer 4th Battalion, Ibadan; and S. L. Akintola, Premier of Western Nigeria."

    Apart from Alhaji Sir Ahmadu Bello, "the Sardauna of Sokoto and Premier of Northern Nigeria, others killed in the north included Brigadier S. Ademulegun, Commander of the 1st Brigade NA; Colonel R. A. Shodeinde, Deputy Commandant, Nigerian Defense Academy; Ahmed Dan Musa, Senior Assistant Secretary (Security) to the North Regional Government; and Sergeant Duromola Oyegoke of the Nigerian Army. There were rumors that the senior wife of Sir Ahmadu Bello and the wife of Brigadier Ademulegun were also killed."

    There were a number of political leaders whose lives were spared but were nevertheless arrested and detained in Lagos and Kaduna: "Sir Kashim Ibrahim—Governor of Northern Nigeria; Aba Kadangare Gobara—Assistant Principal Private Secretary to the Premier of Northern Nigeria; Alhaji Hassan Lemu—Principal private secretary to the Premier of Northern Nigeria; and B. A. Fani-Kayode—at the time Deputy Premier of Western Nigeria."

    Sources: Madiebo, *The Nigerian Revolution and the Biafran War*; Luckham, *The Nigerian Military*; Arthur Nwankwo and Samuel Ifejika, *Biafra: The Making of a Nation* (New York: Praeger Publishers, 1969); Nowamagbe Omoigui, "Military Rebellion of 15th January 1966," Part I, Urhobo Historical Society, www.org/niger delta/nigeria_facts/MilitaryRule/Omoigui/1966Comp=Part1.html.

4. Major General Alexander Madiebo (Ret.), commander of the Biafran army, recalls this period this way:

    > The January coup was widely acclaimed all over the country, including the northern Region, where top civil servants celebrated its success and apparently happy ending by holding parties both in their homes and in public places. Acting against my advice that it was improper from the protocol point of view, Katsina [Governor of the Nigerian Northern Region] visited my house

immediately after his appointment. He brought with him his entire entourage of police outriders and patrol cars and a carload of drinks. We all drank to the health of Ironsi. We drank to the health of the new governors. We drank to the survival of a new Nigeria. Katsina would probably say now, I did all that to deceive old Alex into believing all was well. I sincerely believed that he was acting in good faith that night we drank the toasts.

Source: Madiebo, *The Nigerian Revolution and the Biafran War*.

5. The coup plotters had killed Brigadier Zak Maimalari, Lieutenant Colonel Abogo Largema, and the prime minister, Abubakar Tafawa Balewa.

6. Members of his supreme military council included: "Babafemi Ogundipe as Chief of Staff, Nigerian Defense forces; Yakubu Gowon as Chief of Staff, Army; and Military governors of the four regions at the time. These were Chukwuemeka Ojukwu—Military Governor of Eastern Region; Adekunle Fajuyi—Military Governor of Western Region; David Ejoor—Military Governor of Mid-western Region; and Hassan Katsina-Military Governor of the Northern Region."

    Sources: Madiebo, *The Nigerian Revolution and the Biafran War*; Luckham, *The Nigerian Military;* Nwankwo and Ifejika, *Biafra*; Henryka Schabowska and Ulf Himmelstrand, *Africa Reports on the Nigerian Crisis: News, Attitudes, and Background Information: A Study of Press Performance, Government Attitude to Biafra and Ethno-Political Integration* (Upsala: Scandinavian Institute of African Studies, 1978).; Philip Effiong, *Nigeria and Biafra: My Story* (Princeton: Sungai, 2004); Ademoyega, *Why We Struck*; Metz, *Nigeria*.

    Interviews with retired Nigerian soldiers; and Omoigui, "Military Rebellion of 15th January 1966."

7. They were actively being told this, mainly by local and foreign observers and radio and diplomatic types.

8. Nzeogwu was moved to Aba's prison. Of his coconspirator: Major Ifeajuna was transferred to Uyo's prison; Majors Adewale Ademoyega and Tim Onwuatuegwu to Enugu's prison; Captain Gbulie to Abakaliki's prison; and Major I. H. Chukwuka and Captain Nwobosi were both transferred to Owerri's prison.

    Sources: Madiebo, *The Nigerian Revolution and the Biafran War*; Luckham, *The Nigerian Military;* Nwankwo and Ifejika, *Biafra*; Ademoyega, *Why We Struck*; and Omoigui, "Military Rebellion of 15th January 1966."

9. The most bizarre story is the one that says the riots were provoked by a brand of bread named Nzeogwu that had a picture depicting him as St. George the crusader slaying a dragon drawn in the likeness of the Sardauna of Sokoto.

Countercoup and Assassination

1. Madiebo, *The Nigerian Revolution and the Biafran War*, p. 43; Luckham, *The Nigerian Military*.

2. Ibid.

3. Madiebo, *The Nigerian Revolution and the Biafran War.*

4. Ibid.

5. Ibid., p, 62; Luckham, *The Nigerian Military*; interviews with retired Nigerian soldiers; Nwankwo and Ifejika, *Biafra*; Schabowska and Himmelstrand, *Africa Reports on the Nigerian Crisis.*

6. Here are some chilling statistics: Of the 206 individuals murdered during this countercoup (almost ten times as many as during the January 15 coup), 185 were from the East, 19 were from the Mid-Western Region, and 6 from the Western Region. Not a single person from the North lost their life during this blood fest.
   Source: Luckham, *The Nigerian Military.*

7. Achebe, "The Duty and Involvement of the African Writer"; Also Chinua Achebe, *The Education of a British-Protected Child* (London: Penguin Modern Classics, 2009).

The Pogroms

1. Chinua Achebe, "Chinua Achebe on Biafra," *Transition*, pp. 31–38.

2. The hysteria would be heightened by a most sensational news item of that time: A four-engine propeller plane, "a Royal Air Burundi DC-4M Argonaut, flown by . . . Henry Wharton/Heinrich Wartski, crashlanded at Garoua, in Cameroun [*sic*], while carrying a load of arms from Rotterdam." Henry A. Wharton, a German-American, was arrested. The newspapers alleged that the load of arms was en route to Biafra.
   Sources: Tom Cooper, "Civil War in Nigeria (Biafra) 1967–70," *Western & Northern African Database*, November 13, 2003; Metz, *Nigeria.*

PENALTY OF GODHEAD

1. Chinua Achebe, *Collected Poems* (New York: Anchor Books, 2004).

The Aburi Accord

1. Madiebo, *The Nigerian Revolution and the Biafran War,* p. 92; Nwankwo and Ifejika, *Biafra*; Schabowska and Himmelstrand, *Africa Reports on the Nigerian Crisis*; Joe O. G. Achuzia, *Requiem Biafra* (Enugu, Nigeria: Fourth Dimension Publishers, 1986); Metz, *Nigeria.*

2. Lieutenant Colonel Yakubu Gowon—the Nigerian head of state—Colonel Robert Adebayo, Lieutenant Colonel Odumegwu Ojukwu—governor of the Eastern Region—Lieutenant Colonel David Ejoor, Lieutenant Colonel Hassan Katsina,

Commodore J. E. A. Wey, Major Mobolaji Johnson, Alhaji Kam Selem, Mr. T. Omo-Bare.

3. Nwankwo and Ifejika, *Biafra*; Madiebo, *The Nigerian Revolution and the Biafran War*; Schabowska and Himmelstrand, *Africa Reports on the Nigerian Crisis*; Achuzia, *Requiem Biafra*; Metz, *Nigeria*.

4. Ibid. Also J. Isawa Elaigwu, *Gowon—The Biography of a Soldier-Statesman* (Ibadan, Nigeria: West Books Publisher, 1986).

5. Nwankwo and Ifejika, *Biafra*; Achuzia, *Requiem Biafra*; Madiebo, *The Nigerian Revolution and the Biafran War*; Schabowska and Himmelstrand, *Africa Reports on the Nigerian Crisis*; Metz, *Nigeria*.

6. Ibid.

7. Odumegwu Ojukwu. *Encyclopedia Britannica*; retrieved July 20, 2005, using Encyclopedia Britannica Premium Service; interviews with former Nigerian and Biafran soldiers, diplomats, and government officials, Achebe Foundation. T. C. McCaskie, "Nigeria," *Africa South of the Sahara 1998* (London: Europa, 1997); Harold Nelson, *Nigeria: A Country Study* (Washington: U.S. Government Printing Office, 1982); Nwankwo and Ifejika, *Biafra*; Schabowska and Himmelstrand, *Africa Reports on the Nigerian Crisis*; Metz, *Nigeria*; Audrey Smock, *Ibo Politics: The Role of Ethnic Unions in Eastern Nigeria* (Cambridge, MA: Harvard University Press, 1971); Madiebo, *The Nigerian Revolution and the Biafran War*.

8. Ibid.

GENERATION GAP

1. Chinua Achebe, *Collected Poems* (New York: Anchor Books, 2004).

The Nightmare Begins

1. Madiebo, *The Nigerian Revolution and the Biafran War,* p. 93.

2. A memorandum from the American Jewish Congress in 1968 provides some more clarity to this murky milieu:

> A definite step [toward secession] was taken in March when the Government of the Eastern Region announced that all revenues collected on behalf of the Federal Government would be paid to the Treasury of the Eastern Region. The Federal Government, it was alleged, had refused to pay the salaries of refugee civil servants forced to flee their areas of employment, and the East now had some 2 million refugees whose displacement from other parts of Nigeria was "irreversible." Moreover, the Federal Government, it was alleged, had refused to pay the East its statutory share of revenues for months.
>
> Faced with virtual secession, Colonel Gowon finally attempted to deal with grievances about Northern domination and also to appeal to minorities

throughout Nigeria. He proposed that the Northern Region be broken up into six states, the East into three, and the West into two. The new states would coincide, to a large extent, with natural ethnic divisions. Notably, the East would be divided in such a way that the oil reserves would be located in states without an Ibo majority.

Source: Phil Baum, director, Commission on International Affairs, American Jewish Congress, "Memorandum to Chapter and Division Presidents, Chapter and Division CIA Chairmen, CRC's, Field Staff," December 27, 1968.

3. There is confirmation of this analysis from the CIA World Factbook:

Gowon rightly calculated that the eastern minorities would not actively support the Igbos, given the prospect of having their own states if the secession effort were defeated. Many of the federal troops who fought the civil war, known as the Biafran War, to bring the Eastern Region back to the federation were members of minority groups.

Sources: The Library of Congress Country Studies: Nigeria Civil War, http://work mall.com/wfb2001/nigeria/nigeria_history_civil_war.html; CIA World Factbook: Nigeria, the 1966 Coups, Civil War, and Gowon's Government; Metz, Nigeria.

4. The government of Eastern Nigeria was quick to attack Gowon's sardonic tactic of divide and conquer:

To the charge of Igbo domination over reluctant minorities, the Biafran Authorities reply: Because of the well-developed sense of community and cultural assimilation, there are no genuine minorities in the region, only local communities.... [T]he territory of the former Eastern Region of Nigeria is characterized by a high degree of cultural assimilation among the four major linguistic groups of the area: the Igbo, Efik, Ijaw, and Ogoja. Bilingualism and intermarriage, they claim, have made it difficult in many areas even to distinguish Ibos from non-Ibos [sic]. To support their claim that the non-Ibo peoples of the former Eastern Region are fully behind Biafra, officials of that state assert that of the 30,000 Easterners massacred in 1966, some 10,000 were non-Ibos [sic] and of the 2 million who were forced to return home, nearly 480,000 were non-Ibo [sic]. Biafran officials further assert that the former Eastern Region was the only part of Federal Nigeria which did not experience violent ethnic strife.

Sources: Baum, American Jewish Congress, "Memorandum," December 27, 1968; The Library of Congress Country Studies; CIA World Factbook; Metz, Nigeria.

5. The Library of Congress Country Studies; CIA World Factbook; Nwankwo and Ife-jika, Biafra; Achuzia, Requiem Biafra; Madiebo, The Nigerian Revolution and the Biaf-ran War; Schabowska and Himmelstrand, Africa Reports on the Nigerian Crisis.

Part 2

The Nigeria-Biafra War

The Biafran Position

1. Luckham, *The Nigerian Military.*

The Nigerian Argument

2. The American Jewish Congress provides further elucidation. Some used the minorities and their fear of Igbo domination as a reason for preventing the secession of Biafra:

> Supporters of Nigeria fear that Biafran success would encourage ethnic groups in other African countries to attempt secession, thus further balkanizing a continent already divided into a large number of tiny and barely viable nations. They also argue that minority groups in the East, which form 35-40% of the population, do not favor an independent state in which they would allegedly be at the mercy of the more aggressive and numerous Ibos [*sic*]. The Federal Government, they claim, therefore has a moral responsibility not to abandon these peoples to Ibo [*sic*] domination. Mr. William Whitlock, British Under Secretary of State for Commonwealth Affairs, stated before Parliament on August 27 that he believed the 5 million non-Ibos [*sic*] of the East wanted to remain within Nigeria. This view was supported by The Guardian of August 21 (Parliamentary Debates pp. 32, 18).
>
> One leading supporter of the Nigerian cause, Father James O'Connell, Professor of Government at Ahmadu Bello University, sees the conflict as one between the Ibos [*sic*] of the East and the minorities in the rest of Nigeria. The latter, he claims, now control the Federal Government, sit on the richest oil fields, and provide the majority of the soldiers for the Federal army. Within the context of the new 12-state structure which Colonel Gowon has decreed, these minorities see a chance to escape from domination by the major ethnic groups which they experienced in the three regions of the old Federation. O'Connell suggests they are as desperate to maintain a united Nigeria as the Ibos [*sic*] are to have their own country.

Source: Baum, American Jewish Congress, "Memorandum," December 27, 1968.
3. Ibid.

The Role of the Organization of African Unity

4. Ibid.
5. James D. D. Smith provides this historical observation of the role of intermediaries such as the Organization of African Unity in serving as effective agents of conflict resolution:

Intermediaries have their own difficulties when they become involved in cease-fire negotiations, and the way they conduct themselves has serious implications on their ability to be effective. Indeed, third parties may even be an obstacle to cease-fire [negotiations]. . . . These obstacles are not the same as those which stand in the way of a cease-fire. Here, we are concerned with those obstacles preventing the existence of a workable cease-fire proposal or agreement, which may or may not lead to an actual cease-fire. The acceptable proposal or agreement is a necessary but insufficient requirement for an actual cease-fire. In the case where it is only the appearance of the desire for cease-fire which is sought, proposals may be deliberately defective.

Source: James D. D. Smith, *Stopping Wars: Defining the Obstacles to Cease-Fire* (Boulder, CO.: Westview Press, 1995).

6. It is sad to note, with the benefit of forty years of hindsight, that of the aforementioned six nations only Ghana and Cameroon were spared destabilizing national crises similar to Nigeria's that either broke up the respective country or toppled political interests.

7. Enahoro, who was federal commissioner (minister) for information and labor under General Yakubu Gowon's military government, remembers his encounter with Eni Njoku this way:

I have always held that the civil war was unnecessary and avoidable. The delegation of the Midwest Region, which I led at the 1966 conference, held behind-the-scenes discussions with leaders of each of the other delegations; we made proposals, which the leader of the Eastern delegation, Prof Eni Njoku, agreed to go to Enugu to try and sell the plan to the then Military Governor of the Eastern Region, Colonel Ojukwu. The Conference therefore adjourned for a short period; but Professor Njoku and the Eastern delegation never returned to the Conference, and that was the end of our efforts.

Source: Pini Jacobs, "Chief Anthony Enahoro Speaks," *Sahara Reporters*, January 2, 2006.

8. Sara S. Berry, Elbert, George A., Uphoff, Norman Thomas; reply by Stanley Diamond. "Letters: An Exchange on Biafra," *New York Review of Books*, April 23, 1970.

9. Ibid. Baum, American Jewish Congress, "Memorandum," December 27, 1968; Morrow, "Chinua Achebe, An Interview," *Conjunctions*; Metz, *Nigeria*; Achebe, "Chinua Achebe on Biafra," *Transition*; The Library of Congress Country Studies.

10. Julius Nyerere, *Biafra, Human Rights and Self-Determination in Africa* (Dar es Salam: Government Printer, April 13, 1968).

11. Achebe, "Chinua Achebe on Biafra," *Transition*.

12. From francophone West African writers.

13. Details from Dr. Okechukwu Ikejiani.

The Triangle Game: The UK, France, and the United States

1. The triangle game of the former imperial powers and the United States has been extensively discussed by a number of authors, Michael Leapman, Rick Fountain, and university scholars among them.

2. Michael Leapman writing about cabinet papers that recall the starving children of the Biafran war: "British Interests, Nigerian Tragedy," *Independent Sunday,* January 4, 1998.

3. Rick Fountain, "Secret Papers Reveal Biafra Intrigue," BBC News, January 3, 2000.

4. "Britain: Loss of Touch?" *Time*, March, 29, 1969.

5. The eminent journalist Leapman provides a rare look into the schemes and policy intrigues of the Wilson cabinet:

> General Gowon imposed a blockade on Biafra, which meant that no oil could be exported anyway. This was a blow for the British economy, already floundering in the crisis that led to devaluation later in the year. Now the prime object of Whitehall was to get the blockade lifted. An important lever fell into British hands when Gen. Gowon asked for more arms: 12 jet fighter-bombers, six fast patrol boats, 24 anti-aircraft guns. . . . George Thomas, Minister of State at the Commonwealth Office, was sent to Lagos. The Commonwealth Office note to Wilson about the mission was explicit: "If Gowon is helpful on oil, Mr. Thomas will offer a sale of anti-aircraft guns."
>
> The plan went awry. Gen. Gowon would not lift the blockade but he got his guns anyway; planes and boats were refused, but the Nigerians were permitted to take delivery of two previously ordered patrol boats—which ironically helped enforce the ban on Shell-BP's oil shipments. That victory came, but not quickly. During 1967 the words "famine" or "hunger" appeared nowhere in the hundreds of official documents devoted to the conflict. They would not emerge until 1968, when I and other reporters went to Biafra and witnessed the scenes for ourselves.
>
> By then the policy was too set to be altered. Too many reputations depended on the war's outcome. The conflict went on for another two years. Millions of children starved. How many would still be alive if that one slim chance had been grabbed back in August 1967 and Option E, E for ethical, had prevailed?

> *Source*: Leapman, "British Interests," *Independent Sunday*.

6. Metz, *Nigeria*; Frederick Forsyth, *The Biafra Story: The Making of an African Legend* (London: Penguin, 1969); John de St. Jorre, *The Nigerian Civil War* (London: Hodder and Stoughton, 1972); N. U. Akpan, *The Struggle for Secession 1966–1970: A Personal*

Account of the Nigerian Civil War (London: Frank Kass and Co., 1972); Elechi Amadi, *Sunset in Biafra: A Civil War Diary*, African Writers Series (London: Heinemann, 1973); Falola and Heaton, *A History of Nigeria*; Madiebo, *The Nigerian Revolution and the Biafran War*, p. 14; Effiong, *Nigeria and Biafra*.

7. John W. Young, *The Labour Governments 1964–70*, Vol. 2: *International Policy* (Manchester: Manchester University Press, 2009).

8. As quoted in Alain Rouvez, Michael Coco, and Jean-Paul Paddack, *Disconsolate Empires: French, British, and Belgian Military Involvement in Post-Colonial Sub-Saharan Africa* (Lanham, Md.: University Press of America, 1994), p. 148.

9. Senators Edward Kennedy of Massachusetts, Strom Thurmond of South Carolina, Charles E. Goodell of New York, and Donald E. Lukens of Ohio were well-known American legislators who "became strong supporters of the Biafran regime, and urged relief organizations and the State Department to supply desperately needed funds [at least for humanitarian efforts]." Collectively, they put significant bipartisan pressure on the Nixon administration to act on the growing humanitarian catastrophe in Biafra.

10. Karen E. Smith, *Genocide and the Europeans* (Cambridge, England: Cambridge University Press, 2010), p. 71; Roger Pfister, *Apartheid South Africa and African States: From Pariah to Middle Power, 1961–1994* (London: I. B. Tauris, 2005), pp. 52–53.

11. Jacques Foccart, *Foccart parle: entretiens avec Philippe Gailland* (Paris: Fayard, 1997).

12. Pfister, *Apartheid South Africa and African States*, pp. 52–53.

13. A 1968 article published in the journal *Africa Today* provides a self-congratulatory overview of the role of the United States in the war:

> The United States is the only great power that has followed a neutral course. She has supported humanitarian efforts to bring relief to starving civilians, and even recently released several transport planes to religious relief agencies as dramatic testimony of concern for saving human lives. While the Nigerians have been unhappy over the opposition of the United States to a "starve them into submission" policy, they have recognized that the United States has not given military support to the Biafran secession or encouraged in principle diplomatically. However, other great powers have committed themselves. The French now privately back the Biafrans through Gabon with arms, and the Russians and British supply Lagos with arms, planes, and bombs.

> *Source*: Council on Religion and International Affairs, *Worldview* 12 (1969).

14. A letter written by Mrs. Betty C. Carter of Washington, D.C., to Dean Rusk, dated July 25, 1968, illustrates this point:

> Yesterday evening while eating dinner and watching the news I was unable to finish eating upon seeing the faces of starving children, babies, men, and women in Biafra. I felt nauseated because of having so much when these

people were in obvious pain and in dire need of food. I cannot bear to see anyone in need when I have something to share. Though it is not possible for me to go to Biafra at this time, I felt the least I could do was write to you and express my concern for these people and ask that the U. S. and other concerned governments and the United Nations press for a cease fire. I am sending a check to the World Church Service today to help the starving Biafrans.

Source: "BIAFRA-NIGERIA 1967–1969 POLITICAL AFFAIRS," Confidential U.S. State Department Central Files, A UPA Collection from LexisNexis.

15. The signatories to the declaration were the leaders of fifteen organizations at the vanguard of American organized labor, women's groups, and the civil rights movements. The list now reads like a who's who of African American civil rights history, with names such as: Roy Wilkins, executive director, National Association for the Advancement of Colored People (NAACP); Dorothy Height, president, National Council of Negro Women; and James Farmer, chairman, National Advisory Board, Congress of Racial Equality. Other leaders who signed the document included: A. Philip Randolph, president of the Brotherhood of Sleeping Car Porters and vice president of the American Federation of Labor–Congress of Industrial Organizations; and Bayard Rustin, executive director, A. Philip Randolph Institute.

Sources: *The Crisis Magazine* 75, no. 8 (October 1968), p. 291. This is the official publication of the NAACP. See also: Baum, American Jewish Congress, "Memorandum," December 27, 1968; *1968 Annual Report*, National Association for the Advancement of Colored People.

16. Ibid.

17. Arthur Jay Klinghoffer, "Why the Soviets Chose Sides," *Africa Report* (February 1968), p. 4. Also: Interviews with Nigerian and Biafran former military officers.

18. The Soviets have broadened their technical assistance and trade programs, and have announced plans to erect a $120 million steel mill and, if Gowon is agreeable, intend to expand their embassy staff and open consulates in other Nigerian towns to put them in closer contact with labor and student groups.

Source: "Britain: Loss of Touch?" *Time*, March, 29, 1969.

19. Ibid. Robert Guest, in *The Shackled Continent: Power, Corruption, and African Lives* (Washington, DC: Smithsonian Books, 2004), writes:

Visitors to the Ajaokuta steel plant in Nigeria are surprised to see goats grazing among the gantries and children playing by the silent rolling mills. Nigeria flushed away a total of $8 billion trying to build a steel industry at Ajaokuta and elsewhere [which] operated fitfully, at a loss, and usually at a small fraction of capacity when the present government came on board.

See also: *The Economist* 354, iss. 8152–55; Daniel Jordan Smith, *A Culture of Corruption: Everyday Deception and Popular Discontent in Nigeria* (Princeton: Princeton University Press, 2008); Colin Nicholls, et al., *Corruption and Misuse of Public Office* (New York: Oxford University Press, 2011); Yingqi Wei and Balasubramanyam, V. N., eds., *Foreign Direct Investment: Six Country Case Studies*, New Horizons in International Business Series (Northampton, Mass: Edward Elgar Publishing, 2004); *Africa Confidential* 42–43 (2001); Mary Dowell-Jones, *Contextualizing the International Covenant on Economic, Social and Cultural Rights: Assessing the Economic Deficit* (Herndon, Va.: Martinus Nijhoff Publishers/Brill, 2004).

20.   The [Nigerian] House of Representatives asked the Federal Government to investigate the alleged "massive" looting of equipment at the Ajoakuta Steel Company Limited and the National Iron-Ore Mining Company, Itakpe, and bring the perpetrators to book. The House, in a resolution in Abuja, observed that the Ajaokuta steel plant had cost Nigerian tax payers over $4.6bn without producing one sheet of steel in its many years of existence.

        Source: John Ameh, "Reps move to halt looting of Ajaokuta Steel Company equipment," *Punch*, October 30, 2009.

21.   Achebe, "Chinua Achebe on Biafra," *Transition*.

22.   On this point, the American Jewish Congress goes even further:

        The crazy-quilt grouping of Great Britain, the Soviet Union, and the UAR (Egyptian pilots fly most of the MIG's for the Nigerian Air Force), on one side, and France, China and Portugal on the other (Portugal allows the use of the island of Sao Tome for relief flights) makes clear, at least, the unmitigated and cynical pursuit of selfish interests on the part of the Great Powers, while hundreds of thousands of Africans die each month.

        Source: Baum, American Jewish Congress, "Memorandum," December 27, 1968.

        The tragedy is also captured succinctly here by the American scholar Stanley Diamond:

        Commentators of such divergent views as Richard Sklar and Auberon Waugh have pointed out [that] it is unlikely that the war would have been declared or, if declared, that it would have followed its tragic course, had the interests of the Big Powers not been decisive. In so critical an area as Nigeria, which attained formal independence as recently as 1960, imperial and internal dynamics can hardly be divorced from each other.

        Source: Diamond, Reply, *New York Review of Books*.

The Writers and Intellectuals

1.   The following passage from Kurt Vonnegut highlights his keen sense of perception and irony and captures, ultimately, the cruel absurdity of war:

> The young general [Ojukwu] was boisterous, wry, swashbuckling—high as a kite on incredibly awful news from the fronts. Why did he come to see us? Here is my guess: He couldn't tell his own people how bad things were, and he had to tell somebody. We were the only foreigners around.
>
> He talked for three hours. The Nigerians had broken through everywhere. They were fanning out fast, slicing the Biafran dot into dozens of littler ones. Inside some of these littler dots, hiding in the bush, were tens of thousands of Biafrans who had not eaten anything for two weeks and more.
>
> What had become of the brave Biafran soldiers? They were woozy with hunger. They were palsied by shell shock. They had left their holes. They were wandering.

> *Source*: Kurt Vonnegut, "Biafra: A People Betrayed," *Wampeters Foma & Granfalloons* (New York: Delacorte Press, 1979).

2.   Ezenwa-Ohaeto, *Chinua Achebe*, p. 143.
3.   Todd F. Davis, *Kurt Vonnegut's Crusade, or, How a Postmodern Harlequin Preached a New Kind of Humanism*. SUNY Series in Postmodern Culture (Albany, N. Y.: State University of New York Press, 2006), p. 141.
4.   Ezenwa-Ohaeto, *Chinua Achebe*, p. 143.
5.   The term "intellectual warrior" was coined by Biafran writers to describe Stanley Diamond during the war. Christopher Okigbo might have been the first to use the phrase.
6.   Achebe, *The Education of a British-Protected Child*.
7.   Ezenwa-Ohaeto, *Chinua Achebe*, p. 143.
8.   Ibid.

The War and the Nigerian Intellectual

1.   Version of events told during writers' discussions.
2.   Achebe, "Chinua Achebe on Biafra," *Transition*.
3.   Alexander O. Animalu, *Life and Thoughts of Professor Kenneth Onwuka Dike* (Nsukka, Enugu State, Nigeria: Ucheakonam Foundation, 1997); also, conversation with Onwuka Dike at his home in Dedham, Massachussetts, shortly after the war.
4.   A few of the roving ambassadors for Biafra were: Dr. Nnamdi Azikiwe (who later left the breakaway republic), Dr. Kingsley Ozumba (K. O.) Mbadiwe, Professor Eni

Njoku, Chukwuma Azikiwe, Dr. Hilary Okam, Dr. Okechukwu Ikejiani, as well as Cyprian Ekwensi.

5. Animalu, *Life and Thoughts of Professor Kenneth Onwuka Dike*; also, conversation with Dike at this home.

6. Author's recollections.

7. Ibid.

8. Marie Umeh, "Emerging Perspectives on Flora Nwapa: Critical and Theoretical Essays," *Africa World Press* (February 1998). Also Femi Nzegwu, "Flora Nwapa," *The Literary Encyclopedia*, first published October 20, 2001, http://www.litencyc.com/php/speople.php?rec=true&UID=3364, accessed February 6, 2012.

The Life and Work of Christopher Okigbo

1. Chinua Achebe, *Hopes and Impediments* (Garden City, NY: Doubleday, 1989), p. 118.

2. Obiageli Okigbo, *A Biographical Sketch of Christopher Okigbo (1932–1967)* © Christopher Okigbo Foundation, 2010; Donatus Ibe Nwoga, *Critical Perspectives on Christopher Okigbo* (Washington, D.C.: Three Continents Press, 1984); Dubem Okafor, *Dance of Death: Nigerian History and Christopher Okigbo's Poetry* (Trenton, NJ, and Asmara, Eritrea: African World Press, 1998); James Wieland, *The Ensphering Mind: History, Myth and Fictions in the Poetry of Allen Curnow, Nissim Ezekiel, A. D. Hope, A. M. Klein, Christopher Okigbo and Derek Walcott* (Washington, DC: Three Continents Press, 1988); Uzoma Esonwanne, ed., *Critical Essays on Christopher Okigbo* (New York: G. K. Hall & Co., 2000); Sunday Anozie, *Christopher Okigbo: Creative Rhetoric* (London: Evan Brothers, and New York: Holmes and Meier, 1972).

3. Chinua Achebe and Dubem Okafor, eds., *Don't Let Him Die: An Anthology of Memorial Poems for Christopher Okigbo* (Enugu, Nigeria: Fourth Dimension Publishers, 1978).

4. Ibid.

5. Francis Ellah, our colleague in Ibadan and beyond, remembers Okigbo this way:

> Chris was a very sociable type. . . . [H]e talked all the time, telling everyone he met what he thought of the person. Chris read classics but nobody knew that his poems meant anything. We read them and then he published a few of them, and they turned out to be monumental works. The last time I saw Chris was when I came back from London, and he regaled us with a detailed account of his exploits. At one time, when he was librarian at UNN [University of Nigeria], and I had just started work with the Foreign Service, I built a home near Enugu campus and was within three hundred yards to Chris Okigbo's home on the campus. This brought us closer together. Then, of course, I met his older brother, Pius.

> *Source*: May 30, 2005, © The Achebe Foundation. Interview number 6: Senator Francis J. Ellah.

6. Eyewitness account.
7. Ibid.
8. Author's recollection.
9. Achebe and Okafor, eds., *Don't Let Him Die*.

The Major Nigerian Actors in the Conflict: Ojukwu and Gowon

1. On the Biafran side, aside from General Odumegwu Ojukwu: Major General Philip Effiong, chief of General Staff; Brigadier Tony Eze; Brigadier Pat Amadi; Colonel Joe ("Air Raid") Achuzie; Colonel Nsudo; Colonel Iheanacho; Colonel Archibong; Brigadier Patrick Amadi, Biafran army; Colonel Patrick Anwunah, chief of logistics and principal staff officer to Ojukwu; Colonel David Ogunewe, military adviser to Ojukwu; Patrick Okeke, inspector general of Biafran police; Sir Louis Mbafeno, chief justice of Biafra; and the young and talented Matthew Mbu, Biafran foreign minister.

   On the Nigerian side, apart from Major General Yakubu Gowon, the Nigerian head of state, there were: Obafemi Awolowo, deputy chairman, Supreme Military Council; Brigadier Emmanuel Ekpo, chief of staff, supreme headquarters; Brigadier Murtala R. Muhammed; Brigadier Mobalaji Johnson; Lieutenant Colonel Shehu Musa Yar'Adua; Brigadier Hassan Katsina, chief of staff, Nigerian army; Brigadier Emmanuel Ikwue, chief of air staff; Rear Admiral Joseph Wey, chief of naval staff; Dr. Taslim Elias, attorney general; H. E. A. Ejueyitchie, secretary to the Federal Military Government; Anthony Enahoro, commissioner for information; Olusegun Obasanjo; Colonel Benjamin Adekunle; Theophilus Y. Danjuma; and the twelve state governors.

   Sources: Luckham, *The Nigerian Military*; Nwankwo and Ifejika, *Biafra*; Achuzia, *Requiem Biafra*; Madiebo, *The Nigerian Revolution and the Biafran War*; Schabowska and Himmelstrand, *Africa Reports on the Nigerian Crisis*; Metz, *Nigeria*.

2. Gowon and Ojukwu were the two main protagonists of the Nigerian Civil War, yet they only ever met face-to-face once, and that meeting took place before the war. They never gave themselves the opportunity to actually sit down and discuss their views on the war, but even if such a conversation had taken place, there would likely have been no positive result. At least one thing becomes clear when their respective points of view are juxtaposed and analyzed: In their own minds, both Gowon and Ojukwu saw their own positions as non-negotiable.

   Source: Smith, *Stopping Wars*, pp. 131–32.

THE ARISTOCRAT

3. Ojukwu, *Encyclopedia Britannica*, retrieved July 20, 2005; interviews with former Nigerian and Biafran soldiers, diplomats, and government officials, Achebe Foundation;

McCaskie, "Nigeria"; Nelson, *A Country Study*; Nwankwo and Ifejika, *Biafra*; Schabowska and Himmelstrand, *Africa Reports on the Nigerian Crisis*; Smock, *Ibo Politics*; Metz, *Nigeria*.

4. Kalu Ogbaa, *General Ojukwu. The Legend of Biafra* (New York: Triatlantic Books, 2007).

5. Frederick Forsyth, as quoted in Ralph Uwechie, *Reflections on the Nigerian Civil War: Facing the Future* (published in cooperation with Trafford Publishing [Bloomington, IN], 2004), p. 146; © Ralph Uwechie.

6. *Biafra: Fighting a War Without Guns,* BBC documentary; producer: Michael Stewart; editor: Laurence Rees (1995).

7.   Despite all odds, Gowon and Ojukwu had ample opportunity to resolve the crisis without further bloodshed, but their personal dispositions toward each other would not let them put their egos behind them in the pursuit of a course nobler than the feelings of two individuals.

        Source: Kalu N. Kalu, *State Power, Autarchy, and Political Conquest in Nigerian Federalism* (Lanham, MD: Lexington Books, 2008).

THE GENTLEMAN GENERAL

8. J. Isawa Elaigwu, *Gowon: The Biography of a Soldier-Statesman* (London: Adonis & Abbey Publishers, 2009); Achebe Foundation interviews. Number 15: General Yakubu Gowon in conversation with Pini Jason October, 16, 2005.

9. Madiebo, *The Nigerian Revolution and the Biafran War.*

10. Gowon was invited to Great Britain for a state visit soon after the war ended—the first Commonwealth African head of state to be treated this way—for a three-day affair. Gowon pulled all the stops and mesmerized the British.

11. Nigerian Institute of International Affairs, *Nigeria: Bulletin on Foreign Affairs* 8, iss. 6–10 (1978).

12. Henry Robinson Luce, "General Gowon: The Binder of Wounds," *Time* 95 January 26, 1970.

13. Statement attributed to Lieutenant Colonel Ojukwu published in the *Nigerian Outlook* (Enugu) March 21, 1967, as quoted in Luckham, *The Nigerian Military*, p. 77, fn. 1.

14. Ojukwu is often referred to by his detractors as a warmonger, but his life experiences and actions prior to the war challenge that assumption:

        One of the most compelling ironies of Nigerian history is the fact that it was Ojukwu who freed Chief Obafemi Awolowo (of starvation is a legitimate weapon of war infamy) from Calabar prison even though historical revisionists would love this inconvenient fact to just disappear somehow and give the credit to Gowon. In addition, Ojukwu's choice of Ado Bayero, the Emir of the ancient city of Kano in Northern Nigeria as chancellor of the University of Nigeria, Nsukka, stemmed not only from a deep affection for Kano and its people, a city he had spent several years in, but clearly a feeling that Nigeria's diversity was a strength and not a weakness!

Source: Ogbaa, General Ojukwu.

15.   There has been great debate about Gowon's role in the July 1966 coup. In his land-mark study, The Nigerian Military, Robin Luckham sheds a great deal of light on the feelings of Eastern military officers concerning Gowon's involvement. He finds these sentiments difficult to substantiate, but his analysis serves as an important illumination of the thoughts and mood of the Eastern military elite (see chapter II, "July 1966: The Junior Officers' and NCOs' Coup," in the section Three Different Views of the Coup, pp. 62–63).

There are several sources, mainly Nigerian, that report that Gowon had an indeterminate role in the coup; other international sources, such as the follow-ing, are more candid in their opinions. The Economist of July 26, 1975, reported: "Brigadier Murtala Mohammed [sic], who has now taken over as Nigeria's leader, was an instigator of General Gowon's own 1966 coup and nearly got the top job then. He is alleged to have been involved in plots against General Gowon since then."

According to editor Roy Godson, in Menace to Society: Political-Criminal Collabo-ration Around the World (New Brunswick, NJ: Transaction Publishers, 2003): "On July 29, 1966, a company of Hausa Army officers attacked and killed [Aguiyi Ironsi] and installed their own man, Major General Yakubu Gowon, in August 1966." ("Slic-ing Nigeria's National Cake," by Obi N. I. Ebbe, p. 141).

16.   Asked in 2005 whether he thought the war was inevitable, Gowon had this to say:

No! It was the action of the leaders! When it got to the stage whereby the leaders would not agree then a decision had to be taken. There would not have been a civil war had there not been secession! If there was no decision to break away from the country, certainly there wouldn't have been any reason to start fighting. The civil war was as a result of the East and the leadership of Ojukwu deciding to break away. Now, I had a duty and responsibility. I swore allegiance to Nigeria, and Nigeria is composed of all the various parts. And the East was part of Nigeria. But the Ojukwu leadership, because of whatever reasons it had, and, of course, I know there were very strong reasons why he made certain decisions; but I know it was personal ambition more than anything else. Yes, unfortunate events had occurred, and I can assure you, if anyone had any sleepless night, it is because of the sort of thing that happened in Nigeria from 1966 up to that time.

Honestly, if you think that one enjoyed seeing the harrowing experiences of the Igbo in various parts of the country, especially in the Northern part of the country in 1966, I can assure you, you are wrong. Well God knows! And that was why one had to use certain expressions at the time in order to keep control of the people. I was accused of using the words: "God had called another Northerner, again, to lead." But it was the only way I could bring sanity to bear on a situation galloping out of control. And we were able to bring the situation under control. Now I accept that those were very trying experiences for the Igbo that can make anybody say: well, you don't want us, so we will go. At least, with our honest and sincere effort to get the situation under control, no matter what anyone would say, you can rest assured that we tried not to allow the situation to get to the stage whereby it resulted in civil war.

Source: Achebe Foundation interviews. Number 15, part 2: General Gowon in conversation with Pini Jason, October 31, 2005.

Ojukwu's own take on the calamity that befell our nation is also salient:

Events of the time made war possible . . . not me. My good friend, Jack; he was thirty-three then, and so was I. That, in addition, made war almost inevitable. My good friend, Jack, had a smattering knowledge of the Eastern Region, but I grew up in it, and that created its own conflict. And so on and so forth. There are so many things. . . . My good friend, Jack: His people sent me a Christmas present of a headless corpse. He heard about it. . . . I received it! There's conflict even in that experience, and so on and so forth.

But to be honest, war could have been avoided; after all, all you need to stop war is to say, I won't fight! So it could have been avoided. But having fought it, my prayer is that we move forward, and learn from the past lessons of the war. We cannot wish it away. Whenever the history of Nigeria is written, whatever that is, there must be something written on the war. If you leaf through that book and there's no mention of it, then throw the book away, because that is not the history of Nigeria. . . . But you'll draw from the book the requisite lessons; if it has something on the war.

Source: Achebe Foundation interviews. Number 10, part 1: Dim Chukwuemeka Odumegwu Ojukwu in conversation with Professor Nnaemeka Ikpeze and Nduka Otiono, July 25, 2005.

17.   In *Understanding Civil War: Evidence and Analysis, Vol. 1, Africa,* Collier et al. were not able to neatly wrap their highly respected theories of the genesis of civil war around the Nigerian situation:

Compared to the theory [the Collier-Hoeffler model], the reality of Nigeria's conflicts is often puzzling, but it is precisely for this reason that this case offers several insights that may further our understanding of civil war. One insight is that several variables in the CH model, such as ethnic dominance and natural resource dependence, have to be re-operationalized. Another is that the way in which the government responds to protest matters in the process of conflict escalation and can trigger or prevent a civil war.

> *Source*: Annalisa Zinn, "Theory Versus Reality: Civil War Onset and Avoidance in Nigeria Since 1960," in Paul Collier and Nicholas Sambanis, eds., *Understanding Civil War: Evidence and Analysis, Vol. 1, Africa* (Washington, DC: World Bank Publications, 2005), p. 117.

18. Jacob Bercovitch and Karl R. Derouen Jr., "Enduring Internal Rivalries: A New Framework for the Study of Civil War," *Journal of Peace Research* 45, no. 1 (2008): 55–74.

19. Nathaniel H. Goetz provides an example of this "locking in period":

> Neither of the belligerents [Gowon and Ojukwu] was willing to concede the superiority of humanitarian over political considerations, which made it impossible to reach any agreement about the routes and methods to be used for moving relief supplies through the Federal blockade. In these circumstances, the humanitarian agencies felt compelled, given the gravity of the nutritional situation inside the enclave [of Biafra] in the summer of 1968, to step up their "clandestine" airlift of relief supplies.

> *Source*: James M. Clevenger, "The Political Economy of Hunger: Famine in Nigeria, 1967–1970," master of social sciences thesis, University of Birmingham, UK (June 1975), as quoted in Nathaniel H. Goetz, "Humanitarian issues in the Biafra conflict," Working Paper No. 36, New Issues in Refugee Research, United Nations High Commissioner for Refugees (April 2001).

20. Writing about MacArthur's Pacific challenges, James R. Locher III suggests that the American general's failure to address a number of pressing issues similar to Gowon's (albeit on a much larger scale) *"resulted in divided effort, the waste of diffusion and duplication of force, [and] undue extension of the war with added casualties and cost."* (Emphasis added.) James R. Locher III, *Victory on the Potomac: The Goldwater-Nichols Act Unifies the Pentagon*. Williams-Ford Texas A&M University Military History Series (College Station, TX: Texas A&M University Press, 2004). Author interview with Archie D. Barrett, May 19, 2000.

21. Supported by the work of Smith, *Stopping Wars*.

22. Raph Uwechue. *Reflections on the Nigerian Civil War: Facing the Future* (Bloomington, IN: Trafford Publishing, 2004); Laurie S. Wiseberg, "An Emerging Literature: Studies of the Nigerian Civil War," *African Studies Review* 18, no. 1 (April 1975), pp. 117–26.

23. Ibid. A *Time* magazine article from 1968, appropriately titled "A Bitter African Harvest," elaborates:

> Ojukwu has also said no to a British offer of $600,000 in relief funds. His reason: Britain sells arms to Gowon. Therefore, says Ojukwu, to give food at the same time would only "fatten the Biafrans for slaughter with British-made weapons." Meanwhile his countrymen need an estimated 200 tons of protein

food a day to survive, and are getting only about 40. Ojukwu insists that the only way to protect Biafra's sovereignty is to fly the food in. He proposes mercy flights during the daytime, but these require the cooperation of federal Nigeria, which has threatened to shoot down the planes.

Source: "A Bitter African Harvest," *Time*, July 12, 1968.

24.   Francis Ellah worked in the Biafran Ministry of Transport and Communications, served as secretary to the Atrocities Commission, and supervised the establishment and activities of the Biafran Students' Union.

Source: Achebe Foundation interviews: Senator Francis Ellah in conversation with Professors Ossie Enekwe and Nduka Otiono. © Chinua Achebe Foundation.

THE FIRST SHOT

1.   Chinua Achebe, *Collected Poems* (New York: Anchor Books, 2004).

The Biafran Invasion of the Mid-West

1.   Madiebo, *The Nigerian Revolution and the Biafran War*; Metz, *Nigeria*.
2.   Ibid.
3.   C. Odumegwu Ojukwu, *Biafra: Selected Speeches with Journals of Events* (New York: Harper & Row, 1969).
4.   De St. Jorre, *The Nigerian Civil War*.
5.   Information from former classmates in Ibadan and Umuahia and their family members.
6.   It was generally believed that both Lieutenant Colonel Odumegwu Ojukwu of the Eastern Region (Biafra) and Lieutenant Colonel David Ejoor of the Mid-Western Region met secretly on several occasions to discuss the crisis before and even after the declaration of Biafra. In a recent interview, Ejoor (now a retired major general) admitted that all of these actions were taken "to prevent battle on Benin soil and to protect everybody's interest, including the Igbo-speaking citizens [of the Region], even though [he] primarily supported the Federal Government."

  Source: S. E. Orobator, "The Biafran Crisis and the Midwest," *African Affairs* 86, no. 344 (July 1987), pp. 367–83; *African Affairs* is published by Oxford University Press on behalf of The Royal African Society.

7.   Others included Ojukwu, General Philip Effiong, Major Emmanuel Ifeajuna, Major Sam Agbamuche, Major Phillip Alale, and Major Okonkwo.
8.   Nwankwo and Ifejika, *Biafra*; The Library of Congress Country Studies; *CIA World Factbook: Nigeria, the 1966 Coups, Civil War, and Gowon's Government*; Achuzia, *Requiem Biafra*; Madiebo, *The Nigerian Revolution and the Biafran War*.
9.   See Appendix for details of the speech.
10. Achebe Foundation interviews: Nigerian soldiers from the former Mid-Western Region. © Achebe Foundation, 2008.

11. Ibid. Nwankwo and Ifejika, *Biafra*; Achuzia, *Requiem Biafra*; Madiebo, *The Nigerian Revolution and the Biafran War*; The Library of Congress Country Studies; *CIA World Factbook*.

12. "Victor Banjo's Third Force [was] a movement opposed to both Gowon's Federal Military Government and Ojukwu's separatist regime in Biafra, 'which thinks in terms of a common denominator for the people.'"

     Source: Holger G. Ehling, ed., *No Condition Is Permanent: Nigerian Writing and the Struggle for Democracy* (Amsterdam: Rodopi, 2001), p. 51.

13. Achebe Foundation interviews: Biafran and Nigerian soldiers. © Achebe Foundation.

14. Interview with Odumegwu Ojukwu in *New Nigerian*, July 21, 1982.

15. Olusegun Obasanjo, *My Command: An Account of the Nigerian Civil War, 1967–1970* (London: Heinemann Educational Books, 1980); Wole Soyinka, *The Man Died: Prison Notes of Wole Soyinka* (London: Africa Book Centre, 1972) ; David A. Ejoor, *Reminiscences* (Lagos, Nigeria: Malthouse Press, 1989); Nwankwo and Ifejika, *Biafra*; Achuzia, *Requiem Biafra*; Madiebo, *The Nigerian Revolution and the Biafran War*.

Gowon Regroups

1. Anthony Clayton, *Frontiers Men: Warfare in Africa Since 1950* (London: Routledge, 2004), p. 94.

2. Ibid.

3. Michael Leapman of *The Independent,* in a brilliant article on the subject, provides great illumination of the British reaction to the Mid-West offensive:

> [T]he Biafrans scored a military success (their only one, as it turned out) when they marched into the Mid-West Region and occupied Benin. This provoked a rethink in Whitehall. The Commonwealth Office set out five choices. A and B involved maintaining or increasing arms to Nigeria, C was to stop all supplies, D to promote a peace initiative and E a combination of the last two. Thomas wrote to Wilson [the prime minister], holidaying in the Scillies, recommending Option E. That view might have prevailed had not Sir David Hunt, British ambassador in Lagos and a keen advocate of the Federal cause, flown to Britain and persuaded the government to continue providing arms.
>
>   Soon the war turned in Gowon's favor and in November the flexible Thomas wrote to Wilson again, proposing this time that arms supplies be stepped up: "It seems to me that British interests would now be served by a quick Federal victory."

    Source: Leapman, "British Interests, Nigerian Tragedy," *The Independent,* on cabinet papers that recall the starving children of the Biafran war.

4. Interview with retired Nigerian army officer who prefers to remain anonymous.

5. Nigerian Radio news broadcasts monitored from Enugu. There has been no credible corroboration of these claims that I found.

The Asaba Massacre

1. Ibid. One year later Muhammed's forces would invade Onitsha, where he lay siege to the largest market in West Africa. During the "Otuocha market massacre," as it came to be known, over five hundred innocent women and children visiting or working in the market were killed.

2. Interviews with Nigerian and Biafran army officials.

3. Monsignor Georges Rocheau (sent down on a fact-finding mission by His Holiness the Pope), April 5, 1968, as reported in *Le Monde* (the French evening newspaper) and Forsyth, *The Biafra Story*, p. 210.

4. Austin Ogwuda, "Gowon faults setting up of Oputa Panel," *Vanguard*, December 9, 2002.

5. General Haruna, who was under cross-examination by the Ohanaeze Ndigbo (a pan-Igbo group) counsel, Chief Anthony Mogbo, senior advocate of Nigeria (SAN), said whatever action he or his troops took during the war was motivated by a sense of duty to protect the unity of the country.

    Source: Ogwuda, "Gowon faults setting up of Oputa Panel."

Biafran Repercussions

1. Madiebo, *The Nigerian Revolution and the Biafran War*; Nwankwo and Ifejika, *Biafra*; Achuzia: *Requiem Biafra*.

2. Ibid.

Blood, Blood Everywhere

1. Clayton, *Frontiers Men*, p. 94.

The Calabar Massacre

1. Rev. David T. Craig, writing in the *Presbyterian Record* of December 1967 (Scotland), gave more revelation of Nigerian acts of genocide under the caption of "Operation Calabar": "A group of Efik people (the local inhabitants) brought

two young men in civilian dress to the soldiers. The young lads looked like secondary school students. With the Northern soldiers was an Efik-speaking soldier. It was his duty to question prisoners in the Efik language. His job was to see if any spoke Efik with an Ibo [*sic*] accent. These two young lads did. The soldiers took aim and they were shot on the spot." (Emphasis in original.)

Source: "The Violations of Human and Civil Rights of Ndi Igbo in the Federation of Nigeria (1966–1999): A Call for Reparations and Appropriate Restitution, A Petition to the Human Rights Violations Investigating Committee, by Oha-na-Eze (The Apex Organization of the Entire Igbo People of Nigeria) for and on Behalf of the Entire Ndi Igbo, October 1999," http://magazine.biafranigeriaworld.com/oha-na-eze/october-1999-human-civil-rights-petition.html.

2. The quote is from Alfred Friendly Jr., "Pressure Rising in Nigeria to End Civil War as Military Standoff Continues," *New York Times*, January 14, 1968; see also, M. S. Armoni, *The Minority of One*, Vol. 10 (1968); Forsyth, *The Biafra Story*.

3. *The Times* (London), August 2, 1968.

4. Ibid.

5. "The Violations of Human and Civil Rights of Ndi Igbo in the Federation of Nigeria (1966–1999), October 1999."

6. The American Jewish Congress reports:

Some Nigerian commanders, notably Colonel Benjamin Atakunle [*sic*], maintain that the denial of food to Biafran-held areas and to Ibo [*sic*] people in Federally-controlled areas, is a legitimate and necessary strategy. As Colonel Atakunle [*sic*] himself told a Dutch newspaper: "I want to see no Red Cross, no Caritas, no World Council of Churches, no Pope, no missionary, and no UN delegation. I want to prevent even one Ibo [*sic*] having even one piece to eat before their capitulation.

Source: Quoted in Baum, American Jewish Congress, "Memorandum," December 27, 1968, from the *London Economist*, August 24, 1968, as cited in the *Village Voice*, October 17, 1968.

7. Thirty-four years later, in a Nigerian *Guardian* newspaper article published on July 25, 2004, with the caption "I Did Not Dislike Igbos, But I Had A War to Win," Adekunle provides his perspective on his duties as a soldier for the federal forces:

Brigadier-General Benjamin Adekunle has finally dispelled the notion that he is a hater of the Igbo. "I don't dislike Igbos. But I learned one word from the British and that is "sorry." I did not want this war. I did not start this war— Ojukwu did. But I want to win this war. So I must kill Igbos. Sorry!"

He is referring to the 30-month Nigerian Civil War that lasted between 1967 and 1970. This explanation is contained in the book, "The Nigeria-Biafra

War Letters: A Soldier's Story (Vol. i)," an explosive account of his role in the war. Brigadier Adekunle was the Commander of the "Third Marine Commando," the dreaded force that operated in controversial circumstances during the war.

> Source: www.igbofocus.co.uk/html/biafra_news.html#I-did-not.

8. Achebe, *Transition*, pp. 31–38.
9. Clayton, *Frontiers Men*, p. 94.
10. Hugh McCullum reports:

By this time, it appeared as if the Igbo people had lost all their cities including the oil centre of Port Harcourt and the capital, Enugu. Soon 5 million people were squeezed into a tiny oval-shaped enclave of 2,000 sq km around the market town of Umuahia, the new capital . . . touting his now infamous 'final offensive,' [underestimating the Biafrans] "Gowon boasted that war would be over in two weeks. The war in fact turned into a bloody and bitter one . . ." painfully stretching out over a 30 month period.

> Source: Hugh McCullum. "Biafra Was the Beginning." *AfricaFiles*, no. 8 (May 27, 2004) © AfricaFiles; www.africafiles.org/article.asp?ID=5549.

11. African-American Institute, *Africa Report* 14 (1969).
12. Solange Chaput-Rolland, *The Second Conquest: Reflections II* (Montreal: Chateau Books, 1970); Peter Schwab, *Biafra, Interim History* (Ann Arbor: University of Michigan Press, 2008).
13. Newspaper clippings; radio broadcasts monitored in Biafra; travelogues seen during diplomatic trips.

BIAFRA, 1969

1. Chinua Achebe, *Collected Poems* (New York: Anchor Books, 2004).

The Republic of Biafra

THE INTELLECTUAL FOUNDATION OF A NEW NATION

1. Dictionary.com Unabridged, based on the *Random House Dictionary* © Random House, Inc. 2012. http://dictionary.reference.com/browse/republic?s=t.
2. For the full text of the Ahiara Declaration, please visit: http://www.biafraland.com/Ahiara_declaration_1969.htm.
3. Ezenwa-Ohaeto, *Chinua Achebe*, p. 140.
4. Author's recollection of events.

The Biafran State

1. "Republic of Biafra," *The Columbia Encyclopedia*, 2008. Encyclopedia.com, April 2, 2010; Nwankwo and Ifejika, *Biafra*; Achuzia, *Requiem Biafra*; Madiebo, *The Nigerian Revolution and the Biafran War*; www.worldstatesmen.org/Nigeria.htm; Metz, *Nigeria*.

2. Nwankwo and Ifejika, *Biafra*; Achuzia, *Requiem Biafra*; Madiebo, *The Nigerian Revolution and the Biafran War*; Schabowska and Himmelstrand, *Africa Reports on the Nigerian Crisis*; Biafra @ a glance, www.kwenu.com/biafra/biafra.htm; Biafra Foundation, http://biafra.cwis.org/pdf/BiafraNewsAgency23.pdf, p. 6; Metz, *Nigeria*.

3. Johnston Akunna Kalu Njoku, *Enyi Biafra: Regimental Drill, Duty Songs, and Cadences from Biafra* (Glassboro, NJ: Goldline & Jacobs Publishers, 2009).

4. Europa Publications, *Regional Surveys of the World 2004 Set: Africa South of the Sahara 2004* (London: Routledge, 2004).

5. Information from Professor Obiora Udechukwu.

THE BIAFRAN FLAG

6. Robert A. Hill et al. (eds.), *The Marcus Garvey and Universal Negro Improvement Association Papers, Vol. X: Africa for the Africans, 1923–1945* (Berkeley: University of California Press, 2006); Tony Martin, *Race First: The Ideological and Organizational Struggles of Marcus Garvey and the Universal Negro Improvement Association* (Westport, CT: Greenwood Press, 1987), p. 43; Vincent Bakpetu Thompson, *Africa and Unity: The Evolution of Pan-Africanism* (New York: Longman Publishing Group, 1977).

THE BIAFRAN NATIONAL ANTHEM

7. Njoku, *Enyi Biafra*.

8. John Albert Lynn writes in *The Bayonets of the Republic* about the importance of songs in the establishment of new states and posits that songs were engaged during the French Revolution for the purposes of "indoctrination and as a medium of political education." Lynn further reports that nations often turn to songs to stir the spirit of patriotism and evoke emotions of nationhood and dreams of prosperity and liberty: "[Songs] improve the public spirit," the French revolutionaries understood, "exciting the courage of the defenders of the Patric."

Source: John Albert Lynn, *The Bayonets of the Republic: Motivation and Tactics in the Army of Revolutionary France, 1791–94* (Boulder, CO: Westview Press, 1996).

9. Nnamdi Azikiwe, *Origins of the Nigerian Civil War* (Apapa, Nigeria: Nigerian National Press, 1969).

10. William Peterson, *Ethnicity Counts* (Piscataway, NJ: Transaction Publishers, 1997).

11. Jean Sibelius (December 8, 1865–September 20, 1957); Nwankwo and Ifejika, *Biafra*; http://www.nationalanthems.info/bia.txt; http://www.sibelius.fi/english/ela mankaari/index.htm; Biafra @ a glance: http://www.kwenu.com/biafra/biafra.htin.

12. Alex Duval Smith, "Emeka Ojukwu: Soldier who led his people into the war of Biafran independence," *The Independent*, December 13, 2011.

13.   In *The Origins of the Civil War*, Nnamdi Azikiwe reports, "The music of Sibelius, 'Be Still My Soul,' was appropriated, and my ode to 'Onitsha Ado N'Idu: Land of the Rising Sun' was plagiarized and adapted to suit the secessionists."

14.   Nwankwo and Ifejika, *Biafra*; http://www.nationalanthiems.info/bia.txt; http://www.sibelius.ri/english/elamankaari/index.htm; Biafra at a glance.

15.   Ibid.

THE MILITARY

16.   Clayton, *Frontiers Men*, p. 93.

17.   *Biafra,* BBC documentary (1995).

18.   Clayton, *Frontiers Men*, p. 93; *Biafra,* BBC documentary (1995).

19.   We are told that Henry A. Wharton and Ron Archer were two American pilots who were particularly effective in flying relief supplies and ammunitions into Biafra. Their expert knowledge of the West African terrain made it possible for them to evade Nigerian military radar and still land on Uli airstrip undetected. It was said that Mr. Wharton, in particular, had become such a success and asset to the Biafrans that the military government of Nigeria had placed a huge bounty on his head.

One of the most legendary expatriate pilots of the conflict, Rolf Steiner, worked seamlessly with Biafra's Fourth Commando Division. Military lore held that Steiner was not paid for these exploits but required only free food and board. This endeared him deeply to Ojukwu, who not only heaped military favors on Steiner but made him a Biafran citizen. Steiner, a veteran French legionnaire of both the Vietnam and Algerian conflicts, provided Biafra much needed military reconnaissance as well as tactical, technical, and strategic guidance.

Taffy Williams, a controversial South African of Welsh descent, was called a "professional soldier of fortune." It was said he came to the aid of the Biafrans as a result of what he felt was the injustice of the pogroms. "Taffy Williams, who looked something like Peter O'Toole from *Lawrence of Arabia*, gregarious for a clandestine fighter," was much admired by the Biafrans and decorated with the honorary title of major of the People's Army.

Sources: Achebe Foundation interviews: Nigerian and former Biafran soldiers © Achebe Foundation, 2008; Peter Schwab, ed., *Biafra* (New York: Facts on File, 1971); Madiebo, *The Nigerian Revolution and the Biafran War*; "World: Nigeria's Civil War: Hate, Hunger and the Will to Survive," *Time*, August 23, 1968; Rolf Steiner, *The Last Adventurer* (Boston: Little, Brown, 1978).

20.   Operation Biafran Babies. The Swedish military aviation page; www.canit.se/-griffon/aviation/text/biafra.htm.

21.   A *Time* magazine reporter wrote an article published in 1969, during the war, describing the encounter:

Last week, as the Biafran rebellion against Nigeria neared its second anniversary, Von Rosen and his flyers attacked the Nigerian airport at Benin, reported damage to one MIG and several civilian planes sitting on the ground. That raid and two earlier forays, which damaged British- and Russian-made Nigerian planes at Enugu and Port Harcourt, eased the pressure on Biafra's landing strip at Uli. With no Nigerian bombers overhead for a change, transports were shuttling in.

Source: "Biafra: How to Build an Instant Air Force," *Time*, June 6, 1969.

22.   Madiebo, *The Nigerian Revolution and the Biafran War*, p. 100.

23.   After he returned home from Biafra last year, Von Rosen continued to worry about the underdog. . . . The plight of the Biafrans rekindled his sympathies for the outgunned and inspired an improbable, wildly romantic scheme: to marshal pilots and planes and create an instant air force for the planeless Biafrans. . . . [Von Rosen] approached Malmö Flygindustri, builders of the MFI-9B, and received permission to take up one of the trainers for familiarization flights. He searched quietly for pilots and demanded, with reason, that they be experienced. . . .

The Biafran government put up $60,000 for the purchase of five second-hand MFl-9Bs in a third-party transaction handled through a Zurich bank. Biafran Leader Odumegwu Ojukwu appointed Von Rosen an air force colonel and approved an additional $140,000 for refitting the planes in friendly Gabon and for the pilots' salaries. Finally Von Rosen told his wife, Gunvor, of his plans—up to a point. "He told me he was going to Biafra," Countess von Rosen said, . . . "but he didn't say he would be bombing MIGs."

Source: "Biafra: How to Build an Instant Air Force," *Time*, June 6, 1969, the pogram-war-starvation.blogspot.com/2007/12/biafra-how-to-build-an-instant-air-force.html.

24.   Pfister, *Apartheid, South Africa, and African States,* pp. 52–53.

25.   McCullum, "Biafra Was the Beginning," *AfricaFiles.*

26.   We have the following amazing description of what landing at Uli was like from a 1969 story in *Time*:

As they near ground level, crews must maneuver in darkness for all but the final 30 seconds before touchdown. The runway is really only a section of the road between Uli and Mgbidi that has been widened to 75 feet. "That's a nice wide road," comments one flyer, "but a damned narrow runway." Airplanes' wheels have no more than a 20-ft. margin on either side. Wingtips brush treetops, and to avoid running out of runway, pilots reverse their propellers and "stand" on their brakes. Not infrequently, an incoming pilot discovers that the control tower has blithely sent a plane out above or below him.

Source: "Biafra: Come on Down and Get Killed," *Time*, March 21, 1969.

27.   Interview with anonymous American relief pilot.

Ogbunigwe

28. During his last wartime speech Biafran head of state Chukwuemeka Odumegwu Ojukwu summarized many of the technological feats of the Biafran state:

> In three years of war, necessity gave birth to invention. During those three years, ... [w]e built bombs, rockets, and we designed and built our own refinery and our own delivery systems and guided them far. For three years, blockaded without hope of import, we maintained all our vehicles.
>
> The state extracted and refined petrol, individuals refined petrol in their back gardens. We built and maintained our airports, maintained them under heavy bombardment. . . . We spoke to the world through a telecommunications system engineered by local ingenuity.
>
> In three years, we had broken the technological barrier, became the most advanced Black people on earth.

> *Source*: Excerpt from last wartime speech of Chukwuemeka Odumegwu Ojukwu, head of Biafran state; Emma Okocha, "Odumegwu Ojukwu—The Last Campaign of the Biafran General," *Vanguard*, February 15, 2010.

29. E. O. Arene, *The "Biafran" Scientists: The Development of an African Indigenous Technology* (Lagos, Nigeria: Arnet Ventures, 1997); Bayo Onanuga, *People in the News, 1900–1999: A Survey of Nigerians of the 20th Century* (Lagos, Nigeria: Independent Communications Ltd., 2000); pay special attention to entry on Ezekwe; Michael Robson, "Douglas A/B-26 Invader/Biafran Invaders"; www/vectaris.net/id307.html.

30. Vincent Chukwuemeka Ike, *Sunset at Dawn: A Novel about Biafra* (London: Collins and Harvill Press, 2006).

Biafran Tanks

31. Morrow, "Chinua Achebe, An Interview," *Conjunctions*.

32. I hope I am not misunderstood: No nation is truly independent; clearly not. You can manage certain things, but you do rely on others, and it's a good thing the whole world should be linked in interdependence. As human beings you can be independent, but as members of society you are related to your fellows. In the same way, nations can manage certain affairs on their own and yet be linked to others.

33. After the war many of the scientists who developed the aforementioned devices were absorbed by the federal government into the Projects Development Institute (PRODA) and the Scientific Equipment Development Institute (SEDI-E), both in Enugu. The institutes were initially fairly successful under the expert leadership of talented scientists such as Gordian Ezekwe, but they suffered from poor federal investment and support, and have, like so many other institutions in Nigeria, fallen into disrepair. See: www.proda-ng.org/index.html.

A Tiger Joins the Army

34. Theresa Emenike, "Welcome to Amaigbo"; www.amaigbo.plus.com/files/amaigbo2 .html.

35. Adeyinka Makinde, *Dick Tiger: The Life & Times of a Boxing Immortal* (Tarentum, PA: Word Association Publishers, 2005); www.boxrec.com/media/index.php/Dick_ Tiger.

36. Adeyinka Makinde, *Dick Tiger: The Cyber Boxing Zone Encyclopedia—Lineal Champion*; www.cyberboxingzone.com/boxing/tiger-d.htm.

37. Robert M. Lipsyte recalls how it happened:

> We wrote the letter.... "I am hereby returning the M.B.E. because every time I look at it I think of millions of men, women, and children who died and are still dying in Biafra because of the arms and ammunition the British government is sending to Nigeria and its continued moral support of this genocidal war against the people of Biafra."

> *Source*: Robert M. Lipsyte, "Pride of the Tiger," in Jeff Silverman, ed., *The Greatest Boxing Stories Ever Told: Thirty-Six Incredible Tales from the Ring* (Guilford, CT: Globe Pequot Press, 2004), p. 299.

Freedom Fighters

38. Ezenwa-Ohaeto, *Chinua Achebe*, p. 136.

39. In the years before and directly after the Chinese Communist Party's ascension to power in 1949, the relationship between the civilian populace and the People's Liberation Army remained supportive, appreciative, and mutually beneficial. Mao Zedong compared the army to a fish and the people to the water which is its element: The army exists immersed within the populace, and without the support and affection of the people, the army cannot succeed. During the early years of the Communist era, the People's Army did indeed enjoy the support of the civilian populace.

   The PLA was a tool employed by the Communist Party, which implemented egalitarian policies such as division of land and shattered the exploitative system of feudal land tenure, providing a unifying ideology behind which peasants and soldiers alike might rally. It was an army built of volunteers, so peasants did not fear conscription for themselves or their sons when the army was near. Because the PLA was a successful army, and representative of the inspirational ideology of the Communist Party, it became a matter of pride to be a soldier or to have a family member enlist. The People's Army was a volunteer army, a force of men fighting for their political beliefs, their future livelihood, and their newly claimed land.
   Source: People's Liberation Army; www.people.ucsc.edu/-myrtreia/essays/PLA .html.

40. Zdenek Červenka confirms this: "The behind-the-lines guerrilla forays were led by hand-picked members of the Biafran Organization of Freedom Fighters (BOFF)...."

The recruits were young [and] had been screened for character and high motivation."

Source: Zdenek Červenka. *The Nigerian War, 1967–1970: History of the War: Selected Bibliography and Documents* (Bonn, Germany: Bernard & Graefe, 1971), p. 141.

Traveling on Behalf of Biafra

1. Introduction of the francophone literary movement known as *La Négritude*; www .French.about.com/library/bl-negritude.htm.
2. Ibid. Heather Carlberg, "Negritude. Political Discourse—Theories of Colonialism and Postcolonialism"; www.postcolonialweb.org/poldiscourse/negritude/html.
3. *La Négritude*; www.French.about.com/library/bl-negritude.htm.
4. Based on events I witnessed and some I was told about; also see www.oikoumene .org//.
5. "Another Try at Biafra Talks," *Miami News*, May 27, 1968.
6. Local St. Simons, Georgia, lore. Also extensively documented in history books.

REFUGEE MOTHER AND CHILD (A MOTHER IN A REFUGEE CAMP)
1. Chinua Achebe, *Collected Poems* (New York: Anchor Books, 2004).

Life in Biafra

1. Sara S. Berry, George A. Elbert, Norman Thomas Uphoff; reply by Stanley Diamond. "Letters: An Exchange on Biafra," *New York Review of Books*, April 23, 1970.
2. The material from the following section is adapted from "Chinua Achebe on Biafra," *Transition*, pp. 31–38.
3. *Resurgence* 2, iss. 11 (1970); see also the editorial, "In the Curve of Africa, Fear, Relief, Surrender," *St. Petersburg Times*, January 13, 1970.

The Abagana Ambush

1. "Smash Biafra" was a term used widely during the war.
    Sources: "On September 3, Nigeria was preparing an air, sea and land offensive in a drive to smash Biafra": Ms. Kalindi Phillip on behalf of *African Recorder* 6 (New Delhi: Asian Recorder & Publication, 1967); also see *The Spectator*, vol. 244 (London: F. C. Westley: Literary Collections, 1980): "In public the British Labour government claimed that it armed Nigeria to forestall the Russians; in secret a junior British

minister wrote to the Nigerians ordering them to purchase Russian siege artillery in order to smash the Biafran army."

2. Norman Tobias, "A-I Skyraider-Acre, Siege of, 1799," *The International Military Encyclopedia*, vol. 1 (Gulf Breeze, FL: Academic International Press, 1992); Colin Legum and John Drysdale, *Africa Contemporary Record: Annual Survey and Documents, Vol. 2* (Oxford, UK: Africa Research Ltd., 1970).

AIR RAID

1. Chinua Achebe, *Beware Soul Brother*, African Writers Series (London: Heinemann, 1972).

The Citadel Press

1. Ernest Emenyonu, ed., *Emerging Perspectives on Chinua Achebe* (Trenton, NJ: Africa World Press, 2003).
2. Achebe, "Chinua Achebe on Biafra," *Transition*, pp. 31–38.

Staying Alive

1. Chinua Achebe and Dubem Okafor, eds., *Don't Let Him Die: An Anthology of Memorial Poems for Christopher Okigbo* (Enugu, Nigeria: Fourth Dimension Publishers, 1978).
2. Achebe, "Chinua Achebe on Biafra," *Transition*.
3. In a story by Tony Edike on June 29, 2009, in the *Nigerian Vanguard,* we are informed:

> About 183 different types of unexploded explosives recovered from nine states affected by the Nigerian-Biafran Civil War were yesterday detonated by the Ministry of Defense, 39 years after the war ended.
>
> Two of the bombs dropped during the war were recovered from the residence of a renowned author, Chinua Achebe, according to the experts.
>
> The exercise, which took place at Onyeama Hills on Enugu-Onitsha Expressway and witnessed by the Minister of Defense, Dr. Shettima Mustafa, the Enugu State Deputy Governor, Sunday Onyebuchi, and members of the armed forces and representatives of the United Nations, was handled by a team of experts under the Humanitarian De-Mining project.

4. Achebe and Okafor, *Don't Let Him Die*.

Death of the Poet: "Daddy, Don't Let Him Die!"

1. Achebe and Okafor, *Don't Let Him Die.*
2. Achebe, "Chinua Achebe on Biafra," *Transition.*
3. Ibid.
4. Achebe and Okafor, *Don't Let Him Die.*

Mango Seedling

1. Chinua Achebe, *Collected Poems* (New York: Anchor Books, 2004).

Refugees

1. Interview with Professor Christie Achebe, Brown University, Rhode Island, April 2010.
2. A wild-game hunting enthusiast's information guide provides this startling information about hunting bullets:

> The [VLD wild game bullet] penetrates up to 3 inches before it starts to expand. This delayed expansion results in a wound channel that is deep inside the vital area of any big game. After the bullet starts to expand it will shed 80% to 90% of its weight into the surrounding tissue, traveling as deep as 18 inches. This results in a massive wound cavity that creates the greatest possible amount of tissue damage and hemorrhaging within the [organs]. This massive and extensive wound cavity results in the animal dropping fast.

> *Source*: Long Range Store, Best of the West Productions; www.longrangestore .com/Berger_VLD_Hunting_Bullets_p/70100000.htm.

3. A *Time* journalist who toured the children's hospitals at Okporo and Emekuku had this to say:

> In villages that are nearly deserted, old men and women, along with sickly children, die quietly in their huts. At the missionary hospital in Emekuku, a mob of starving children gathers at the door. The hospital has room for only 100 of them: the strongest-looking children are taken in, and the least hopeful cases turned away. "This started out as an epidemic in March," says a London-trained Biafran doctor, Aaron Ifekwunigwe. "Now it is a catastrophe."

> *Source*: "A Bitter African Harvest," *Time.*

4. Dan Jacobs, *The Brutality of Nations* (New York: Alfred A. Knopf, 1987).

5. Goetz, "Humanitarian Issues in the Biafra Conflict"; see also Caroline Moorehead, *Dunant's Dream* (New York: HarperCollins, 1988), pp. 615–16.

WE LAUGHED AT HIM

1. Chinua Achebe, *Collected Poems* (New York: Anchor Books, 2004).

The Media War

1. Achebe, *The Education of a British-Protected Child*.
2. House of Lords official report, August 27, 1968.
3. Hugh McCullum provides this perspective: "For the first time in history and just by accident, the mass media zeroed in on an African humanitarian disaster. New technology and a new generation of young, bright, media-savvy church people and NGOs made this possible."
   Source: McCullum, "Biafra Was the Beginning."

Narrow Escapes

1. In *Social History of Rape*, Paul Tabori confirms this abomination:

   A young British doctor who worked in the pediatric hospital told the reporter: "The soldiers on duty in the area of the pediatric hospital at Okporo were such monsters that I never let the nurses go anywhere without an escort. Especially the white ones. . . . Two Biafran nurses who would only give their names as Theresa and Caroline said they were raped several times."

   Source: Paul Tabori, *Social History of Rape* (London: New English Library, 1971).
2. "Elephant Grass: Common Name: Napier grass, Uganda grass; Genus: Pennistum; Species: purpureum; Parts Used: leaves for animal fodder. . . . In the savannas of Africa it grows along lake beds and rivers where the soil is rich. Local farmers cut the grass for their animals, carrying it home in huge piles on their backs or on carts."
   Source: www.blueplanetbiomes.org/elephant_grass.htm.

VULTURES

1. Chinua Achebe, *Collected Poems* (New York: Anchor Books, 2004).

Part 3

The Fight to the Finish

1. Captain Steve Lewis, "Che Guevara and Guerrilla Warfare: Training for Today's Nonlinear Battlefields," *Military Review* (September–October 2001), p. 101 Also, interview of retired Nigerian and Biafran Army officers © Achebe Foundation 2008-2011; See also the military theory, theorists, and strategy Web page of the Air War College. This is the intellectual and leadership center of the American air force. http://www.au.af.mil/au/awc/awcgate/awc-thry.htm.

The Economic Blockade and Starvation

1. Chukwuemeka Odumegwu Ojukwu. *Biafra: Selected Speeches and Random Thoughts of C. Odumegwu Ojukwu* (New York: Harper & Row, 1969).
2. Metz, *Nigeria*; Forsyth, *The Biafra Story*; de St. Jorre, *The Nigerian Civil War*; Akpan, *The Struggle for Secession 1966–1970*; Amadi, *Sunset in Biafra*; Falola and Heaton, *A History of Nigeria*; Madiebo, *The Nigerian Revolution and the Biafran War,* p. 14; Ademoyega, *Why We Struck*; Effiong, *Nigeria and Biafra*.
3. Seymour M. Hersh, *The Price of Power: Kissinger in the Nixon White House* (New York: Summit Books, 1983), p. 136.
4. "Negotiators who have been meeting for four weeks in Addis Ababa made marked progress in clearing the logjam holding up large-scale relief. Meeting with Emperor Haile Selassie, moderator of the talks, they agreed to create both air and land corridors for shipments of food to Biafra's starving civilians."
    Source: "Nigeria: Biafra's Two Wars," *Time*, August 30, 1968.
5. Writing for the United Nations High Commissioner for Refugees' series, New Issues, Professor Nathaniel H. Goetz of Pepperdine University succinctly captures the complexity of the standoff:

    > Politically, the possibility of a land corridor seemed impossible. One of the many disagreements between the warring parties was simple, yet it illustrates both the mistrust and complexity of what was occurring: Ojukwu forbade the necessary food to reach the country through a neutral corridor for fear Nigerian troops would poison it.... On June 5, an ICRC DC-7 aircraft was shot down by the Federal air force over Biafra, killing the three aid workers onboard. Because of this incident, serious disputes over the conduct of relief operations arose and the airlift was again suspended.

    Source: Goetz, "Humanitarian Issues in the Biafra Conflict."

The Silence of the United Nations

1. Hammarskjöld was "a Renaissance man," reportedly with interests as varied as banking, economics, literature—he loved the work of Emily Dickinson and Hermann Hesse—politics, Christian theology, fine art, linguistics, gymnastics, outdoor sports such as skiing.

    Source: "Dag Hammarskjöld —Biography"; Nobelprize.org, December 14, 2011; www.nobelprize.org/nobel_prizes/peace/laureates/1961/hammarskjold-bio.html.

2. Metz, *Nigeria*.

3. Edward Newman, Ramesh Thakur, and John Triman, in their benchmark study for the United Nations, *Multilateralism Under Challenge: Power, International Order, and Structural Change* (New York: United Nations University Press, 2006), suggest that the UN's response to humanitarian disasters prior to 1970 was "undeveloped" at best:

    > Surprising as it may now seem the United Nations system was very slow to manifest any broad responsibility for disaster response....
    >
    > The United Nations system was not utilized to manage a systemic and multilateral response to a broad range of humanitarian disasters until about 1970. In the well-publicized Nigerian-Biafran conflict (1967–1970), the major relief players trying to get aid to civilians in secessionist Biafra were the International Committee of the Red Cross (ICRC) and its Red Cross partners, and Joint Church Aid, a faith-based private consortium. While other relief actors like the French Red Cross acted independently, no UN organ or agency was a major player in that drama.
    >
    > After Biafra ... the General Assembly created the UN Disaster Relief Office. By 1992 this office morphed into the UN Department of Humanitarian Affairs.

4. The *New York Times* article read in part:

    > The Nigerian Federal Government readies [another] "final offensive" in war with Biafra; Government spokesman says East must be subdued by end of February or growing international aid will make Federal victory impossible.

    Source: Alfred Friendly Jr., "Nigerians Are Preparing for Another 'Final' Offensive; War With Biafra, 19 Months Old, Still Bogged Down; Mood in Once-Cocky Lagos Turns Glum as Foe Revives," *New York Times*, February 5, 1969.

5. Jeffrey D. Blum, "Who Cares About Biafra Anyway?" *Harvard Crimson*, February 25, 1969.

6. Special to the *New York Times*, "Biafrans Warned of Enemy's 'Desperate Effort'; Ojukwu Asserts That British May Lose Holdings," February 12, 1969.

7. Ezenwa-Ohaeto, *Chinua Achebe,* quoting from Chinua Achebe, "A Letter [on Stanley Diamond]," in C. W. Gailey, ed., *Dialectical Anthropology: Essays in Honor of Stanley Diamond, Vol. 1* (Gainesville, FL: University Press of Florida, 1992), p. 134.

8. John W. Young, *The Labour Governments 1964–70, Vol. 2: International Policy* (Manchester, UK: Manchester University Press, 2009); Arthur Agwuncha Nwankwo, *Nigeria: The Challenge of Biafra* (London: R. Collings, 1972); Ruby Bell-Gam and Uru Iyam, David, *Nigeria,* vol. 100 of World Bibliographical Series (Oxford: Clio Press, 1999); P. J. Odu, *The Future That Vanished* (Bloomington, IN: Xlibris Corporation, 2009), p. 168.

9. "Britain: Loss of Touch?" *Time.*

10. Speaking to journalists in Umuahia, Ojukwu

> suggested that the feasible way to bring Nigeria to the bargaining table was "diplomatic victory whereby Nigeria would be faced with the specter of isolation." Was Wilson the man to bring off such a diplomatic victory? Replied Ojukwu: "I do sincerely hope that this trip is no gimmick and that he is genuinely out for peace. It is true that his previous actions do not justify this hope. Yet for the sake of Nigeria, Biafra, Africa and Britain, one can only hope."

> Source: "Nigeria: Twin Stalemates," *Time,* April 4, 1969.

Azikiwe Withdraws Support for Biafra

1. African-American Institute, *Africa Report* (1969).

2. Chinua Achebe Foundation interview: Dr. Okechukwu Ikejiani, March 6, 2005.

The Recapture of Owerri

1. Madiebo reports that Colonel Ogbugo Kalu achieved this surprising feat in three phases—by galvanizing the Fifty-second Brigade under Colonel Chris Ugokwe, the Third Brigade of the Fourteenth Division under Lambert Iheanacho, and the Sixty-eighth Battalion under Major Ikeji—and then surrounding the complacent troops of the Nigerian army while preventing reinforcements from reaching the Nigerians.

    Source: Madiebo, *The Nigerian Revolution and the Biafran War,* pp. 301–10.

2. During a visit to the United States in 2003, Colonel Achuzia described how he earned the nickname "Air Raid":

> I never knew I was called "Air Raid." It was when Chief Ngbada of Abakiliki and others called me to come over to their region which was also mine (I was

born in Abakiliki) to help repel the invading feds that a drama unfolded that made me know I was called Air Raid. In Abakiliki, I spent three days in a fierce battle to repel the feds from reaching Uwana—the home of Akanu Ibiam. It was brisk and very successful. On my way back, and approaching a military check point, I heard shouts of Air Raid, Air Raid everywhere. Market women were running into the bush. People were taking cover left right and center. As a war commander, I got down from my vehicle to take a look at where the plane was coming from. It was then that my orderly told me that people were running because of me. That I was also known as "Air Raid." I immediately asked that the rumor should be dispelled immediately and people should go about their normal business. It was a sobering experience for me.

Source: Godson Ofoaro, "Ngige and Achuzia came to town," *Nigeriaworld*, November 10, 2003; nigeriaworld.com.

Ugochukwu Ejinkeonye, one of Nigeria's prized journalists, interviewed the former Biafran war leader in 2005 and discovered an Achuzia, then seventy years old, who was far from his austere reputation, amiable and reflective:

Achuzia had assumed office as the Secretary-General of Ohaneze Ndigbo, the apex socio-cultural organization in Igboland, and by this time had developed a reputation for his frankness in public statements, and the passion with which he canvassed the Igbo position on matters of national and regional interests.

Ejinkeonye found the retired colonel astutely unrepentant for his role in the Nigeria-Biafra war, even while he espoused his strong belief in a "one, united Nigeria, where equity, justice, fairness and mutual respect for one another are unreservedly operational at all levels of governance and social interactions."

Achuzia's perspective on the quality of the Nigerian army and why the war was fought is both instructive and alarming:

How can there be unity in an army that is packaged on what you call federal character (Nigerian version of Equal Opportunity)? People don't join the army because they see it as a vocation; most of the people in the army are surrogates of certain people who put them there for their nefarious purposes. When we have a proper, well-oriented country, we will put together an army that will be for the protection and the defense of the people against external aggression. . . . The Igbo fought when the pogrom started, and they were being killed and pushed out of the federation. So, to ensure that they stayed in the federation, they had to fight or else, it would have meant being dispossessed of their land. So where were we expected to run to when the hostilities started— to Cameroon? So these were the reasons. Again, you must try to differentiate the reasons for the Civil War from the reasons why Nigeria had a coup, and some people carried out "Operation *Wetie*," and the civil strife the country has experienced since the 1950s.

Source: Chinua Achebe Foundation interviews: Colonel Joseph Achuzia in conversation with Ugochukwu Ejinkeonye, November 28, 2005.

3. Interviews with anonymous retired Biafran soldiers.

Biafra Takes an Oil Rig: "The Kwale Incident"

1. "Eni is an outgrowth of Agip (Azienda Generale Italiana Petroli), an oil and gas company set up by the fascist Italian government in the 1920s." "Eni," *Encyclopdia Britannica Online*, April 8, 2009.

2. "Biafra: Reprieve for Eighteen," *Time*, June 13, 1969; Anthony Hamilton Millard Kirk-Greene, *Crisis and Conflict in Nigeria: A Documentary Sourcebook, Volume 2* (London: Oxford University Press, 1971); Ben Gbulie, *The Fall of Biafra* (Enugu, Anambra State, Nigeria: Benlie Publishers, 1989); *Indian Journal of International Law* 14, iss. 1–15, 15, iss. 4.

3. Interview with anonymous former Biafran intellectual.

4. "Biafra: Reprieve for Eighteen," *Time*.

5. Ibid. Also Kirk-Greene, *Crisis and Conflict in Nigeria*; Gbulie, *The Fall of Biafra*; *Indian Journal of International Law*.

6. Gabonese and Ivorian diplomats made this real possibility clear to Ojukwu. Also see the following: *West Africa*, iss. 2718–43 (London: West Africa Publishing, 1969), p. 661; Africa Bureau, *Africa Digest* 16 (London: Africa Publications Trust, 1969), p. 72.

7. "Pope Paul VI met Federal Nigerian and Biafran representatives separately during his visit to Kampala early in August. A Vatican spokesman said that the Pope had raised the possibility of negotiations to resolve the conflict."
    Source: Commonwealth Parliamentary Association. General Council, Royal Institute of International Affairs, *Report on World Affairs* 50, iss. 3 (1968).

8. *The Daily Register* (Red Bank), August 1, 1969; see also *Africa Research Bureau* 6 (London: Africa Research, 1969).

9. Robert D. Schulzinger, *A Companion to American Foreign Relations*, volume 24 of Blackwell Companions to American History, Blackwell Handbooks in Linguistics (New York: John Wiley & Sons, 2006); Auberon Waugh and Suzanne Cronjé, *Biafra: Britain's Shame* (London: Joseph, 1969); Peter Schwab, *Biafra* (New York: Facts on File, 1971), digitized by the University of Michigan Press, September 16, 2008.

10. Russell Warren Howe and Sarah Hays Trott, *The Power Peddlers: How Lobbyists Mold America's Foreign Policy* (Garden City, NY: Doubleday, 1977); Christian Chukwunedu Aguolu, *Biafra: Its Case for Independence* (self-published, 1969); Hersh, *The Price of Power*.

11. Kari A. Frederickson, *The Dixiecrat Revolt and the End of the Solid South, 1932–1968* (Chapel Hill: University of North Carolina Press, 2001).

12. Ibid.

13. *West Africa* magazine, iss. 2718–43 (1968, 1969).

1970 and The Fall

1. Martin Meredith, *The Fate of Africa: A History of the Continent Since Independence* (New York: PublicAffairs, 2011), p. 205; Henry Robinson Luce, *Time* 100, iss. 14–26 (New York: Time, 1972); Blaine Harden, "2 Decades Later, Biafra Remains Lonely Precedent," *Washington Post*, June, 27, 1988.

2. Chinua Achebe Foundation interviews, Number 15: General Yakubu Gowon, October 2005, ©The Chinua Achebe Foundation.

3. Mort Rosenblum, "Gowon Assails International Relief Agencies: Biafran Crisis Builds Up," *Observer-Reporter* (Washington County, PA), Associated Press, January 14, 1970; "Lagos Spurns Promises of Aid," *The Montreal Gazette*, Reuters, January 15, 1970; Jean Strouse, *Newsweek* 75, iss. 1–8; United Press International, "Nigeria Eases Relief Ban: Million Biafrans Near Starvation," *Palm Beach Daily News*, January 15, 1970; Nancy L. Hoepli, ed., *West Africa Today* 42, iss. 6 (1971).

     According to Carl Ferdinand and Howard Henry, "Three days after thousands of Biafran soldiers surrendered, Nigeria's leader, General Yakubu Gowon, assailed the international relief agencies coordinated through Joint Church Aid (JCA) and said: 'Let them keep their blood money.'"

     Source: *Christianity Today* 14, iss. 1–13; vols. 1-13 (Chicago: American Theological Library Association, 1969).

4. Ibid.

5. Dirk Kruijt and Kees Koonings, eds., *Political Armies: The Military and Nation Building in the Age of Democracy* (London, New York: Zed Books, 2002).

6. Various estimates place the number killed at over two million people.

The Question of Genocide

1. "Death Tolls for the Major Wars and Atrocities of the Twentieth Century"; www.users.erols.com/mwhite28/warstat2.htm. The following sources provide death tolls for the Biafran war: *Compton's Encyclopedia*: 1,500,000 starved; Charles Lewis Taylor, *The World Handbook of Political and Social Indicators* (WHPSI): 1,993,900 deaths by political violence, 1966–70; George Childs Kohn, *Dictionary of Wars*: nearly 2,000,000; William Eckhardt in *World Military and Social Expenditues, 1987–88* by Ruth Leger Sivard: 1,000,000 civilians + 1,000,000 military = 2,000,000; Dan Smith, *The State of War and Peace Atlas*: 2,000,000; Jacobs, *The Brutality of Nations*: 3,000,000.

2. Robert Leventhal, "Responses to the Holocaust: A Hypermedia Sourcebook for the Humanities," Department of German, University of Virginia, 1995; www2.iath .virginia.edu/holocaust/genocide.html.

Another undeniable authority, the United States Holocaust Memorial Museum, reminds us:

> On December 9, 1948, in the shadow of the Holocaust and in no small part due to the tireless efforts of [a Polish-Jewish lawyer, Raphael] Lemkin, the United Nations approved the Convention on the Prevention and Punishment of the Crime of Genocide. This convention establishes "genocide" as an international crime, which signatory nations "undertake to prevent and punish." It defines genocide as:
>
> "[G]enocide means any of the following acts committed with intent to destroy, in whole or in part, a national, ethnical, racial or religious group, as such:
>
> (a) Killing members of the group;
>
> (b) Causing serious bodily or mental harm to members of the group;
>
> (c) Deliberately inflicting on the group conditions of life calculated to bring about its physical destruction in whole or in part;
>
> (d) Imposing measures intended to prevent births within the group;
>
> (e) Forcibly transferring children of the group to another group."

Source: http://www.ushmm.org/wlc/en/article.php?moduleId-10007043.

The Arguments

1. The American Jewish Congress suggests that compounding this overwhelming evidence, according to the Biafrans, is:

> The Federal government has refused to discuss peace . . . unless and until Biafran leaders renounce their proclamation of secession. Biafrans have refused this demand because they believe they can gain their aims through conventional or guerrilla warfare, and also because they are convinced that Nigerian military commanders intend to perpetuate genocide against the Ibos [*sic*] people.

Source: Baum, American Jewish Congress, "Memorandum," December 27, 1968.

2. Ibid.

3. Herbert Ekwe-Ekwe, *The Biafra War: Nigeria and the Aftermath* (Lampeter, Ceredigion, UK: Edwin Mellen Press, 1991). As quoted in "The Violations of Human and Civil Rights of Ndi Igbo in the Federation of Nigeria (1966–1999)," October 1999.

4. Jacobs, *The Brutality of Nations*.

5. Ibid.
6. Arthur Meier Schlesinger, *Dynamics of World Power: A Documentary History of U.S. Foreign Policy, 1945–1973, Volume 1* (New York: Chelsea House, 1983).
7. Ibid.
8. Baum, American Jewish Congress, "Memorandum," December 27, 1968.
9. Ibid.
10. Ibid.
11. *Biafra*, BBC documentary (1995).
12. Ibid.

The Case Against the Nigerian Government

1. Jacobs, *The Brutality of Nations*.
2. With just the right kind of inflection bound to mesmerize his admirers, Gowon played that role to the hilt, quoting Lincoln in speech after speech and talking about "binding up the nation's wounds."

    Source: Luce, "General Gowon."

3. Nigerian leader Allison Ayida produced his viewpoint on starving children . . . :
    "Starvation is a legitimate weapon of war, and we have every intention of using it on the rebels."

    Source: Forsyth, *The Biafra Story*.
    Also see: Thierry Hentsch, *Face au blocus: histoire de l'intervention du Comité international de la Croix-Rouge dans le conflit du Nigéria, 1967–1970* (Geneva: Droz, 1973); Ekwe-Ekwe, *Biafra Revisited*; Ojukwu, *Biafra*.

4. Stanley Diamond's extensive reporting from Biafra around this time has preserved his observations for posterity:

    Direct reports from the former Biafran enclave (East Central State) indicate the following:

    1) No systematic distribution of food and relief supplies is taking place; indeed no adequate effort is being made. This was already evident by the end of January, 1970. On the 24th the London *Observer* had reported that only eighty food distribution centers remained in the enclave; before the surrender there had been 3,000. . . .

    2) Biafran currency has not been converted, nor is it accepted as legal tender. This works a particular hardship on the majority of impoverished peasants who must buy seed yams for the current growing season. A new cycle of hunger and dependency seems to have begun.

    3) The more than 60,000 federal troops are billeted in secondary schools

and private homes throughout the former Biafran enclave. Most if not all secondary schools are so occupied, prolonging the educational crisis.

4) Foreign correspondents are barred from Eastern Nigeria. Dispatches filed from Lagos on the situation in former Biafra are confused and contradictory.

The general policy seems to be one of attrition and isolation of the Ibo-speaking [*sic*] peoples in particular, with the promise of reward being held out for certain minority groups.

In the notes to his reply, Diamond quotes from K. W. J. Post's article, "Is There a Case to Be Made for Biafra?" *International Affairs* 44 no. 1 (January 1968), pp. 26–39:

Post states further that with the failure of Biafran secession, "a restoration of the old spoils system is certainly on the cards. Similarly the northern leaders may emerge again, heading an axis of the six new states [in the north]; the old NPC [Northern Peoples' Congress] was always something of a coalition of local interests and there is no reason why this should not emerge again under some of the old leaders, probably those from Kano and Bornu."

Diamond further quotes in his notes from Dr. E. C. Schwartzenbach, *Swiss Review of Africa* (February 1968):

The [Nigerian] war aim and solution of the entire problem was to discriminate against the Ibos [*sic*] in the future in their own interest. Such discrimination would include above all the detachment of those oil-rich territories in the Eastern Region which were not inhabited by them at the beginning of the colonial period, on the lines of the projected twelve-state plan. In addition, the Ibos' movement would be restricted, to prevent their renewed penetration into the other parts of the country. Leaving them any access to the sea, the Commissioner declared, was quite out of the question.

He also cites in the notes an unpublished "memorandum on the background, cause, and consequences of the Nigerian civil war issued in November 1968 by more than sixty British subjects, including Sir Robert Stapledon, the last British governor of the Eastern Region (1959–60)":

Each medal has its reverse. But, whatever the verdict, there can be no conceivable justification for what happened to the Ibos [*sic*] in the North in 1966. No objective consideration of their case can avoid the fact that, as rational and sentient human beings, they were made to feel themselves rejected by the most brutal possible means from the North and from Nigeria as a whole. The irony for Biafra was to be that, having seen her people driven out by the rest of Nigeria and hunted back to their homeland, she found Nigeria at war with her to preserve the integrity of a Federation where her people could no longer live.

Source: Reply by Stanley Diamond to Sara S. Berry, George A. Elbert, and Norman Thomas Uphoff, "Letters: An Exchange on Biafra," *New York Review of Books*, April 23, 1970.

5. "The Violations of Human and Civil Rights of Ndi Igbo in the Federation of Nigeria (1966–1969)," October 1999; Achebe, *The Trouble with Nigeria*, p. 45–46; Jane Guyer and LaRay Denzer, *Vision and Policy in Nigerian Economics: The Legacy of Pius Okigbo. West African Studies* (Ibadan, Nigeria: Ibadan University Press, 2005).

6. Ibid.

7. Guyer and Denzer, *Vision and Policy in Nigerian Economics*.

8. "Twin Stalemates," *Time*.

9. This school of thought is exemplified by the well-regarded scholar Martin Meredith, who believes: "The aftermath of the war was notable for its compassion and mercy, and the way in which the memories of Biafra soon faded."

Source: Meredith, *The Fate of Africa*, p. 205.

Gowon, expectedly, gives himself high marks for the role of his government following the conflict:

What you should remember about the time—and, at least, give us some credit for it—is that we did not take what would be considered normal action under such circumstances. In such an instance, all the senior officials involved—politicians as well as in the military—would have been strung up for their part in the war. This is what happened at the end of the Second World War in Germany; it happened in Japan at the end of the campaign in that part of the world. This is the civilized world's way of doing things. But we did not do even that. We did set up committees to look into cases such as where rebel officers had been members of the Nigerian armed forces, and their loyalty was supposed to be to the federal government. When the war ended, we reabsorbed practically everyone who was in the army. But there were officers at a certain senior level that we insisted had to accept responsibility for their role in the secession. It was the only thing to do. Probably I could have given pardon; however, I was not the one who gave pardon to Ojukwu.

Source: Chinua Achebe Foundation interview: Gowon in conversation with Pini Jason, 2005.

10. I shared my views about reintegration with *Transition* magazine during the war period, and they reflect the mind-set of a lot of Biafrans following the war:

The Nigerians say, "You come back; we will integrate you." This is nonsense—we know they will not—there is so much bitterness on both sides. This talk of integration is so much eyewash and is intended for foreign consumption. The point I am making is that it is not so much what the crimes are of the people persecuted—they may have committed crimes, but the point is they have been persecuted, and on a scale that is almost unbelievable. For a month or two the people were in a state of shock, a sort of total paralysis. It is really no use talking of unity; you don't unite the dead, you only unite the living, and there must be a minimal willingness on the part of those who are to be united.

Source: Achebe, "Chinua Achebe on Biafra," *Transition*, pp. 31–38.

Gowon Responds

1. Chinua Achebe Foundation interview: Gowon in conversation with Pini Jason, 2005.

Part 4

Nigeria's Painful Transitions: A Reappraisal

1. Robert I. Rotberg, *Nigeria, Elections and Continuing Challenges* (New York: Council on Foreign Relations, 2007).
    West Africa, iss. 4321, iss. 4328–31 (London: West Africa Publishing, 2002) reports:

    > The Nigerian elections are shaping up as a possible contest of ex-military leaders seeking to recycle their personal relevance, and they all appear to have substantial followings among the civilian political elite.

    The News, vol. 28 (Lagos: Independent Communications Network, Ltd., 2007): noted:

    > Nigerian politics is becoming more disappointing by the day. Instead effacing issues and ideology, our leaders are busy fighting among themselves to be in power just to satisfy their bloated ego and retain their loot.

2. Osita G. Afoaku, "The Politics of Democratic Transition in Congo (Zaire): Implications of the Kabila 'Revolution,' " *Journal of Conflict Studies* XIX, no. 2 (Fall 1999), published by the Gregg Center for the Study of War and Society, University of New Brunswick; Smith, *Genocide and the Europeans*, p. 71; interviews and discussions with several African and French historians and intellectuals; Pfister, *Apatheid South Africa*, pp. 52–53.

3. In a House of Commons speech made on November 11, 1947; cited at http://wais .stanford.edu/Democracy/democracy_DemocracyAndChurchill%28090503%29 .html.

4. The data on the scale of corruption in Nigeria is for the forty years since indepen- dence, 1960–2000. Daniel Jordan Smith, *A Culture of Corruption: Everyday Deception and Popular Discontent in Nigeria* (Princeton: Princeton University Press, 2008), p. 131; Chinua Achebe, "Open Letter to President Olusegun Obasanjo Rejecting the Com- mander of the Order of the Federal Republic of Nigeria (CFR)," October 15, 2004; Virginia Baily and Hoskins, Veronica, eds., *Africa Research Bulletin: Political, Social, and Cultural Series* 42 (2005–2006); Felix Ukah, *Anambra Political Crises: Eye-Witness Account* (Anambra, Nigeria: Computer-Edge Publishers, 2005).

5. Elie Wiesel, *The Kingdom of Memory: Reminiscences* (New York: Random House Digi- tal, 2011).

State Failure and the Rise of Terrorism

1. "The Failed States Index, 2011," *Foreign Policy* (July/August 2011); http://www .foreignpolicy.com/failedstates.

2. Quotation of Professor Robert Rotberg in James J. F. Forest, *Countering Terrorism and Insurgency in the 21st Century: International Perspectives. Combating the Sources and Facili- tators, Vol. 2* (Westport, CT: Praeger Security International, 2007), p. 97.

3. Ibid.

4. R. Borum, "Understanding the Terrorist Mind-set," *FBI Law Enforcement Bulletin* (July 2003), pp. 1–10, and as discussed in Michael A. Bozarth's PowerPoint presenta- tion, "Genesis of Terrorism: An Exploration of the Causes of Terrorism and of the Conditions That Produce Them," Department of Psychology, University of Buffalo. Copyright 2006

5. A Hausa term that is loosely translated into English as "Western education is a sin."

6. Farouk Chothia, "Who Are Nigeria's Boko Haram Islamists?" BBC Africa Service, January 11, 2012; http://www.bbc.co.uk/news/world-africa-13809501.

AFTER A WAR

1. Chinua Achebe, *Collected Poems* (New York: Anchor Books, 2004).

Postscript: The Example of Nelson Mandela

1. Equatorial Guinea is Africa's third-largest oil producer, after Nigeria and Angola. It has the highest per capita income on the African continent and is ranked twenty- eighth in the world. According to the Organization for Economic Development

(OECD): "[A] household survey for poverty evaluation (EEH) carried out by Equatorial Guinea in 2006 [found that] 76.8 percent of the population is poor, which translates into a head-of-household poverty ratio of 66.4 percent. This is a very poor ratio for a country where average income per capita was greater than USD 20 000." The scale of corruption in that country is staggering. This story should be particularly enlightening: Angelique Chrisafis, "France Probes Africa's Big Spenders," *Mail and Guardian*, February 10, 2012, http://mg.co.za/article/2012-02-10-france-probes-africas -big-spenders/.

See also: BBC News, "President's son buys $35m US home," November 8, 2006, http://news.bbc.co.Uk/2/hi/africa/6129992.stm; "A Murderous Dictator, His Rapper Son and a $700m-a-Year Oil Boom," *The Independent*, March 16, 2004, http://www .independent.co.uk/news/world/africa/a-murderous-dictator-his-rapper-son-and-a -700mayear-oil-boom-6172555.html.

Appendix: Brigadier Banjo's Broadcast to Mid-West

1.   www.dawodu.com/banjo.htm.

INDEX

Achebe, Chinua
There was a country

$27.95

10/12 PG